Spheres of Action: Art and Politics

Tate Publishing

Spheres of Action: Art and Politics

Edited by Éric Alliez and Peter Osborne

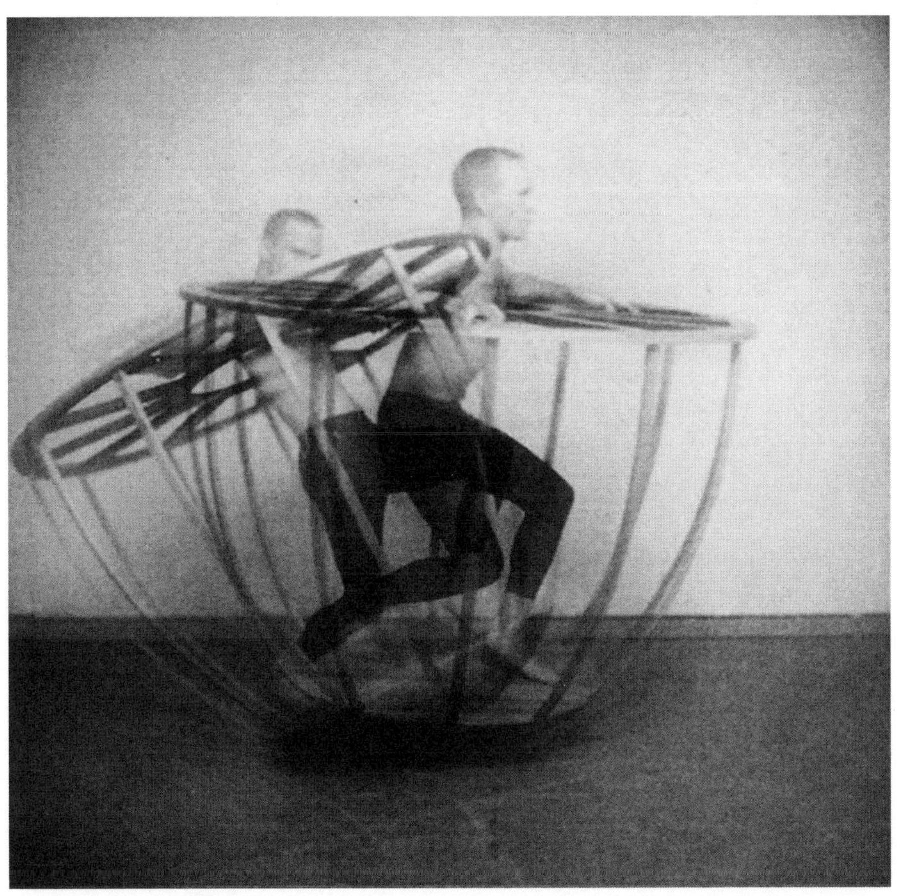

First published 2013 by order of the Tate Trustees
by Tate Publishing, a division of Tate Enterprises Ltd,
Millbank, London SW1P 4RG
www.tate.org.uk/publishing

A catalogue record for this book is available from
the British Library

ISBN 978 1 85437 975 7

Designed by ARPA (A Research Projects Agency)
Printed and bound in China by Toppan Leefung Printing Ltd

Front cover and frontispiece:
Jana Sterbak, *Proto-Sisyphus* 1990

Introduction
Peter Osborne and Éric Alliez

Philosophical writing about the arts has a long history in the Western tradition, but it is only since the second half of the eighteenth century – within the ambit of Enlightenment and Revolution – that art has been connected to politics in something like an inherent manner. 250 years is a long time in politics, less so within the longue durée of philosophical thought; the rhythms of art's histories lies somewhere in between. To write of 'art and politics' today from a theoretical perspective involves, necessarily, engaging with these disparate temporalities – philosophy, art, politics – in their inconstant but constitutive conjunctions within the present. And the present offers a variety of standpoints from which to do this. In the European context, these largely remain standpoints associated with the territorial bases of what appear, in the language of cultures, as 'national traditions'; however transnational these traditions may actually be, in the origin, dissemination and development of their intellectual contents. Such national traditions are even less self-sufficient today than they were 250 years ago, at the outset of what appears, retrospectively, as the passing convergence of two discrete but overlapping lines of thought: aesthetics as a discourse on art and nature (pre-eminently, beauty and the sublime), and the philosophy of art as a discourse on modern art, in an increasingly insistent difference from all things 'natural' (truth in history, dissonance, shock and the inorganic – to name but a few categories of the modern).

In the course of the eighteenth century, elements of British criticism, French encyclopedism and German philosophy combined, in varying quantities, to make up the three main 'sources and component parts' of these two discourses.[1] Refracted back through the prisms of national context, during the nineteenth century, these discourses recombined, to produce something approaching national images of thought about art. At the outset of the 21st century, though, only the shadows of those images remain, in the main, as animating vehicles for the classification and marketing of individual works and collective 'heritage' alike. The traditions themselves – at least, the living ones – are increasingly visibly post-national in their constituent elements: nationally post-national, one might say – as everything around us.

In this book, we have brought together three sets of essays about art and politics from debates with their homes in three different European states: France, Italy and Germany (Parts I–III, respectively). The distinctiveness of each set derives not from any singular national intellectual tradition – however broadly defined – but from its nationally specific articulation of transnational discourses: internationally circulating discourses received and transformed into 'culture' as part of the histories of particular states.[2] And in the cases presented here, they are not just 'part of' the cultural histories of these states, but situated 'in and against' – as well as between – them. For these are politically oppositional or 'alternative' streams of thought, in line with the received, classically modern function of art and aesthetic as *critical* discourses and practices of one kind or another. Different kinds of critical discourse have different relations to politics. The three sets of essays in this book offer snapshots of three different, (post-)national articulations of the relations between philosophy, art and politics; and their different temporal rhythms.

Something similar to the relational logic of this trans- and thereby de-nationalising, postnational situation may be applied to the illusory self-sufficiency of philosophical discourse, within which the relationship between art and politics has been thought in the mainstream of the European tradition, as part of the philosophical discourse of modernity. In thinking the relationship between art and politics, philosophy necessarily opens itself up to a living 'outside', however hard it tries to cover this over with a blanket of conceptual appropriation. The de-nationalising effect of a certain transnationalisation of intellectual traditions is mirrored here in the disruptive effect upon philosophical discourse of a certain 'transdisciplinarisation'. In all three cases, the philosophical discourse of modernity is subject to a demand for the transdisciplinary intensification of the relationships between life and thought. However, such a demand cannot be reduced to the projection of a new vitalism. Rather, it points towards a new, post-Romantic redefinition of 'the critical' itself. This is the common ground of our three uncommon cases of writing about 'art and politics' in France, Italy and Germany, today.[3]

France

A post-Romantic redefinition of the critical requires recovering for criticism those political energies displaced into 'aesthetics' at the outset of modern philosophy, in the immediately aftermath of Immanuel Kant's thought. Indeed, a case can be made that in its immediate post-Kantian formation 'aesthetics' simply *is* the name for the displacement of political desire into a philosophical discourse about the structure of production of feelings through form. Such form, or formative force *(Bildende Kraft)*, is associated with a *vis poetica* that determines a new organic form for everyone.[4] That this is a displacement, rather than an expansion or an overflow, has traditionally been attributed to the political 'under-development' of Germany in the eighteenth century, and what was effectively a kind of censorship of politics by history.

Famously, in the analysis of the young Karl Marx, the proximity of the historical underdevelopment of Germany to the political modernity of France had as its cultural consequence the compensatory hypertrophy of German philosophy.[5] Aesthetics, in its proto-Romantic determination, was at once an internal reaction against, and a medium for the reflective continuation of, this hypertrophy of ideas. As an attempt to bridge the gap between ideality and the actual, it was simultaneously a representative of the will to politics within idealist philosophy, and of idealist philosophy within discourse on the arts. It thereby became the representative of the displaced presence of the desire for politics within the arts themselves. This 'German' ideology projected the sublime, or sublimity, into a 'perfect beauty', manifesting the *Bildenden Künste* (formative or 'plastic' arts) as the *Ineinsbildung* (imagistic unity) of the infinite in the finite.

But what of that displacement of politics which *is* aesthetics in France? For Marx, France was the geopolitical signifier of modernity: democratic revolution. Yet, in the course of the nineteenth century, the failure of revolution became the functional correlate in French culture of political underdevelopment in Germany. Thus was the ground laid in France too for the establishment of the problematic of aesthetics as the displacement of a 'failed' political desire. Its result, the intensification of aesthetics into aestheticism, usurped the cultural space of post-revolutionary classicism, while providing a new terrain on which to reformulate old problems. That what Jacques Rancière thinks of as the transition from a representational to an aesthetic 'regime of art' (from Aristotelian poetics to Kantian aesthetics) might be argued to have taken place, emblematically, in France itself (Charles Baudelaire) some eighty years after Germany (Gotthold Ephraim Lessing) goes some way towards accounting for what appears from the outside as a residual classicism in French philosophical aesthetics. Rancière himself affirms this modern classicism, via Friedrich Schiller, as an alternative to both the catastrophism of François Lyotard's post-holocaust sublime and Gilles Deleuze and Félix Guattari's post '68 'molecular revolution'.[6] In fact, one might say that a kind of superior poetics is engaged, and largely assumed, by Georges Didi-Huberman in his post-phenomenological critique of art history and by Rancière in his critique of the philosophy of art – the two disciplines with which contemporary French aesthetics is in permanent critical dialogue, through its reconfigurations of the aesthetic image in relation to the image of thought. A set of such reconfigurations make up Part I, below.

In the anglophone context, *post*-aesthetic uses of semiotics, psychoanalysis and cultural theory have dominated discourse on contemporary art since the 1970s. In France, however, it is the *image* that remains the central articulating concept of aesthetics, art history, art criticism and philosophy of art. The philosophical question of the relationship between image and word (*forme du visible* versus *forme de l'énonçable*) continues to delineate the parameters of debate. And with regard to contemporary art, discussion thus focuses on the *aesthetic image*, the image in its aesthetic determination as (conceptually) *under*determined, a disarticulation or undoing of meanings.

Ultimately, this is as true of Nicolas Bourriaud's 'relational aesthetics' (and more recently, his 'altermodernity') as it is of Rancière's 'pensive image' or Didi-Huberman's 'symptom-image'.

But do some contemporary artworks *undo* or *remake* the aesthetic image itself? Is the conception of art as a political redistribution of the sensible constrained by or liberated from the aesthetic? What is the effect of photography and film on the indetermination of the image? Can the aesthetic image escape the symbolic determinations of sex? Can the aesthetic image distinguish itself from or within the spectacle of capital-become-image? And might an *art of forces* actively engaged with semiotics disengage itself from the very notions of image and form? These are the main questions that animate the essays in the first, 'French' part of this collection.

Italy

Our second, 'Italian', section is about 'Art and Immaterial Labour'. The conjunction is at once innocent and presumptuous. If, as Theodor Adorno once suggested, the general problem with using the word 'and' in titles is that it 'permits everything to be connected with everything else and is thus incapable of hitting the mark', nevertheless, as he also acknowledged, there are rare occasions on which its 'banality' exhibits a strange 'cunning' and carries with it an essential rightness. 'Art' and 'immaterial labour' seem to belong together today – indeed, to be on the cusp of turning into each other – even if it is unclear quite why. 'Good titles', Adorno argued, 'are so close to the work that they respect its hiddenness.' In such cases, 'the colourless word "and" sucks up the meaning [of the conjunction] into itself' when it 'would have turned to dust if it had been conceptualised'. Yet, conceptualise it here we must, at least in a provisional manner.[7]

The 'rightness' of the belonging together of 'art' and 'immaterial' both belies and reinforces the opacity of their conjunction. In fact, the identification of art with immaterial labour has become so strong in certain quarters that it is not so much affirmed by the statement of their connection as problematised by it, thrown into doubt. When placed against the background of a presumed identity, the 'and' functions to separate the two terms, to assert their difference. This presumed identity derives, on the one hand, from the recent history of art – or at least a particular canonical (mis)description of it – and, on the other, from a certain promiscuousness inherent within the concept of immaterial labour itself.

In 1973, in her book *Six Years: The Dematerialization of the Art Object*, the US art critic Lucy Lippard famously declared the years from 1966 to 1972 to have been the years of the 'dematerialization of the art object', by virtue of the primacy of 'so-called conceptual art or information or idea art'.[8] In 1992, the Italian philosopher and 'autonomist' political activist Antonio Negri published 'Lavoro immateriale e soggettività' ('Immaterial Labour and Subjectivity'), with Maurizio Lazzarato, in the Italian journal *Deriveapprodi*. It extended Marx's concept of productive labour into unwaged activities, through the notion of the 'informational', cultural and intellectual content of commodities.[9] Thus, one might say, after twenty years, post-Marxist economics caught up with contemporary art. However, things are not quite as simple as this picture suggests.

According to these two narratives, conceptual art 'dematerialised' the *object* (specifically, the *art* object), while information technology made *labour* 'immaterial'. There is a disjunction here between object and act, which restages the classical modern philosophical antinomy of the subject: the subject can only know itself as an object, yet as such, it fails to know itself as that which knows, since it knows not as an object, but only in and as an act. This disjunction makes the identification of art and immaterial labour appear differently depending on one's starting point. From the standpoint of the thesis of the 'dematerialised' art object (or at least, the dematerialisation of its artistic significance), it is the immateriality of the new forms of labour that establishes the connection with art, tracking the dematerialisation of the object back to the immateriality of its source. The notion of thinking as a form of art labour is clearly expressed in, for example, Sol LeWitt's 1969 'Sentences on Conceptual Art'. From the standpoint of immaterial labour, on the other hand, this 'immateriality' is generalised beyond the 'economy' to *all* spheres of life, art included. There is little specificity to art labour from this standpoint. Indeed, at times, it appears as a model for the new concept of labour itself.

It is not clear that these art-critical and political-economic problematics are compatible, or indeed that each is individually coherent. Hence the transformative potential of their crossing, at the point of a subversive reflection on the purported becoming-labour of art and becoming-art of labour – a point at which each risks, retrospectively, 'turning to dust'.

However, reflecting the Italian context of our contributors, it should be noted that the topic of Part II is not '*Conceptual* Art and Immaterial Labour', but more simply 'Art and Immaterial Labour'. The debates that accompanied the 'dematerialisation' of art thesis (whereby New York followed up its 'theft' of the idea of modern art in the 1950s, with claims on the ownership of 'conceptual art' in the 1960s)[10] have largely remained confined to the Anglo-American artworld, where the question of the relations between an art 'after philosophy' and an art 'after Conceptual Art' continues to set the terms of critical debate.[11] In the context of 'post-autonomist' Italian politics since the 1980s, on the other hand, it has been the idea that new, 'immaterial' forms of labour involve new *modes of production of subjectivity* that has driven the debate. Despite the connection to new communications technologies, the connection of 'immaterial labour' to art is thus, philosophically, at base an 'aesthetic' one, insofar as the production of a new kind of subjectivity is precisely the function conventionally claimed for the aesthetic in the aftermath of Kant's work.[12] Yet this suppressed Kantian aspect to the Italian problematic reflects the influence of the post-structuralist French thought of the 1980s, rather than German idealism or Romanticism directly. A Deleuzo-Guattarian problematic, with Foucauldian leanings, provides much of the philosophical framework for recent Italian left-political thought. This Franco-Italian philosophical-political exchange, staged in the French journals *Futur Antérieur*

(1990–8) and its successor, *Multitudes*, in its early years (2000–9), has been a complex one. It poses very different questions for aesthetics to the ones raised by the so-called 'dematerialisation of art' thesis.

In the Franco-Italian left-political and philosophical debates since the 1980s, a plurality of positions on a new 'immaterial' and 'biopolitical' constitution of labour and life, respectively – in 'societies of control' (Deleuze), of 'security' (Foucault), or in the 'Empire' of cognitive capitalism (Michael Hardt and Negri) – are associated with a plurality of political calls for 'new aesthetic paradigms'. Here, everything begins with Deleuze and Guattari's 1972 *Anti-Oedipus*. In his Preface to that book, Foucault suggested that it should be approached as an 'art' of living and thinking, rather than as a 'philosophy'. As such, according to Foucault, it articulates the reality-conditions of May '68 at their most disruptive by 'using political practice as an intensifier of thought', to unfetter selves from the negative, in order to invest the transformative force of desire's connections in a reality that is no longer dissociable from it, and its 'machines' of production and anti-production.[13]

However, the Italians would not have been able to invest in these new 'becomings' without investigating and investing the mutations of contemporary capitalism from within, in order to elaborate a new social constructivism. Such an investigation and an investment renewed the link between 'theory' and 'practice' through the study of new forms of labour and new types of struggle in all domains of life. In Italy, the aftermath of May '68 was prolonged and intensified for ten years, culminating in the '77 Movement, through which the Italian *Autonomia* produced their own Copernican revolution: a 'Marx Beyond Marx'.[14] 'Marx beyond Marx' effectively meant leaving the socialist and post-socialist critique of capitalist valorisation for the communist affirmation of a 'self-valorisation' that could no longer be ascribed to the 'worker' as such – think of the movements of *emarginati,* women and students; of a *fully* socialised worker. Capital appeared now as an 'apparatus of capture' of the creative potential of life, proceeding by means of a 'machinic enslavement' of the 'processes of subjectivation' that it puts to work. 'Apparatus of capture', 'machinic enslavement', 'processes of subjectivation' – these are the key locutions in the emphatically Franco-Italian pages of Deleuze and Guattari's *A Thousand Plateaus* (1980), which swarm with direct and indirect references to the writings of Mario Tronti, Negri and Franco 'Bifo' Berardi.[15]

It is surely a curious 'Marxism' that overturns the capital–labour dialectic by opposing to the self-valorisation of capital the self-valorisation of social forces. Yet this is a Marxism to which Deleuze nonetheless laid claim, while Guattari ended up 'deterritorialising' the Marxian reference so absolutely in his 'permanent molecular revolution' (a collection of his articles entitled *La Révolution moléculaire* appeared in 1977) that it vanished completely as a literal reference. But can an analysis of what Guattari called 'Integrated World Capitalism' really do without a 'beyond Marx'? In any case, the notion of labour comes out utterly transformed, extending in two directions: 'intensive surplus labour *that no longer even takes the route of labour*, and extensive labour that has become *precarious and floating*'.[16]

The convergences and differences between the essays in Part II carry with them the political, as well as the theoretical, stakes of the movement from which they depart. What is spoken of today in terms of 'immaterial' labour entails a relation to art that aims to problematise the modern-romantic aesthetic notions on the basis of which, for so long now, not politics itself but 'the political' has been defined. Needless to say, this does not mean speaking of aesthetics as a surrogate politics, but rather of a new political problematisation of the concept of aesthetics, beyond the received conception of art-form.[17]

Germany

Not just a political problematisation of aesthetics, but its *direct politicisation* was, of course, the project of the 'historical' avant-gardes of the 1920s and 1930s: Dada, Surrealism, Futurism, and Soviet constructivism and Productivism, in particular.[18] Debates about avant-gardes, and the theory of avant-garde, sprang into life in the 1970s in response to both the New Left politics of the day and the recovery of the left traditions of the interwar years (1918–39) that it instigated – especially in West Germany, where the whole question of 'the past' had been subjected to a profound political amnesia during the Adenauer years (1949–63), which followed the Allied military occupation.[19] Recently, these debates have come back to life once again, after a period of some two decades during which many had consigned them to the dustbin of history – along with history itself, paradoxically.[20] The 'perpetual present' of postmodernism did not last long. With a turn in art-critical writing from the 'postmodern' to 'the contemporary', the question of the present has acquired a novel historical complexity and urgency, within which the question of avant-gardes has been reopened on a new social and geo-political basis.

Our third, 'German', set of essays, on 'Art, War, Avant-Garde', positions art within the social, understood as a field of both psychic and political conflict – of war, terror, struggle, taboo, repression, iconoclasm and repetition. This field is viewed, at once, from the 'utopian' egalitarian standpoint of the historical avant-garde and with a certain, psychoanalytically informed, nihilistic disillusion. Here, reflection on the history of avant-gardes through the prism of twentieth-century German history remains the route to an understanding of the present. However, the theoretical terms of these reflections are the result of a more complicated set of exchanges: on the one hand, between German and French philosophy, and on the other, between philosophy and 'media'. The 'transdisciplinarisation' of philosophy to which we referred at the outset, which accompanies the transnationalisation of national 'traditions', is manifest here in the innovative forms of a post-Frankfurtian critical theory.

In the anglophone context of the last thirty years, the phrase 'critical theory' has been used in two quite different ways. On the one hand, it refers to the project of the Frankfurt School, in its various formulations, over a fifty-year period from the early 1930s (the early Max Horkheimer) through to 'middle period' Jürgen Habermas in the 1980s. On the other hand it has come to denote a far broader but nonetheless discrete tradition, with its roots in Marx, Friedrich Nietzsche, Sigmund Freud and Ferdinand de Saussure, and its primary manifestations in France in the period from the late 1950s to the end of the 1990s. Roland Barthes, Jacques Lacan, Louis Althusser, Michel Foucault, Jacques Derrida and François Lyotard appear as its main representatives here. In the first case, the phrase is both self-designating and the object of explicit theoretical reflection. In the latter case, however, it was the result of the reception of a theoretically heterogeneous body of work into the literary departments of the Anglo-American academy, where 'criticism' was an established professional activity. Consequently, while the conceptual emphasis in the reception of the Frankfurt School has been on criticism or critique (*Kritik*) – the main opposition being between 'Traditional and Critical Theory' (the title of Horkheimer's famous essay from 1937) – the emphasis in the reception of the French tradition was placed heavily on 'theory', the main opposition being between theoretical and a- or anti-theoretical (historically, *aesthetic*) interpretative practices. Yet 'theory', here, is not a name for an alien philosophy (in the way in which 'critical theory' was initially an alias for a certain philosophical reception of Marxism) but a purportedly *post*-philosophical pursuit, occupying the place, but not the mode, of what Heidegger referred to – in opposition to the metaphysical thought of philosophy – simply as 'thinking'. This theory functioned in a transdisciplinary manner, although it did not theorise itself as such.[21]

What these two bodies of thought share is a suspicion of the self-sufficiency of philosophy, an orientation towards inter-and transdisciplinarity, an openness to the general text of writing, and a critical attitude towards the institutions of Western capitalist societies. Where they differ is in their relations to the philosophies of Hegel and Heidegger. The former, Frankfurt variant is self-consciously post-Hegelian and anti-Heideggerian, while the latter Parisian one is insistently anti-Hegelian and generically post-Heideggerian. As Jean-Luc Nancy put it at the end of the 1980s: '"French" thought today proceeds in part from a "German" rupture with a certain philosophical "France" (which is also a rupture with a certain "Germanity").'[22] It was this displaced Germanicism of French thought that was the object of attack in Habermas's polemic, *The Philosophical Discourse of Modernity* (1985) – a book that appeared in the wake of the extraordinary success in Germany of Peter Sloterdijk's *Critique of Cynical Reason* (1983), an importation of French Nietzscheanism back into the German context, which in certain respects prepared the ground for the reception of Deleuze's thought in Germany.

The philosophically 'Germanic' character of much French theory is well established. Less attention has been paid to the influence of French thought – including that which proceeds from 'a German rupture with a certain philosophical France' – on the German critical tradition. Yet some of the most productive developments within the orbit of Frankfurt critical theory have been driven by a reflective intensity in the relationship to intellectual and artistic events in France. This is true not only of Walter Benjamin in the 1930s, but also of aspects of early Horkheimer and Adorno's thought of the 1940s. More recently, there is a 'post-Frankfurtian' German thought of the

1980s, 1990s and beyond that has been profoundly influenced by currents of French theory of the 1960s and 1970s: French Nietzscheanism, structuralism, Barthes, Foucault, situationism, Deleuze/Guattari and Jean Baudrillard. This problematises the nationalism of German philosophy in a quite different way from Habermas's personal identification with American pragmatism (his philosophical Marshall Plan) and his concern to reformulate normative issues within the terms of post-analytical philosophy. It is notable that these currents have all been concerned in some way with an aesthetic reactivation of political action; and that they have been able to flow more freely, in Germany, in art schools and institutes of media studies than in philosophy departments.

The 'German' essays in Part III are all marked by different aspects of the French thought of the 1960s: *vitalism, structuralism* and *deconstruction*, in Sloterdijk, Peter Weibel and Boris Groys, respectively. And the medium for their reception of these currents has been a distinctive variant of German media philosophy, nurtured in the art school and media institute in Karlsruhe.

German media philosophy is not a philosophy 'of' media, but a redefinition of contemporary philosophy from the standpoint of a new concept of media. This involves a de-definition of the conventional conception of media, as a sociological and communicational concept, and its reinvention via the treatment of power relations as 'the medium of the media'. This redefinition transforms the study of 'media' into a series of transdisciplinary aesthetics operations.[23] It is the distinctive contribution of what we are tempted to call the 'Karlsruhe' (as opposed to the Weimar) School of German media philosophy to have added a further twist to this theoretical operation: a problematisation of aesthetics that is at once technological, historical and political. It has thereby enacted something like a corresponding *'de-definition' of aesthetics*, from the standpoint of political action.[24] It is the connection of the aesthetic back to political action that raises the heritage of the historical avant-gardes within this (post)media philosophy, and also, with it, fascism: the spectre of the transformation of the political de-definition of aesthetics into a meta-aesthetic redefinition of politics itself.[25] Each of the thinkers in Part III refuses to confine the artistic and political logics of the historical avant-gardes to the interwar years; and while concerned with its aesthetics aspects and psychic investments, refuses to reduce politics to aesthetics. Rather, all three find the logic of the historical avant-gardes, transformed and reactivated within the present, in radically different spheres and modes of action.

1 Cf. V. I. Lenin, 'The Three Sources and Three Component Parts of Marxism' (1913), in *Collected Works*, vol.19, Progress Publishers, Moscow 1972, pp.23–8. The deeper history of the relationship between the two discourses runs back to the Italian Renaissance, during which the science of optics gave new intellectual life and prestige to the ancient discourse of aisthesis and medieval classifications of the system of the arts were revised to the advantage of painting.

2 See David Lloyd and Paul Thomas, *Culture & the State*, Routledge, New York & London, 1998.

3 For more about the transdisciplinarity of those philosophical discourses that have engaged with problems of art and politics since the 1960s, see the website of the AHRC research project 'Transdisciplinarity in the Humanities' (2011–2013), which we are working on in the Centre for Research in Modern European Philosophy (CRMEP) at Kingston: http://fass.kingston.ac.uk/research/crmep/projects/transdisciplinarity.

4 Friedrich Schlegel, 'Atheneum Fragments', in *Philosophical Fragments*, trans. Peter Firchow, University of Minnesota Press, Minneapolis 1991, fragment no.338, p.69.

5 Karl Marx, 'Contribution to the Critique of Hegel's Philosophy of Law: Introduction' (1843–44), in Karl Marx and Frederick Engels, *Collected Works*, vol.3, Lawrence and Wishart London 1975, pp.175–87.

6 Jacques Rancière, 'The Sublime From Lyotard to Schiller: Two Readings of Kant and their Political Significance', *Radical Philosophy*, no.126, July/August 2004, pp.8–15; and 'Deleuze, Bartleby and the Literary Formula', in Jacques Rancière, *The Flesh of Words: The Politics of Writing*, Stanford University Press 2004, Ch.2.

7 Theodor W. Adorno, 'Titles' (1962), in *Notes to Literature*, vol.2, trans. Shierry Nicholsen Weber, Columbia University Press, New York 1992, pp.3–11; quoted here, pp.4–5. There is an interesting resonance with Adorno's brief analysis of the 'and' in Deleuze's remarks on the 'and' in his 1976 interview 'Three Questions on Six Times Two', in Gilles Deleuze, *Negotiations, 1972–1990*, trans. Martin Joughlin, Columbia University Press, New York 1995, pp.37–45 – a discussion that reprises his earlier thoughts on conjunction and disjunction, developed in the courses of an elaboration of the 'serialism' of structuralism. See Gilles Deleuze, *The Logic of Sense* (1969), trans. Mark Lester with Charles Stivale, Columbia University Press, New York 1990. Intriguingly, the 'and' is at the heart of some debates central to contemporary European philosophy.

8 Lucy Lippard, *Six Years: The Dematerialization of the Art Object from 1966 to 1972* (1972), California University Press, Berkeley 1997. Lippard had previously expounded the thesis in a more restricted context, in Lucy Lippard and John Chandler, 'The Dematerialization of Art', *Art International*, February 1968.

9 Antonio Negri and Maurizio Lazzarato, 'Lavoro immateriale e soggettività', *Deriveapprodi*, No.0, 1992. The most commonly used source for the notion is a later essay by Lazzarato: Maurizio Lazzarato, 'Immaterial Labour' (1996), trans. Paul Colilli and Ed Emory, in Paolo Virno and Michael Hardt (eds.), *Radical Thought in Italy: A Potential Politics*, University of Minnesota Press, Minneapolis 1983, pp.133–46.

10 See Serge Guilbaut, *How New York Stole the Idea of Modern Art*, trans. Arthur Goldhammer, University of Chicago Press, Chicago 1985; Peter Osborne, 'Survey', in Peter Osborne (ed.), *Conceptual Art*, Phaidon, London 2002.

11 Joseph Kosuth, *Art After Philosophy and After: Collected Writings, 1966–1990*, MIT Press, Cambridge MA 1991; Alexander Alberro and Sabeth Buchmann (eds.), *Art After Conceptual Art*, MIT Press/Generali Foundation, Cambridge MA/Vienna, 2006.

12 See Gilles Deleuze, *Kant's Critical Philosophy: The Doctrine of the Faculties* (1963), trans. Hugh Tomlinson and Barbara Habberjam, University of Minnesota Press, Minneaoplis 1984, Ch.3.

13 Michel Foucault, 'Preface', in Gilles Deleuze and Félix Guattari, *Anti-Oedipus: Capitalism and Schizophrenia* (1972), trans. Robert Hurley et al, University of Minnesota Press, Minneapolis 1983, pp.xii, xiv.

14 See Antonio Negri, *Marx Beyond Marx: Lessons on the Grundrisse* (1979), trans. Harry Cleaver et al, Autonomedia/Pluto, New York/London 1991.

15 Gilles Deleuze and Félix Guattari, *A Thousand Plateaus: Capitalism and Schizophrenia*, trans. Brian Massumi, University of Minnesota Press, Minneapolis 1987.

16 Ibid., p.518, translation modified.

17 See Félix Guattari, *Chaosmosis: An Ethico-Aesthetic Pardigm* (1992), Indiana University Press, Bloomington 1995.

18 This classificatory terminology of the 'historical' avant-garde, understood to have attacked aristic autonomy (as opposed to the 'neo-avant-garde' of the postwar years, which was internal to an autonomous art) is that of the German literary and art historian and theorist, Peter Bürger. See Peter Bürger, *Theory of the Avant-Garde* (1974; 1980), trans. Michael Shaw, University of Minnesota Press, Minneapolis 1984. Despite the influence of Walter Benjamin (whose 1929 essay on Surrealism was influenced by his trip in Moscow in 1926–7), Bürger himself focuses on Dada and Surrealism to the neglect of the distinctiveness and, arguably, the deeper historical importance of the Soviet avant-gardes.

19 See Adorno, 'The Meaning of Working Through the Past' (1960), in Theodor W. Adorno, *Can One Live After Auschwitz? A Philosophical Reader*, ed., Rolf Tiedemann, Stanford University Press, Stanford 1993, Ch.1.

20 Francis Fukuyama, *The End of History and the Last Man*, Penguin, Harmondsworth 1992 (based on an essay first published in 1989); Lutz Niethhammer, *Posthistoire: Has History Come to an End?* (1989), trans. Patrick Camiller, Verso, London and New York 1992.

21 This paragraph draws on Peter Osborne, 'Philosophy After Theory: Transdisciplinarity and the New', in Jane Elliott and Derek Attridge (eds.), *Theory After 'Theory'*, Routledge, London and New York 2011, pp.19–33, p.25.

22 Jean-Luc Nancy, 'Introduction', in Jean-Luc Nancy et al (eds.), *Who Comes After the Subject?*, Routledge, New York and London 1991, p.3.

23 For a sample of recent German media philosophy, see the Dossier, 'What is German Media Philosophy?', *Radical Philosophy*, no.169, July/August 2011, pp.7–16 – the record of an event at The Institute of Contemporary Arts, London, in May 2011, organised by the editors of this volume. Two of the contributors to this dossier, Lorenz Engel and Bernhard Siegert, are co-directors of the Internationale Kolleg für Kulturtechnikforschung und Medienphilosophie (IKKM), in Weimar.

24 Boris Groys, currently at New York University, was previously Professor of Philosophy and Art Theory at the School of Fine Arts in Karlsruhe (1994–2007), of which Peter Sloterdijk is the Rector. Peter Weibel has been the Director of the Center for Art and Media Technology (ZKM) in Karlsruhe since 1999. During 2003–4, Groys directed the research programme, *The Post-Communist Condition*, in cooperation with ZKM.

25 The idea of fascism as an 'aestheticisation of politics', whereby humankind has reached the point at which 'it can experience its own annihilation as a supreme aesthetic pleasure', derives from Walter Benjamin. Walter Benjamin, 'The Work of Art in the Age of its Technological Reproducibility. Second Version' (1935–6), in *Selected Writings, Volume 3, 1935–1938*, trans. Edmund Jephcott et al, Harvard University Press, Cambridge MA and London 2002, p.122.

The Aesthetic Image

1
Notes on the Photographic Image
Jacques Rancière

In the relation between art and image, photography has played a symptomatic and often paradoxical role. Baudelaire made of it the sinister instrument of the triumph of technical reproduction over artistic imagination. And yet we also know of the long struggle of photographers (*pictorialistes*) to affirm that photography was not merely mechanical reproduction, but rather an interpretation of the world. But scarcely had they won their battle to endow the technical medium of photography with the status of artistic medium, when Benjamin turned the game on its head. He made mechanical reproduction the principle of a new paradigm of art: the productions of the mechanical arts were for him the means towards a new sensible education, the instruments of the formation of a new class of experts in art, namely in the art of interpreting signs and documents. Cinema was a series of tests of our world. Atget's photos were indices to interpret; Sander's collections were notebooks for teaching combatants in the social struggle to readily identify allies and adversaries. The photographic medium participated in the construction of a sensible world where men of the age of the masses could affirm their existence as both possible subjects of art and experts in its use.

It seems, nevertheless, that the destiny of the art of photography has no more confirmed Benjamin's diagnostic than that of Baudelaire. To support this claim, we can point to two phenomena more or less contemporary to one another that concern both photography and its interpretation. On the one hand, the 1980s saw photography invade art museums and exhibitions, taking on the dimensions of monumental paintings. These large-format photographs, amidst the proliferation of installations and video installations, assure, in a certain sense, the continuity of the pictorial surface. But, at the same time, what they present to us on this surface seems to turn its back on the forms of the pictorial revolutions of the twentieth century. Without even speaking of extreme examples like Jeff Wall's revival of the historical tableau, we can think of the multiplication of portraits and the new status of the portrait, illustrated by, for example, photographer Rineke Dijkstra's monumental por-

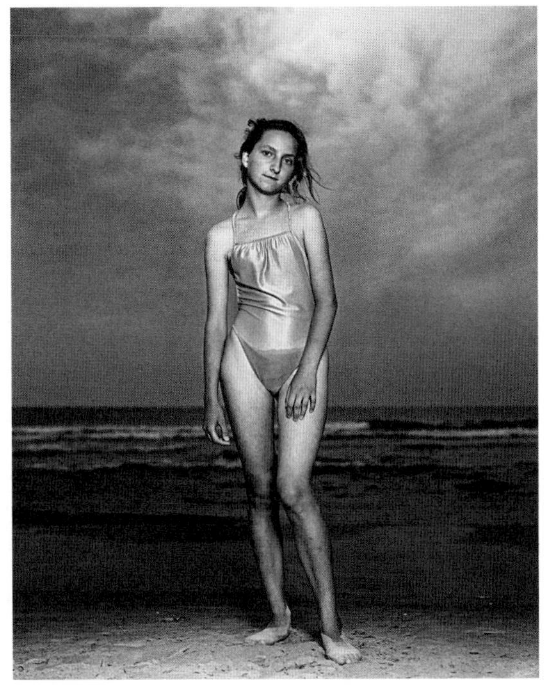

Rineke Dijkstra
Kolobrzeg, Poland, July 26 1992, 1992

traits of otherwise indifferent individuals, represented without any particular aura: slightly awkward-looking adolescents onworking-class beaches, young mothers still burdened by their babies, or apprentice toreadors, whose red-faced figures clash with the bullfighter's traditional suit of lights. On the one hand, these full-length portraits present themselves as documents on social types or age groups undergoing transformation. On the other, the absence of expression, combined with the formalism of the pose and the size of the image, gives these indifferent figures something mysterious: something that for us also inhabits the portraits of Florentine and Venetian nobility which populate the museums. The teenager in the green swimsuit photographed on a Polish beach, with her slender body, her swaying hips, and her unfurled hair (above) is like an awkward replica of Botticelli's Venus. Photography is thus not content to occupy the place of painting. It presents itself as the rediscovered union between two statuses of the image that the modernist tradition had separated: the image as representation of an individual and as operation of art.

How should we think this new coincidence and tension between the grand pictorial form and simply the images of indifferent individuals? The interpretation seems, at first sight, split between two extremes: at the one end, an exacerbation of the sensible presence of the photographed subject, in its provocative power with respect to modernist logic; at the other, an integration of this photographic realism – or hyperrealism – into the modernist scheme. In the first instance, we think of course of Barthes and *Camera Lucida*, the absolute reference for thought on photography in the 1980s. Barthes's manoeuvre was to break the representation of the indifferent in two. The indifferent is, on the one hand, that which is identifiable by the intersection of a certain number of general traits. On the other, it is the absolute singularity of that which imposes its brute presence, and affects by this brute presence. We recognise here the principle of the opposition between the *studium*, conceived as the informative content of the photograph, and the *punctum*, conceived as its affective force, irreducible to transmission of knowledge. This affective force is the transfer of an absolute singularity, that of the represented subject, to another absolute singularity, that of the viewing subject. It is easy to underline the double paradox of this theorisation in light of the ulterior evolution of photography. It privileges a vision of photographic reproduction where it is the *having-been* of the body that comes to imprint itself on the sensitive plate, and from there touches us without mediation. This raising of the stakes concerning the indexical conception of photography was immediately countered by the digital invasion. At the moment when large-format photography is about to overrun the museum walls and affirm itself as a visual art, it transforms the photographic gaze into the gaze of an individual who pages through albums. But this historical contretemps refers us back to a more fundamental torsion concerning the relation between photography, art and modernism. In a certain manner, Barthes contorts the formalist modernist, who opposed the form (artistic/pictorial) to the anecdote (empiricist/photographic). Barthes diverts the opposition by transferring the anecdote to the *studium*, in order to pit it against not the artistic form, but an experience of the unique that refutes the pretension to art as well as the platitude of information. However, this opposition between art and photography is perhaps more profoundly the leave given to another modernity, to which Benjamin's essay bore witness, and that inscribed photography among the instruments of a new social sensibility and a new social consciousness (three elements and not two). It is from this point of view that it seems useful to me to examine more closely the examples through which Barthes operates the opposition between *studium* and *punctum*. Let us take, for example, Lewis Hine's photograph of the two disabled children (below).

Photograph by Lewis Hine, c.1920

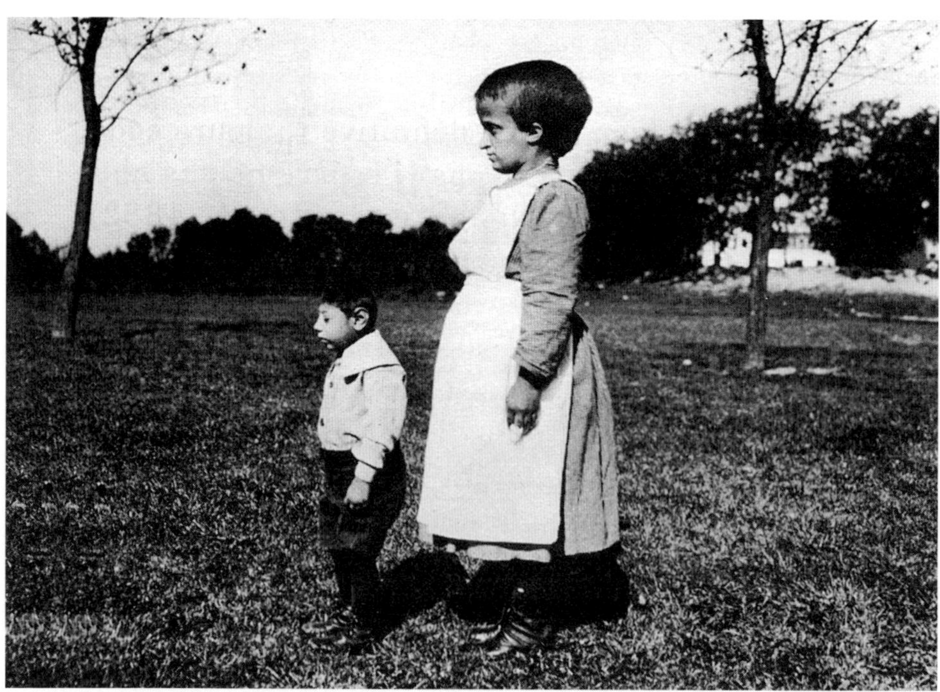

Barthes tells us not to look at the monstrous heads or the pitiful profiles that signify the disability. Instead, he opposes to these the force of fascination that is exerted on him by the details without signification: the boy's Danton collar, the bandage on the little girl's finger.[1] But the *punctum* thus marked, in fact, obeys the same formal logic as the repudiated *studium*. It concerns, in both cases, features of disproportion. The privilege of the *punctum* here is simply to privatise this formal effect. We can read this analysis as the exact reversal of the critical logic previously put to work by the Barthes of *Mythologies*. What was at stake for him there, in a Brechtian logic, was to make visible the social hidden in the intimate, the history dissimulated as the appearance of nature. From this point of view, the very choice of the photograph is significant. The photo of the two disabled children appears as a *hapax* (ἅπαξ λεγόμενον '[something] said only once') in the career of a photographer who devoted numerous series to the representation of work and the campaign against child labour. The 'stupidity' of the detail drawn from the irreducible hardship and misfortune of the two disabled children can be read like a screen placed before other photos of children: that of the Polish child, 'Willie', working in a mill in Rhode Island, or Francis Lance, the five-year-old newspaper 'salesman'. Yet, these 'documentary' photographs are the bearers of a tension between visuality and signification that is perhaps more interesting than the image of the two disabled children. They are in effect made for the purpose of denouncing the scandal of child labour. Yet, Willie's attitude, as he sits nonchalantly (taking his midday rest) in a doffer-box, or Francis Lance's, proudly standing his ground on a train platform with his newspapers tucked under his arm, do not testify to any suffering. What strikes us is precisely the opposite: it is the selfsame ease with which they show themselves capable of both adapting to their work and posing for the camera, thus obliging Lewis Hine to insist, in his commentary, on the dangers of their work, which they themselves seem so unconcerned about.

Impoverished ontology

The activity of the commentator seems to respond, in advance, to the 'Benjaminian' demand. It is, in particular, the relation between the child workers, the camera, the photo and the text that follows this logic, linking the appreciation of the photographic performance to new forms of 'expertise' and to the experimentation of a new sensible world. The Danton collar suffices to silently settle the accounts with this logic. The only sensible world that the photo witnesses is the relation of the absolute singularity of the spectacle to the absolute singularity of the gaze. Much the same can be said about Avedon's photograph of the old slave.[2] Here the procedure is reversed: no detail distracts from a socio-political reading. On the contrary, the mask of the photographed subject speaks of nothing else than the condition of slavery. But the effect is the same: it is slavery in person, as a historical singularity, that offers itself entirely in the singularity of a single face. To declare slavery to be present in person, in front of our eyes, between our hands, is, in fact, to diminish the singularity of the other photographs that speak to us about what took place between the abolition of slavery and our present. For example, a John Vachon photo from his Farm Security Administration project (1936–43) shows us only a sign reading *Colored*, nailed high up on the trunk of a pine tree, next to which is the likely object of its discrimination: a simple drinking fountain. The multiplicity of racial discrimination's forms of sensible existence, and the multiple singularity of these photographs that vary, and thereby tell us of, the visual forms of the metaphor and of the metonymy, come to be crushed against this black mask that presents slavery in person. But this being of slavery identifies itself with its having-been. Avedon's photo represents the slavery that is no longer on the face of a man who, himself, is no longer, at the time when Barthes wrote his commentary. When all is said and done, the singularity of slavery written on a singular face is nothing other than the universality of the having-been; in other words, death.

It is to this singularity that the image of the two disabled children, which conceals those of the playing children of the factories, ultimately comes down. But this singularity of the image is itself determined by the power of words alone. Taking up again the two traits of the *punctum* of this photo, it is first of all the bandage on the finger of the little girl. The French word with which Barthes refers to the bandage is *poupée*. Yet the French reader who does not know this usage of the word immediately has another image. The ordinary sense of the word in French is 'doll'. And the identification of this poignant detail with the *poupée* inevitability evokes a whole series of images: from Hoffmann's automaton, commented on by Freud, to the dismembered dolls that are a part of the surrealist imaginary, and that contributed more than a little to the transformation of Winnicott's transitional object into Lacan's object *petit a*. In short, the effect attributed to the phraseless singularity of the detail is the power of a word. And this power of the word is further accentuated by the proper name that qualifies another poignant detail: the Danton collar. The French reader has no idea what a Danton collar might be. However, the name is immediately associated with that of a revolutionary who had his head sliced off by the guillotine. The *punctum* is nothing other than death foretold.

The analysis of the photo of the two mentally disabled children is therefore linked with that which Barthes devotes to Alexander Gardners's 1865 photo of a handcuffed young man. The photo is beautiful, Barthes tells us, and so is the young man, but that is the *studium*. The *punctum* is that 'he is going to die'.[3] Yet this death foretold is not visible in any of the features of the photograph. Its presumed effect rests on the combination of the brown colouring of the old photographs and the acquaintance with the individual represented, in this case Lewis Payne, condemned to death in 1865 for an attempted assassination of the then American secretary of state. But this affirmation of present death once again employs words to deny what constitutes the visual singularity of the photograph – that is, precisely that its present refuses any readings of the young man's history, of the past that led him there, and of the future that awaits him. The half-nonchalant, half-curious attitude of the young man says nothing about this history, much the same as Willie's relaxed pose said nothing about the hardships of factory work, and the gaze of the Polish teenager on the beach nothing about what reasons she might have had for exposing herself, nor her thoughts as she stands in front of the camera. What they speak to us of is only this capacity to expose one's body at the request of the camera, without, for all that, surrendering to it the thought and the feeling that inhabit it. This tension between exposition and retreat vanishes in the pure relation of the viewer with the death that comes to view him.

This disappearance is not only due to the fact that *Camera Lucida* is first of all a eulogy addressed to Barthes's dead mother. Behind the expression of personal grief, there is the expression of another grief, that of the gaze that endeavoured to tie the appreciation of the beauty of an image to that of the social reality that it expressed. Yet, his second grief also manifests itself in a type of reading which, contrary to Barthes, sees in the new modes of photographic exposition the reaffirmation of a certain idea of the objectivity of the photograph. It is this thesis that was defended in 1988 by a period-defining exhibition entitled 'Another Objectivity' (*Une autre objectivité*).[4] The accompanying text, by Jean-François Chevrier and James Lingwood, redefined, in its own way, the relation between two fundamental aspects of the modernist norm: on the one hand, the fidelity to the law of the medium; on the other, the fidelity to a certain type of exhibition surface, the *forme-tableau* in its formal separation from the multiple social uses of the image. The fact is that the law of the photographic medium does not offer itself up to a simple interpretation. We can liken it to the instrumental conception that makes the camera a means to furnish some objective information about what is in front of it. But, from this, we still have not defined the specificity of the art of photography. We can liken it to the reproducible character of the photographic image. But it is hardly possible to discern the specific quality of an image from the fact that it is reproducible. This is why the theoreticians of photographic objectivity displaced the idea of multiplication in favour of the idea of a multiple unity. Reproducibility thus becomes seriality.

Benjamin based his argumentation on the typologies of August Sander, while Chevrier and Lingwood favoured the works of Bernd and Hilla Becher. But the analogy is problematic. Benjamin expected that Sander's series would help the combatants in the social struggle to recognise allies and enemies. There is manifestly nothing of the sort to be expected from the Bechers' series of water towers or disused industrial sites. They would even fall easily within the scope of Brecht's critique, which was taken up by Benjamin: photos of factories say nothing about the social relations that manifest themselves there. The interest of the series can therefore no longer be looked for in what it enables us to say about social relations. It boils down to an ethical virtue accorded to the multiple as such, in that it rules out the prestige of the one and of the aura, of the unique moment and of the ecstatic contemplation. But this principle is purely negative. Its artistic 'positivity' must thus come from a second manner of thinking the 'objectivity' of the medium. This is summed up, for Chevrier and Lingwood, in the notion of the *forme-tableau*, exemplified by Jeff Wall's backlit photographs. But what relation should we think between these large scenes in the form of historical tableaux and the identical rectangles that make the Bechers' views of water towers and smokestacks resemble pedagogical charts? None, perhaps, if not the Greenbergian idea of the surface that encloses the artist's performance and prohibits him from leaving himself, from showing empathy for his subject or from considering himself as a form of social experimentation. In this sense, the Bechers' industrial sites are a manner of concluding the dream of the artist engineers and factory builders of Peter Behrens's era, in much the same way as Barthes's fascination with the Danton collar served to repress photographer Lewis Hine's engagement on the side of the oppressed and forgotten of the factories and hospices. The reference to the essence of the medium is again here a manner of settling accounts with the epoch where the medium was thought of as the organ of a new collective world. Simply put, this settling of accounts is more complex in the case of the Bechers and the theoreticians of 'objective photography', for whom the repression of the constructivist dream also wants to be the affirmation of a fidelity to the values linked to the industrial universe and the workers' struggle: the sobriety of the documentary gaze that refuses the humanist pathos, the formal principles of the frontal perspective, the uniform framing, and the presentation in series that links scientific objectivity and the disappearance of the subjectivity of the artist.

It remains the case: that which is given to see by the objectivist mindset is fundamentally an absence – disused edifices in the place of social classes and types. Yet, photographing absence can be interpreted in two ways: it can be a manner of showing the programmed departure of the industrial world and worker; but it is just as much a manner of playing on the aesthetic affect of the disused (*desaffecté*) that sends us back to the side of Barthes's 'having-been'. This tension in the objectivist idea of the medium is more perceptible still in the series of containers taken by a follower of the Bechers, Frank Breuer, presented during the 2005 Rencontres photographiques in Arles, in the transept of an ancient church, along with two other series, devoted to warehouses and to logos. From afar the spectator perceived them as abstract scenes or as reproductions of minimalist sculptures. Upon approaching, however, one discovered that the coloured rectangles on a white background were containers stacked in a large deserted space. The impact of the series was down to the tension between this minimalism and the signification that it concealed. These containers were to be, or were to have been, filled with merchandise unloaded at Antwerp or Rotterdam, and probably were produced in a distant country, perhaps by faceless workers in Southeast Asia. They were, in short, filled with their own absence, which was also that of every worker engaged to unload them, and, even more remotely, that of the European workers replaced by these distant labourers.

The 'objectivity' of the medium thus masks a determined aesthetic relation between opacity and transparency, between the containers as brute presence of pure coloured forms and the containers as representatives of the 'mystery' of the merchandise – that is to say, of the manner in which it absorbs human work and hides its mutations. It consists in the relation between presence and absence, in the double relation of a visible form to a signification and an absence of sense. Chevrier bases his argument on the idea of an 'impoverished ontology' of photography. On one level, this is to say that photography does not have the strong ontological consistency that would enable its artistic forms to be deduced from its materiality. But we can give this poverty a more positive signification. If photography is not under the law of a proper ontological consistency, linked to the specificity of its technical mechanism, it lends itself to accomplishing the ideas about art formed by the other arts. This capacity of the mechanical art to realise what other arts had tried to accomplish by their own means was developed at length by Eisenstein, in relation to cinematic editing, which, via the temporal sequencing of shots, realised what painting had tried to accomplish in fragments. Serov, for example, tried to bring out on canvas the energy of the actress Yermolova through cutting, with the help of the lines of the mirrors and of the mouldings of a room, several different framings for the different parts of the body.[5] The editing of the different shots of the stone lions in *The Battleship Potemkin* realised this dream of the painter. Photography allows an accomplishment of the same order by capturing a motionlessness that literature tried to attain through the movement of the phrase or the power of the mystery sought in the contortion of the uses of language. The poverty of photography permits it to realise this inclusion of non-art that literature or painting can only imitate by artistic means.

Exacerbating modernism

This is what can be demonstrated by a photograph situated in the interval between Barthes's 'having-been' and the objectivity of the Becher School. Walker Evans's photograph (overleaf) represents to us a detail of the kitchen in a farm in Alabama. It responds, first of all, to a documentary function at the heart of a major investigation commissioned by the Farm Security Administration. Nevertheless, something happens in the photo that exceeds the task of providing information concerning a miserable situation: a kitchen with neither sideboard nor cupboard, tinplate silverware held in a makeshift rack, a lopsided wooden board nailed to a wall of disjointed and worm-ridden planks. What strikes us is a certain aesthetic disposition marked by disorder: the parallels are not parallel, the silverware is ordered in disorder, the objects on the high beam (functioning as a shelf) are placed in a dissymmetrical manner. This lopsided assemblage composes, in total, a harmonious dissymmetry, the cause of which remains uncertain: is it the effect of chance, the fact that the objects found themselves in front of the objective? Is it the gaze of the photographer, who chose a close-up of a detail, thus transforming a completely random or simply functional layout into an artistic quality? Or is it the aesthetic taste of an inhabitant of the premises, making art with the means available by hammering in a nail or putting a can here rather than there? It is possible that the photographer wanted to show the destitution of the farmers. It is also possible that he simply photographed what was in front of him without any particular intention, and that the photo thus benefits from the beauty of the random. And, it is possible that he took pleasure in seeing

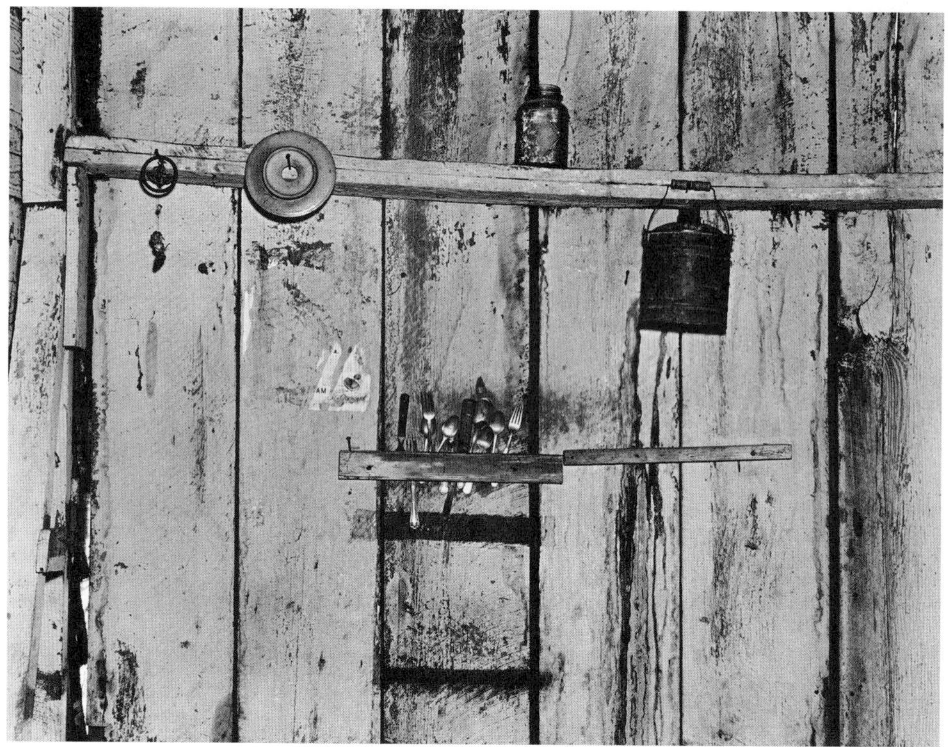

Walker Evans
Kitchen Wall, Alabama Farmhouse, 1936

a quasi-abstract minimalist scene or, conversely, that he wanted to underline a certain beauty of the functional: the sobriety of the plank and of the rack could, in effect, satisfy a certain aesthetic of design, attracted by the simple and brute material, and the art of living and doing transmitted by generations of simple people. All in all, the aesthetic quality of the photograph stems from a perfect equilibrium, a perfect indecision between the two forms of beauty that Kant distinguished: beauty adherent to the form adapted to its function, and the free beauty of the finality without end.

We don't know what was going through Walker Evans's mind in framing his photo as he did. But we do know that he had an idea about art that he inherited, not from a photographer or painter, but from a writer, Flaubert. The idea is that the artist must remain invisible in his work, like God in his creation. But it would be going a bit too far to say that the camera realises on the cheap – that is, by its mechanism alone – that which, for the writer, involves a never-ending work of subtraction. For impersonality is not the same thing as the objectivity of the camera, and the issue is perhaps not so much to subtract but rather to make the 'impersonalisation' of the style coincide with the grasping of the opposite movement: that by which indifferent lives appropriate the aesthetic capacities that subtract them from a simple social identification. The photographer's gaze upon the singular arrangement of the silverware in a poor Alabama kitchen might remind us of the gaze that

Flaubert lent to Charles Bovary as he looked at the head of Minerva, drawn by young Emma for her father on the peeling walls of Father Rouault's farm. This is not merely to say that the camera directly expresses a poetry of the banal that the writer could only make felt through laborious work on each sentence. It is also the power to transform the banal into the impersonal, forged by a literature that hollows out from the inside the apparent evidence, the apparent immediacy of the photo, just as pictorial silence overran the 'Flaubertian' phrase. But this effect of painting on literature and of literature on photography is not the same as a simple shared capacity to transfigure the banality of life into the artistic splendour of indifference. This 'indifference' is also the meeting point, the point of tension, between the subtraction of the artistic effect that characterises the work of the artist and the supplement of aesthetic sensibility that is adjoined to the lives of indifferent beings.

The consideration of both the *punctum* and the objectivism of the *forme-tableau* also lacks this relation between social banality and aesthetic power that inhabits the photographic portrait of the indifferent being. To understand what the 'indifference' of the photograph of the kitchen in Alabama or of the Polish teenager has in common with that of 'Flaubertian' literature, and to what type of 'modernity' this indifference bears witness, one must no doubt integrate these images into a completely different evolution of representation (*figuration*). To sketch out this history, I would like to dwell for a moment on a singular analysis that Hegel devotes, in his *Lectures on Aesthetics* of the 1920s, to Murillo's paintings of the child beggars of Seville, which he saw in the Royal Gallery in Munich. He evokes these paintings in a development whereby he attempts to reverse the classic evaluation of the value of pictorial genres according to the dignity of their subjects. But Hegel does not content himself with telling us that all subjects are equally proper to painting. He establishes a close relation between the virtue of this painting and the activity specific to these young beggars, an activity that consists precisely in doing nothing and not worrying about anything. There is in them, he tells us, a total disregard towards the exterior, an inner freedom in the exterior that is exactly what the concept of the artistic ideal calls for. They are like the young man in one of the portraits at the time attributed to Raphael, whose idle head gazes freely into the distance. Better still, they testify to a beatitude that is almost similar to that of the Olympian gods.[6]

There is one notion in particular in this passage that grabs our attention, that of being carefree. It seems to reply in advance to an analysis of the aesthetic revolution that holds sway today, that by which Michael Fried characterises the theorising and the practice of painting implemented by the contemporaries of Diderot. Presenting the characters in the scene as completely absorbed by their task is, for him, the means by which the painters of that period, following the example of Greuze, posed and resolved the big question of artistic modernity: how can a work be made coherent by excluding the spectator from its space? This 'anti-theatricality' is for him the essence of pictorial modernity, defined not in a 'Greenbergian' manner as simple concentration of the artist on his medium, but rather as definition of the place that it gives to the person who looks upon it. The *forme-tableau* of Jeff Wall's lightboxes or of the large-format cibachromes and chromogenic prints by Rineke Dijkstra, Thomas Struth, Andreas Gursky or Thomas Demand seems to Fried to renew, in exemplary fashion, the tradition of this modernity. But it comes at a price, and the active 'absorption' of the pictorial character, originally illustrated with such impassioned attention by Greuze's characters, increasingly becomes an inability to see and to feel seen. Thus, for example, the tourists in Thomas Struth's photographs of museums are represented in the absence of what they look upon in the Accademia (Michelangelo's *David*) or blurred in the darkness in Tokyo in front of a *Liberté guidant le peuple*, itself separated by a glass pane. Likewise, Rineke Dijkstra's teenagers are valued first of all for the awkwardness proper to their age, for their lack of control over their bodies which makes them unconscious of what they offer to be seen.[7] The window cleaner who, in Jeff Wall's famous 1999 photograph, washes the windows of Mies van der Rohe's pavilion, is not only separated from us by the back that he turns to us and by his relegation outside of the area directly illuminated by the sun; he is also 'deliberately forgetful' of the great event signifying the new day, 'the influx of the warm morning light'.[8] As for the traders at the Hong Kong stock exchange or the workers at the basket factory in Nha Trang, their 'absorption' excludes the spectator all the more effectively as it renders them almost invisible by depriving them of all interiority and making of their attention an entirely mechanical process. It would be off-key, Fried emphasises, to see here any form of representation of capitalist dehumanisation. This 'flattening of absorption' bears witness, on the contrary, to 'the consistency with which this artist resists or indeed repudiates all identification by the viewer with the human subjects of his images – the project of severing calls for nothing less'.[9]

'Objective' photography therefore demonstrates here the exacerbation of a modernist project of separation. The visual attention that is paid by the modest people, in Greuze's paintings, to each other and their surroundings is replaced by their ant-sized representation in Gursky's photographs. But this transformation, in turn, reveals the presuppositions of the analysis: the active absorption of characters by their task is, ultimately, only their passive absorption into the space of the painting. What they are or do matters little, but what is important is that they are put in their place. It is with regard to this positing named absorption that Hegel's insistence on the carefree inactivity of the young beggars becomes meaningful. Inactivity is not laziness. It is the suspension of the opposition between activity and passivity that aligned an idea of art with a hierarchical vision of the world. Murillo's child beggars belonged to the type of picturesque paintings that eighteenth-century aristocrats collected as documents on the exotic life of the working classes. Hegel's analysis removes them from there by giving them a quality which they share with the Olympian gods. This 'carefree' attitude is more striking than the new indifference of subjects and their common capacity to be 'absorbed'. It posits as the exemplary subject of art this 'doing nothing', this common *aesthetic* neutralisation of the social hierarchy and of the artistic hierarchy.

The aesthetic capacity shared by the Olympian god, the young noble dreamer and the carefree street child neutralises the opposition between the subjects of art and the anonymous forms of experience. 'We have the feeling that for a young person of this type any future is possible', says Hegel.[10] It is a peculiar comment, which makes the figures represented in a seventeenth-century painting contemporary beings whose future we consider. The young beggars testify, in fact, for another modernism far removed from that of Michael Fried's absorbed characters, without, for all that, becoming identified with the young velocipede racing experts extolled by Benjamin. The future that they bear is the blurring of the opposition between the world of work and the world of leisure, between the naked forms of life and the experiences of the aestheticised world. It is to this modernity that the assertion of Walker Evans's master, Flaubert, on the indifference of the subject, belongs. This does not mean the possibility for the artist to apply the 'project of severing', symbolic of Greenberg's or Fried's modernism, to any subject. It is realised only in that space where the artist rids himself of all the habitual attributes of the artist style and comes to encounter the attempts of obscure beings to introduce art into their sensible life, or any other of those forms of experience which their social condition is supposed to forbid. Flaubert may ridicule Emma's artistic pretension, but her art is forever linked to this artistic aspiration of a farmer's girl.

It is, similarly, a form of this encounter that James Agee and Walker Evans try to capture, one by brandishing Whitmanian enumerations and Proustian reminiscences to describe the houses of poor peasants, the other by rendering minimalist art and social document indiscernible when framing a dozen or so pieces of cutlery in front of four planks of brute wood. Before our gaze, there is thus neither simple objective information about a situation nor a wound inflicted by the 'it has been'. The photo does not say whether it is art or not, whether it represents poverty or a game of uprights and diagonals, weights and counterweights, order and disorder. It tells us neither what the person who laid the planks and cutlery in this manner had in mind nor what the photographer wanted to do. This game of multiple gaps perfectly illustrates what Kant designated under the name of aesthetic idea: 'a presentation of the imagination which prompts much thought, but to which no determinate thought whatsoever, i.e., no [determinate] concept can be adequate.'[11] The aesthetic idea is the indeterminate idea that connects the two processes that the destruction of the mimetic order left separated: the intentional production of art which seeks an end, and the sensible experience of beauty as finality without end. Photography is exemplarily an art of aesthetic ideas because it is exemplarily an art capable of enabling non-art to accomplish art by dispossessing it. But it is also such through its participation in the construction of a sensible environment which extends beyond its own specificity. What we are shown by the young beggars seen by Hegel, the head of Minerva on the walls of the Normandy farm, the lopsided cans on the beams of the Alabama kitchen, the nonchalant demeanour of the child-worker in his doffer-box, or the swaying hips of the Polish teenager, is that this dispossession which makes art cannot be thought independently of the despecification which removes all of these characters from their social identity. But this despecification itself is not the making of an artistic *coup de force*. It is the correlate of the ability acquired by the characters themselves to play with the image of their being and of their condition, to post it to walls or to set it up before the lens. Judgements about photography are also appreciations of this ability and of what it means for art. This link between artistic purity and aesthetic impurity both fascinated and worried the authors of *Spleen de Paris* and *Madame Bovary*. Walter Benjamin wanted to integrate it in a global vision of the new man in the new technical world. Barthes brought it down to the intimacy of the private gaze. Michael Fried now proposes to bring it down to the interminable task of separation attributed to artistic modernity. But this theoretical *coup de force* would not be possible if the art of photography today was not already the bearer of this tendency to break the historical complicity between the art of the photographer and the aesthetic capacity of his subjects.

Translated by Darian Meacham

1 Roland Barthes, *Camera Lucida*, Hill & Wang, New York 1981, p.51.
2 Ibid., p.34.
3 Ibid., p.96.
4 Jean-François Chevrier and James Lingwood, *Une autre objectivité*, Prato, Paris 1989.
5 S.M. Eisenstein, 'Yermolova', in *Selected Works*, vol.2: *Towards a Theory of Montage*, ed. Misha Glenny and Richard Taylor, British Film Institute, London 1994, pp.82–105.
6 G.W.F. von Hegel, *Vorlesungen über Ästhetik* I, Suhrkamp Verlag, Frankfurt 1986, p.224.
7 Michael Fried, *Why Photography Matters as Art as Never Before*, Yale University Press, New Haven CT 2008, pp.211–12.
8 Ibid., p.75.
9 Ibid., p.173.
10 Hegel 1986, p.224.
11 Immanuel Kant, *Critique of Judgement*, trans. W.S. Pluhar, Hackett, Indianapolis 1987, p.182.

2
People Exposed, People as Extras
Georges Didi-Huberman

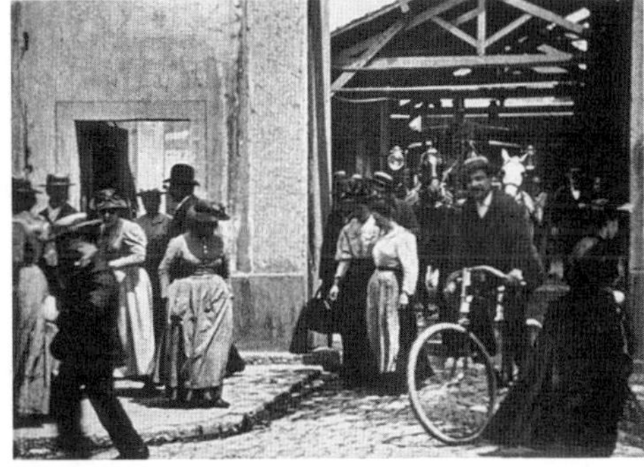

Lumière Brothers
Still from *Workers Leaving the Lumière Factory*, 1895

The title of the first film shown in history is *La Sortie des usines Lumière* – in English, 'Workers Leaving the Lumière Factory'. On 22 March 1895, in the rue de Rennes in Paris, in front of about two hundred spectators, Auguste and Louis Lumière showed for the very first time on a screen the lower classes in full movement. Their own workers had been carefully framed in front of the main gates of the Montplaisir factory, leaving their workshops during a break around midday. Thus, it was while making their exit from the factory that the people made their entrance – and thereby benefited from a new form of exposure – on the stage of the cinematographic era. This is all very simple, as we can see – but quite paradoxical too.

This origin was an origin, as such, only by appearing by *surprise*. The Lumière brothers probably had no intention of placing their 'lower class' employees in the foreground. They were, above all, proud to present to Paris an original process of colour photography called 'autochrome'. However, it is the Kinetoscope projector, appearing at the very end of a showing, that, to their own surprise, most surprised the spectators and filled them with wonder:

> With the help of a Kinetoscope that he invented himself, M. Louis Lumière has shown on a screen a most interesting scene: the personnel from the workshops leaving the factory at lunchtime. This animated scene, which shows all these people in full movement, rushing out onto the street, has produced the most striking effect.[1]

One saw, in a few seconds, about a hundred people appearing, as though this 'people of images' (the workers in Lyon) were suddenly invading the good society of the engineers and of the promoters of the industry (the spectators in Paris) who had come to the showing.

Furthermore, this was an origin only by appearing in the *difference* created between the subjects represented and the mode of their exposure: they are workers shown in the act of leaving their work. There is no violent protest in this exiting: these workers are simply taking advantage of the lunch break for some fresh air, while their boss is, for his part, taking advantage of the good sunlight necessary for the technical creation of his film. But this is where the difference lies, and on several different levels: they turn from being *workers* – that is, makers of photographic materials – to being suddenly *actors* in this first film. One of them, coming out on his bicycle, is called Francis Doublier: some time later he will stand behind the camera enjoying a new social status, that of cinematographic *operator*.[2]

A third paradox appears when we discover that this was an *origin* only by displaying itself completely in the facts of *repetition* and *rehearsal* – two notions contained in a single word in French, *répétition*. The celluloid film of March 1895 was preceded in the summer of 1894 by its 'final rehearsal' on paper – which of course could not be projected on screen; and it was followed by other *répétitions* or versions of the same scene until the end of the century.[3] We should add that, as the film measures only seventeen metres – for a total of about eight hundred photograms or *vues* (views) as they used to be called – the film lasted only one minute, 'and so a repetition of this projection was asked for by the whole wonderstruck audience.'[4]

Finally, this origin, quite strangely, contains nothing with a 'point' of departure: it appears rather like an imprecise territory, a *field* of possibilities both open and relative, not to the intrinsic value of the new technical medium, but to the multiple use-values with which it would gradually become invested. It suffices, first of all, to flick through the catalogue of the '*vues* Lumière' to understand the considerable meaning that the cinematograph has for a history of the exposure of the people: it is the social body in its entirety, under every latitude, that at the end of the nineteenth century becomes the principal object of this new atlas of the world in movement: bull races and baby competitions; political demonstrations and religious processions; the bustling activity of the city, fruit and vegetable markets; dockers at work, fishermen, farmers; children at play; the launching of ships; sports teams and circus performers; washerwomen and Ashanti dancers, wealthy bourgeois men and women in London and wretched coolies in Saigon, and so on.[5]

The question remains: by what means and with a view to what were these 'views' exposed? We know that the figuration of the people was a crucial question for the 'primitive' and 'modern' cinema, beyond – or starting with – 'Workers Leaving the Lumière Factory'.[6] This goes from Griffith to Eisenstein, from Abel Gance to King Vidor. One must mention also Fritz Lang, who worried about the manipulation of crowds in *Metropolis* before Leni Riefenstahl glorified them a few years plus one dictator later, in *The Triumph of the Will.*[7] In this context we can understand the political urgency – and the conceptual difficulty – of an analysis of these 'media' phenomena in the age of conquering totalitarianisms, in the work of thinkers such as Siegfried Kracauer, Bertolt Brecht, Walter Benjamin or Theodor Adorno.[8] It is thus not enough that people be exposed in general: one must go further and ask whether in each case the form of such an exposure – framing, montage, editing, rhythm, narration, and so on – encloses them (that is, alienates them and, finally, exposes them to disappearance) or whether it frees them (by exposing them to appear before us, giving them a power of appearance or apparition).

The imaginary people

'Cinema', wrote Edgar Morin, 'allows us to see the process of penetration of man into the world and the inseparable process of penetration of the world into man' at a precise point, on a dialectical pivotal plane which serves as a conversion operator. This plane is nothing other than the *image* itself, the image in so far as 'it is not only the turntable between the real and the imaginary, but also the radical and simultaneous constituent act of the real and of the imaginary'.[9] If the man of the cinema is indeed that *imaginary man* that Edgar Morin suggested, our diagnosis must certainly not be limited to finding there the man of flight and illusion, the man of the unreal and of ignorance or misrecognition, the apolitical man and the man of indifference to the world. When the group of Lumière workers exited their workshops and went bustling out into the daylight, bigger than life-size on the screen, in front of a group of wonderstruck bourgeois spectators on the rue de Rennes, it was in some way perhaps already a *political meeting*, a meeting created by the image and not cut off from the real, since it linked – for the long duration of the social development of the cinema – the workers with the managers or the customers from the same nascent industry.

In what remains perhaps his most fascinating work, Jean Louis Schefer sketched a poetics and almost a metapsychology of this 'imaginary man' by calling him *ordinary man*, the 'man without qualities' of the cinema. And where our *solitude in front of the image* becomes – through fear, according to Schefer – *consistency or strength of a social body* with which our own solitude would become permeable or soaked, what is

> projected and animated is not ourselves and yet we recognise ourselves in it (as though a strange desire for the extension of the human ... could be at work here) ... It is not possible that my experience of the cinema is totally solitary: this, more than the illusion of movement and of mobility of things that it gives us, is cinema's own particular illusion; ... it seems, because of this beguiling solitude, that a part of ourselves is permeable to effects of sense without ever being able to be born into meaning by our language ... Cinema works on every social being as on a solitary being.[10]

It is probable that the man of the cinema is an 'ordinary' subject – rather than a 'connoisseur' as in archaeology or the plastic arts – inasmuch as he contemplates the movement of human appearances from his own position as an anonymous individual plunged, with his fellow human beings, into the half-light of a screening room. It is thus, also, in so far as this 'strange desire for extension of the human body' works in the dark room like the grains of dust in the beam of light from the projector, between immobile bodies in shadow (the spectators) and moving bodies in the light (the actors). What, then, is the collective being that results from this meeting, the *social being* of cinema? It is impossible, no doubt, to deduce the idea either merely from the cast alone or from the audience alone (this audience that we generally fail to think about, as well as the community and solitude). It is rather the meeting – and not just the 'representation', on the one hand, or the 'reception', on the other – that would make it possible to construct this idea.

This meeting has to do, in each case, with a certain historic state of the relations between poetics and politics. Jacques Rancière traced back to Flaubert the typically modern idea by which 'in the subject-matter of art ... there are no beautiful or ugly subjects any more: Yvetot is on the same level as Constantinople, and a farmer's daughter is on the same level as a society woman.'[11] But one could just as easily go further back and find this economy of figuration in Caravaggio's *Madonna with the Serpent*, in Callot's or in Rembrandt's beggars, or, later, in Goya's *Disasters*. On the basis of this long history in which this 'theatre of the people' is unfurled, Rancière has examined the 'dominant ideas of a time and of an intelligentsia which think [today] that, with regard to the people, enough and even too much has been given', saying this in order to highlight the symptomatic value of recent films such as Bruno Dumont's *Rosetta* or the Dardenne brothers' *L'Humanité*.[12]

This diagnosis by Rancière can be divided into two symmetrical meanings. On the one hand, it seems, the people are exposed to the risk of being hypostasised – and above all reduced – in both a larger and more consensual entity, which is the idea of nation.[13] This is what gives rise to massive identifications, to military choreographies and to patriotic stories, from Busby Berkeley to the sympathetic and triumphant heroes of *Independence Day*. This is what gives the illusion of uniting a 'cast' on show and the 'audience' that judges them.[14] This is what makes it possible, with the help of digital technology, to create armies, whole societies, on the basis of a simple algorithm of cloning, as in *The Matrix* or in *The Lord of the Rings*. In front of such things, the archaic packs of living-dead in the series of films directed by George A. Romero appear like a political alternative to the distressing populism of the living-all-too-living who go about, in a completely interchangeable and alienated manner, in our sitcoms.

On the other hand, the people expose themselves to the risk of being hypostasised in the compressed entity of what is called *pic people*, that is, the 'people of images' – *picture* now, rather than *image* – according to the definition given by *Variety* magazine which specialises in entertainment industry news, celebrity photos and the box office, as its ads show: this magazine gives the term *pic people* to 'all those who participate in the existence of a film', from the humble technicians to the famous actors, and from the producers to the cinema managers.[15] Philippe-Alain Michaud cites this definition with regard to a progression where the notion of 'people' unfortunately gives way, eventually, to the people of the celebrity world and the happy few which the world of showbusiness and the contemporary art world go wild about: the 'beggar' of *Accattone* becomes 'idol'; and martyrdom – even the ancient stylite, all under the American term 'fashion victim' – is seen as a category of 'fashion', in other words as the creation of a stylist.[16]

The concept of *pic people* seems to be characterised by a typically capitalist competition of identificatory props: it is always one star against the other, better than the other; it is the perpetual wonder in front of a body hypostasised in a trademark image – which is neither the image in the anthropological sense, nor a mark in the sense of 'imprint' – of a rather unclear desire. The film buff's passion, with the reserved attitude that often characterises it, enjoys concentrating on 'the best looks, the best actor'; even its reflection regarding a 'politics of actors' renews, by capillary action, the notion of author and thus the authority of the proper name as the symbolic power of Mount Parnassus where the love stories of the gods Gary Cooper, John Wayne or James Stuart are hatched ...[17]

One of the great political powers of the cinema of re-edited/revisited (*remontées*) archives, such as we see in the work of Artavazd Pelechian, Basilio Martín Patino, Jean-Luc Godard or Yervant Gianikian and Angela Ricci Lucchi, consists in going back through history – and thereby performing a work of montage and re-editing – *in search of lost faces*, that is to say faces which have perhaps lost their names today, and which show themselves in their

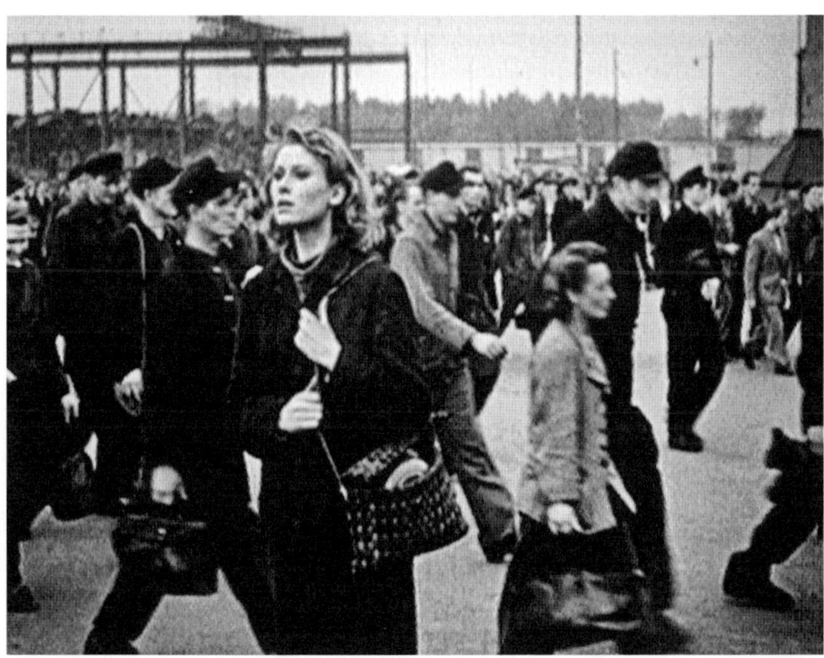

Harun Farocki
Still from *Workers Leaving the Factory in Eleven Decades*, 1995

absence of power and their muteness, but which have lost none of their force when we look at them moving in the flickering light of time-damaged films. It is a way of finding once more an essential quality of the 'primitive' cinema which André S. Labarthe contemplated in the unique face of Falconetti filmed by Dreyer, as well as in the innumerable, nameless faces filmed by Eisenstein; those 'documentary heroes' as he calls them.[18] It is their traces, to a greater or lesser degree, that Harun Farocki sought in an extraordinary collection of *Workers Leaving the Factory* (*Sorties d'usines;* see previous page) where the opening gesture of the Lumière factory workers is diffracted so as to gesture to us, to make a sign to us, with the most contemporary political urgency.[19]

Extras

It seems that the cinema only shows or exposes the people according to the ambiguous status of 'extras' – *figurants* in French. The verb *figurer* means variously 'to appear, to represent, or to be an extra' and is related to the notion of the 'figure'. *Figurant*: it is a banal word, a word for the 'man without qualities' of a setting, of an industry, of a spectacular management of 'human resources'; but, also, it is an unfathomable word, a word from the labyrinths that every figure conceals. The *figurants* – the extras – constitute, above all, in the economy of cinematography, an accessory of humanity which serves as a framework for the role of the central heroes, the real actors in the story, the protagonists, as they are called. For the story which is told they are like the base, the underlying canvas made up of faces, bodies and gestures. They form the paradox, therefore, of being something that is not merely part of the set but human as well. In English, as in Spanish, one calls them 'extras'; in Italian they are *comparsi*, and in German they are *Statisten* – words which indicate the point to which they are not necessary to the story or to the dynamics of the film. They are the dark mass in front of which the 'stars' of the film shine (those considered worthy of being seen, compared as they are to the bright splendours of the night sky, those isolated points in the sky which still carry the names of ancient gods). The *figurants* or 'extras' are the night of the cinema when cinema strives to be an art that makes stars shine. To a certain extent, they are to the world of shows what the miserable wretches – the *misérables* – were to the industrial world of Victor Hugo's time.

The *figurants* or 'extras' would therefore represent something like an accursed share of the high art – and of the huge industry – of cinema. They are situated at the very bottom of the artistic and social ladder where actors who 'play themselves', and where 'secondary characters' and other supporting actors, gain the upper hand.[20] Even journals like *Cahiers du cinéma* only stop briefly to examine 'secondary roles', giving the 'extras' practically no chance of existence at all, poetically and politically speaking: they then disappear underneath the last level which is the 'third man' (*troisième homme*) or the 'minor figure'.[21] In her work on *L'Acteur de cinéma*, Jacqueline Nacache speaks quite justly of the extra as the 'piece-of-furniture-man, the anonymous passerby, the silhouette swallowed up by shadow, the lower-class people of films.'[22]

The extras are the actors of nothing. They are the *non-actors* par excellence, postulated by their semiological and institutional definition: 'All [of the human figures in a film] are not necessarily 'actorly [*actorielles*] figures.' In the first place is the cohort of extras. As individuals, they have no acting (*actantielle*) value: they are 'non-actors' since they do not constitute an acting force in the story. However, as a collective, they can indeed play such a role (like the troops who land on the coast of Normandy in *The Longest Day*).[23] The institutional definition would be as follows:

> The extra is there only for the costume he or she wears, or the spot of moving colour that he or she gives to the décor ... The setting parks him, as a consenting slave of the cinema, submitting him to shouted orders and to military discipline. Should he step out of line, he will put the set in danger (Jerry Lewis in a gag in *The Errand Boy*) ... Each extra is taken on and paid by the production on the basis of his or her 'non-actor' status.[24]

In a professional manual from a film corporation, we can find the following: 'the choice of extras is up to the assistants', who determine the 'number of extras for the décor', combining the director's artistic demands with the economic demands of the producer.[25]

The *figurants*, the 'extras', exist in the plural. If we want to speak of a *figurant* in the singular, we will say in French *un simple figurant*, meaning 'a simple or mere extra'. Simple, mere: because he or she is missing that individuation which makes up the passionate complexity of the character, of the actor, or of the subject of the action. The extras 'figure', and therefore do not act. When they move, they are rather part of a mass effect which drags them into a vast movement, a general design of which each extra is merely a segment, a piece in a mosaic, sometimes just a single point. The word *figurant*s in the plural appears in French around 1740: it was used to refer to a group of dancers who, at the beginning of the ballet, drew different figures with their collective arrangement. Around 1800, the word is used to speak of the characters in plays that only have a 'secondary role' – that is to say, who are there, on stage, but who have absolutely nothing to say. More often than not they exist only by their number, their mass, and their mute lack of differentiation. Around 1907 the word begins to be used in a more general sense to evoke a group of people whose role – in a society or in an historic situation – is neither effective nor meaningful, illustrated in the two expressions 'hidden role' and 'purely decorative role'. *Être figurant*, to be an extra: to be there but only so as not to appear in the spotlight. To melt into the mass and to serve no other purpose than to be at the base of the story, the drama and the action.

In spite of their name, the *figurants* tend to disappear, to not figure, so to speak, since instead they melt into the base, always behind the acting figures. The noise they make is only a murmur. Their appellation is collective. If by chance the names of the extras appear in the credits at the end, their letters are so small and pass by so quickly in front of our eyes that they become a simple column, an unreadable list where each is supposed to 'figure', indistinctly.

The extras are those who have not succeeded in 'making a name' for themselves, and this is why they are so badly paid. They wait for hours on the film set to do what is asked of them, which in general is very little. The make-up artists of course give them hardly any time at all. Their costumes are often chosen to form only a great monochrome, as uniform as possible. The prototype of the extra is no doubt the anonymous foot soldier who, among the hundreds or thousands of his fellows, is just there to figure the battle scene – from which the hero will emerge triumphant or become the wounded hero – and has nothing to do but walk, pointing a bayonet, and pretend to fall down dead at the given moment.

Extras are thus like the innumerable unknown soldiers of commercial cinema. They die forgotten, like dogs. It is no coincidence that the French word *figurants* refers, in slang, to anonymous cadavers exposed in the morgue waiting to be recognised and named – something which rarely happens in such cases. In his *Dictionnaire français-argot* published in 1901, Aristide Bruant cited this lament:

> Your man has not returned home for three days ... Go to the Musée des Refroidis [in other words, 'the Stiffs Museum', slang for the morgue]... He is perhaps one the figurants.

If a friend tells you in French that he or she has *fait de la figuration* in a film – that is, appeared as an extra – and invites you to go to see it, there is a strong possibility that you will hardly see his or her presence on-screen at all. For such is the paradox of the *figurants* or the extras: they have a face, a body, gestures that belong to them, but the setting that calls on them wants them to be faceless, bodiless, and without any personal gestures.

We often have the impression that the extras take their revenge on the lack of differentiation that is imposed upon them with indifference – a discreet but sometimes easily perceptible indifference – which they turn against the story for which they form the decoration. You can see them bored to death, expecting nothing more from cinema, while every actor has the right to expect cinema to allow him at least to appear. Is it for this that the extras always act so badly, as though begrudgingly? Or else is it because the director simply does not know how to look at them, since he has eyes only for the 'true' actors? It becomes painful when the extras are supposed to play a group of people subjected to the same tragic fate as the protagonists, for example in Hollywood representations like *Holocaust* (1978) or *Schindler's List* (1993). It is unbearable in these cases to see that the characters of a film are not equal when confronted by the same fate that touches them. Against this, Claude Lanzmann gave much time to giving faces, words and gestures back to those that the Nazis called *Figuren* in the camps. But is it not an impossible task, or an infinite task, to account for each person's difference, each person's singularity, each person's irreducibility?

We can understand in this context that the extras oblige the film-maker to ask a crucial question, a question that is inextricably linked to aesthetics, ethics and politics. How should one film the *figurants*, the extras? How should one make them appear as actors in a story; how can one refuse to settle for making them indistinct but living shadows? This is the question of the relation established in a film between the little story and the big story, between the local *story* and the *history* in which it takes place. Eisenstein attempted to invert the established relation in Hollywood cinema between the peripeteia and the historic reality: in Hollywood, he said, what you place at the fore is the inevitable trio made up of the husband, the wife and the lover, before choosing – as one chooses one's wallpaper for the house – to place behind them the 'local colour' of the decor and of the extras, be it Imperial Rome, an African safari or Chicago in the 1930s.[26] Against this, it was a matter of giving back to the *figurants* (who are to cinema what the people are to history) their faces, their gestures, their words and their capacity to act; to film them less as a *mass* than as a *community* – that principal actor, active rather than passive – of real history.

In *Battleship Potemkin*, for example, Eisenstein devoted a lot of time to the faces and to the bodies of the extras to capture the way in which the death of Vakoulintchouk arouses a sovereign transformation of personal pain (religious gestures and lamentation) into collective fury (political gestures of imprecation and of calling for vengeance, all filmed close up), and very soon into a revolutionary decision. For *October* (1928), the film crew tirelessly sought extras in the streets, the bistros, the night shelters. Among the eleven thousand people approached, many had been protagonists of the true story itself, the shooting on the Nevsky Prospekt or the taking of the Winter Palace, and it was decided, for the filming, that they should be given real rifles.[27] Eisenstein films them in a wide-angle shot and a high-angle shot, but he places himself also – in the astonishing rhythm of his mixed montage – practically on the ground, to film, for example, the face of a soldier fallen into a puddle.

Finally, in *Strike*, Eisenstein exposes as crudely as possible the body of the people grappling with the exploitation that alienates them: bodies tied up, bodies crushed by work and social suffering. For the last sequences of the film, he had the problem of representing the 'bloody horror' of a mass shooting. The slightest sign of artifice would, in his eyes, have ruined the intensity, and therefore the necessity, of such a scene. In order to get around the aporia of staging extras who fall with varying degrees of conviction under the blank cartridges of the soldiers, he chose to place his extras in the concrete situation of running desperately into a ravine, so that the physical urgency was a reality for each person. The result is a hallucinatory, but somewhat documentary, vision of bodies genuinely precipitated by their own running. Then we see them strewn on the ground, without their having to 'play' any particular role there, while Eisenstein invents the wonderful counterpoint offered by the documentary allegory of the bullock with its throat cut in the abattoir, filmed close up:

> In order to make sure that the extras in the trades council do not look like they are acting ... and above all in order to eliminate the effect of artifice that the screen cannot suffer and that is inevitable even with

> the most brilliant 'death scene', I have used the following procedure ... intended to provoke the maximum effect of bloody horror: the associative alternating between the shooting and the abattoirs. The first, shown in group shots and medium shots, the fall of the 1500 workers into the ravine, the fleeing of the crowd, the shots fired, etc. ... At the same time, all the close ups serve to show the true horror of the abattoirs where the cattle have their throats cut and are skinned.[28]

With his formal choices, Eisenstein wanted to give power back to the masses: to reassert their role as principal actors in the story, but also the specificity of their gestures, of their voice (their clamour, their words). And this is why the extras represented, in his eyes, a fundamental aesthetic issue. The question is still asked today: how should one justly film those who have no name, those who first of all have no voice other than their cry of suffering or revolt? How should one approach non-actors, how should one look them in the eye, listen to their words, and respect their gestures? There is an attempt of this kind in the films of Pier Paolo Pasolini (where we see, in each shot, his tenderness, his respect and even his admiration for every one of the extras), of Jean Rouch, of Alexander Sokurov (where we want to speak to every face that appears in *Russian Ark*), of Atom Egoyan or of Harun Farocki, to name but a few.

By deciding to commemorate the centenary of 'Workers Leaving the Lumière Factory' with a film dedicated to its extras, Mohsen Makhmalbaf, with *Salam Cinema*, came up with a complex set based on a casting call following which five thousand people presented themselves to the director. A film without actors 'about those who would like to work in cinema'. A film about the desire for cinema and about those who, animated by such a desire, see themselves confronted with the very heart of the ethical questions that life asks us: to appear, to figure, or disappear, to remain silent or speak, to remain submissive to an order or to rebel, to be judged or to become a judge, to weigh fiction and lies, art and life, composed emotion and real affect, laughter and tears, intimate secrets and shared history. In the cruel but Socratic process which he employs, Makhmalbaf ends up giving the extras, to whom the film is dedicated, their due: 'You have all played a role. There was room for everyone. Cinema is everyone's business. If cinema speaks about life, then there is enough room.'[29] By this we must understand that a film might only be politically just when it gives a place and a face to the nameless, to those who have no part in the habitual social representation. So, it is a question of *making of the image a common place* where the commonplace of images of the people used to reign.[30]

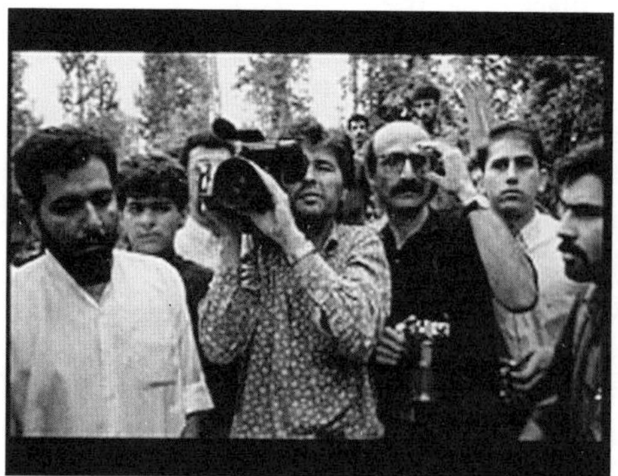

Moshen Makhmalbaf
Production still from *Salam Cinema*, 1995

Translated by Shane Lillis

1 *Bulletin du Photo-Club de Paris* 3, 1895, cited by B. Chardère, *Le Roman des Lumière. Le cinéma sur le vif*, Gallimard, Paris 1995, p.301.

2 Ibid., p.293.

3 Ibid., pp.293–301. G. Sadoul, *Histoire générale du cinéma, I. L'invention du cinéma, 1832–1897*, Denoël, Paris 1948; rev. edn., 1973, pp.284–6. N. Burch, *La Lucarne de l'infini. Naissance du langage cinématographique*, Nathan, Paris 1990, pp.22–8.

4 *Bulletin du Photo-Club de Paris*, p.301.

5 See J. Rittaud-Hutinet, *Auguste et Louis Lumière: les mille premiers films*, ed. Philippe Sers, Paris 1990. P. Dujardin, 'Domitor ou l'invention du quidam', *L'Aventure du cinématographe. Actes du congrès mondial Lumière*, Aléas, Lyon 1999, p.277: 'The time of the cinematograph is indeed the time in which the people appear, whether they are apprehended under the category of the first-comer from the city and the working-class, or whether they are apprehended under the political category of the anonymous individual, that is to say, of that nobody-in-particular who is given the dignity of being a subject by right.'

6 See J.-L. Leutrat, 'Modernité. Modernité?', *Lumière, le cinéma*, Institut Lumière, Lyon 1992, pp.64–70.

7 See P. Sorlin, 'Foule actrice ou foule-objet? Les leçons du premier cinéma', *L'Image. Études, documents, débats*, no.1, 1995, pp.63–74.

8 See M. Girard, 'Kracauer, Adorno, Benjamin: le cinéma, écueil ou étincelle révolutionnaire de la masse?', *Lignes*, no.11, 2003, pp.208–25.

9 E. Morin, *Le Cinéma ou l'homme imaginaire. Essai d'anthropologie sociologique*, Minuit, Paris 1956, pp.ix, 208.

10 J.L. Schefer, *L'Homme ordinaire du cinéma*, Cahiers du cinéma/Gallimard, Paris 1980, pp.11–12, 102.

11 J. Rancière, 'Le bruit du peuple, l'image de l'art (à propos de Rosetta et de L'Humanité)', in A. de Baecque and G. Lucantonio (eds.), *Théories du cinéma*, Cahiers du cinéma, Paris 2001, p.214.

12 Ibid., pp.213–19. Cf. J. Rancière, 'Le théâtre du peuple: une histoire interminable', in *Les Scènes du peuple (Les Révoltes logique, 1975–1985)*, Horlieu Éditions, Lyon 2003, pp.167–201.

13 Cf. J.-M. Frodon, *La Projection nationale. Cinéma et nation*, Odile Jacob, Paris 1998.

14 See L. Gervereau, 'Échantillons ou masses symboliques? Le rôle des foules et du public à la télévision', *L'Image. Études, documents, débats*, no.1, 1995, pp.97–123.

15 P.-A. Michaud, *Le Peuple des images. Essai d'anthropologie figurative*, Desclée de Brouwer, Paris 2002, p.23.

16 Ibid., pp.25–40, 195–248.

17 See L. Moullet, *Politique des acteurs: Gary Cooper, John Wayne, Cary Grant, James Stewart*, Éditions de l'Étoile/Cahiers du cinéma, Paris 1993, R. Bellour, 'Le plus beau visage, le plus grand acteur: Lilian Gish, Cary Grant', *Trafic*, no.65, 2008, pp.82–5.

18 A.S. Labarthe, 'Belle à faire peur', *Lignes*, no.23–4, 2007, p.394.

19 H. Farocki, *Arbeiter verlassen die Fabrik*, video, 1995. Cf. H. Farocki, *Reconnaître et poursuivre*, ed. C. Blümlinger, Théâtre Typographique, Dijon-Quetigny 2002, pp.65–72, 118–19.

20 See J. Nacache, *L'Acteur de cinéma*, Nathan, Paris 2003, pp.92–9.

21 Cf. T. Jousse, 'Seconds rôles: l'album de famille', *Cahiers du cinéma*, nos.407–8, 1988, pp.60–1; N. Rivière, 'Le troisième homme et le second couteau dans le cinéma américain des années quatre-vingt-dix', in G.-D. Farcy and R. Prédal (eds.), *Brûler les planches, crever l'écran. La présence de l'acteur*, L'Entretemps Éditions, Saint-Jean-de-Védas 2001, pp.339–47.

22 Nacache 2003, p.98.

23 A. Gardies, *Le Récit filmique*, Hachette, Paris 1993, p.60.

24 Nacache 2003, p.99.

25 V. Othnin-Girard, *L'Assistant réalisateur*, FEMIS, Paris 1988, pp.77–8.

26 S.M. Eisenstein, 'Les principes du nouveau cinéma russe', *La Revue du cinéma. Critique, recherches, documents*, vol.II, no.9, 1930, p.20.

27 S.M. Eisenstein, 'Une armée de cent mille hommes devant les caméras', trans. A. Vitez, *Octobre*, Le Seuil/Avant-Scène, Paris 1971, pp.149–52.

28 S.M. Eisenstein, 'Le montage des attractions au cinéma', trans. A. Robel, *Œuvres, I. Au-delà des étoiles*, UGE/Cahiers du cinéma, Paris 1974, pp.132–3. On the closeness of this montage to the work of Georges Bataille and Eli Lotar on the human figure in the journal *Documents*, see G. Didi-Huberman, *La Ressemblance informe, ou le gai savoir visuel selon Georges Bataille*, Macula, Paris 1995, pp.280–97.

29 Cf. M. Haghighat and F. Sabouraud, *Histoire du cinéma iranien, 1900–1999*, Éditions BPI/Centre Georges Pompidou, Paris 1999, pp.161–2. See also A. Bergala, *Abbas Kiarostami*,

Cahiers du cinéma, Paris 2004, p.67, who rightly notes how '*Voyage to Italy* (also known as *The Lonely Woman*) [by Roberto Rossellini] and *The Wind Will Carry Us* [by Abbas Kiarostami] end with the same motion: leaving the anonymous people to invade the screen of fiction.'

30 This text is a fragment from a work in progress entitled *Peuples exposés* (*People Exposed*). The first version of the third paragraph was published under the title 'Figurants' in *Dictionnaire mondial des images*, ed. L. Gervereau, Nouveau Monde Éditions, Paris 2006, pp.398–400.

3
Body without Image: Ernesto Neto's Anti-Leviathan
Éric Alliez

> [T]he great Leviathan is that one creature in the world which must remain unpainted to the last.
> — *Herman Melville, Moby-Dick*

> The IMAGE-grip is dislocated and a more fundamental element emerges ... in short, IMAGE is not the work's supreme motive or unifying end.
> — *Hélio Oiticica, Block Experiments*

In the immense emptiness and sepulchral chill of the Pantheon, it seems to emerge, suddenly, a ballooning, billowy suspension of innumerable artificial columns veiled in a delicate white material (stretchable Lycra), whose distended bases, which bulge with faintly perfumed ballast, descend randomly to many levels or reach as far as the ground. This forest of sorts is attached to the vaulting of the building like some monstrous parasite, in a sort of reverse shot to the strict alignment of the building's columns. High up, hanging liana-columns pass through holes in immense sheets of Lycra stretched out between the four branches of the Pantheon in an uneven sinuous network with long, undulating pockets that are constricted or bloated, and to which a number of shafts are also connected. Its capacities exceeded, the eye is led to *contain, at a distance*, this body that is radically heterogeneous both to the place that it invades and to any identifiable reality. It attempts to encompass it by means of an *aesthetic metaphor* – that of some giant, monstrously arborescent octopus-white whale whose entrails are distended and swollen from devouring the Pantheon.

Metaphorisation confers the status of a half-figurative, half-abstract *image* – and therefore the character of a description (such as 'the innumerable suspensions of an inverted and parasitical forest') – on what is otherwise unidentifiable and whose radical alterity, in relation to image-effects, poses the question of knowing if it is *still* of an *aesthetic* order. It is therefore necessary here to recall briefly the two – in our eyes most significant – modalities according to which the aesthetic has recently seen its objects and its stakes redeployed. In the first, aesthetic alterity is a disengagement from vision that engages the gaze in the genesis of visibility at the heart of the visible. It is to this phenomenological 'opening' that Georges Didi-Huberman has lent a second, more dialectical life, between knowing and seeing, that is less 'unrepresentable' to the extent that the labour of the negative in the image substitutes the *visual of a figuring figure* (a superior phenomenology) for the 'invisible'.[1] In the second, the aesthetic is the de-figuring of every representative relationship between the sayable and the visible in the free play of *forms–signs* whose discourse defines forms of visibility as much as modes of intelligibility. It is to this dialectical play of textual excess with regard to the life of forms that Jacques Rancière has given the name 'aesthetic regime', in so far as it participates in a metaphorics that is superior at every point (according the Schillerian principle of a *logos* identical to a *pathos*, etc).[2] One will not fail to notice here that a certain highly contemporary aesthetic turn takes place, or displaces itself, beyond the letter of our two authors, in this *double articulation*. It is in relation to this latter that it is necessary for us, at the outset, to distance ourselves somewhat.

This said, it cannot be denied that our initial descriptive approach to Neto's installation – which seems intent on *metamorphosing* its inevitably optical, distant, static, monumental capturing in view – presents itself as a heterogeneous *chaining together*[3] of metaphors (vegetable, architectural, landscapes, animal, biological ...). But one could *imagine* other equally (in) adequate metaphors to whose descriptions the installation would lend itself (under such and such an *aspect*), whilst evading them globally. And perhaps it should be noted that in their own, 'theatrical' way, photographic images precipitate and aestheticise the putting into image of the installation, by fixing it in spectacularly distanced long or close-up shots. It remains that the multiplication of metaphors or images that are heterogeneous to one another, and the possibility of interpreting them as the index of a mode of assemblage or of proliferating chains that are not of the order of the image, nonetheless poses the question of their (non-)relation to the image. Relation, non-relation, or relation of non-relation ... relaunched by *Leviathan Thot*, the title of the installation, at first an enigmatic linking of two names, in turn poses the question of its relation to statements (*énoncés*).

However, everything changes from the moment that the spectator becomes ambulant: he or she becomes a sensori-motor *component* of this body, which ingests him or her, and into which s/he is plugged. The spectator experiences this body – which is defined only by the set of tensions which animate it (tractions, suspension, stretching, inflation) – in a coenesthetic and tensive manner. But make no mistake: coenesthetic deambulation is not a way of experiencing the immediacy of the naked, sensible presence of a body suspended in space or the properties of a hybrid material that would carry us along in the special effects of a *materia informis*. Hence it *is not* the bearer of an aesthetic experience, at least in the primary sense of a pure sensible apprehension. It is, rather, the way in which we sense, *in the first place*, a mobilising energetic potential that acts on us in the manner of a field of forces, almost independently of any sort of discursive mediation or imaginary transport. And it is through this potentiality which envelops us with the inkling of forces that pass into sensation, that what one must resolve to call *a powerful non-organic life* is given to us to perceive in our own movement. A powerful non-organic life that 'overflows' the immanent but limited, fleeting but ceaselessly relaunched experience that we have of it, or rather that traverses us.

Via this kinetic entrance into the *œuvre*, a material introduction (*entrée en matière*), deambulation *starts up* what can only be 'interpreted' by beginning to experience the diagram of forces stretched out above our heads and around us – as we would experience 'the intrusion of another world into the visual world of figuration'.[4] Absolutely *disorganised* by the most direct connection between the body thus put in motion, the visible that it expresses (what it sees in the sensation without distance that put it in motion) and the virtual that it constructs in *realising* the strange operation to which it is submitted. One might reproach us with extending the Deleuzean diagram well beyond its pictorial usage. But one will equally understand that Jacques Rancière can reproach Deleuze precisely for 'short-circuit[ing] the work of metaphor' whilst the diagram, following Rancière, 'only makes visible if its labour is rendered equivalent to that of metaphor, if words construct such equivalence' in separating the presence in/side art of 'any epiphany of the present'.[5] But this is to postulate the possibility of an equivalence between the work of forms, even if it is dynamic (the dynamic work of the sayable, hence metaphorisable) and the (non-discursive) work of forces. Now, the dynamic/dialectic of forms–signs animating the 'aesthetic regime' cannot in any way be equivalent to an energetics of forces because this participates in a completely different regime – an *aesthesic regime* whose diagrammatic apparatus must be *invested* as such. It doesn't aim at the negation of forms and the denegation of signs (participating, for example, in the symbolic montage of the Pantheon). Rather, it aims at fusing and deterritorialising them as *forces–signs* (which make the referential territorialisation of signifiance and iconic territorialisation of interpretance of the Pantheon take flight). Carried off in this *semiotics of intensities*, 'information' fissures and is dissociated from the discursiveness in which it was caught (its intelligibility is suspended, scrambled, put into crisis).[6]

The work of the diagram does not consist, then, in putting the chaotic genesis of a pure visibility of forms into presence, even if they are mobilised by a spectator who is equally mobile in an 'environmental participation'. *It tends* to the 'capture of forces', to making insensible forces (anaesthetised in the symbolic semiology of the national monument) sensible (*forces insensibles/ insensibilisés*). The *real* stake of this agency (*agencement*[7]) of forces, in itself a-signifying and non-discursive, is to engage a 'diagnosis of our current becomings' in a *politics of experimentation*, a politics of experimentation which *really* begins with the production of novel conjunctions in the tissue of fluxes of materials and of signs ... It is not that metaphor must be ignored, but instead of having the agency of the 'work' fall back on a metaphorical displacement (an equivalence reductive of forces and idealising of forms, appealing to an

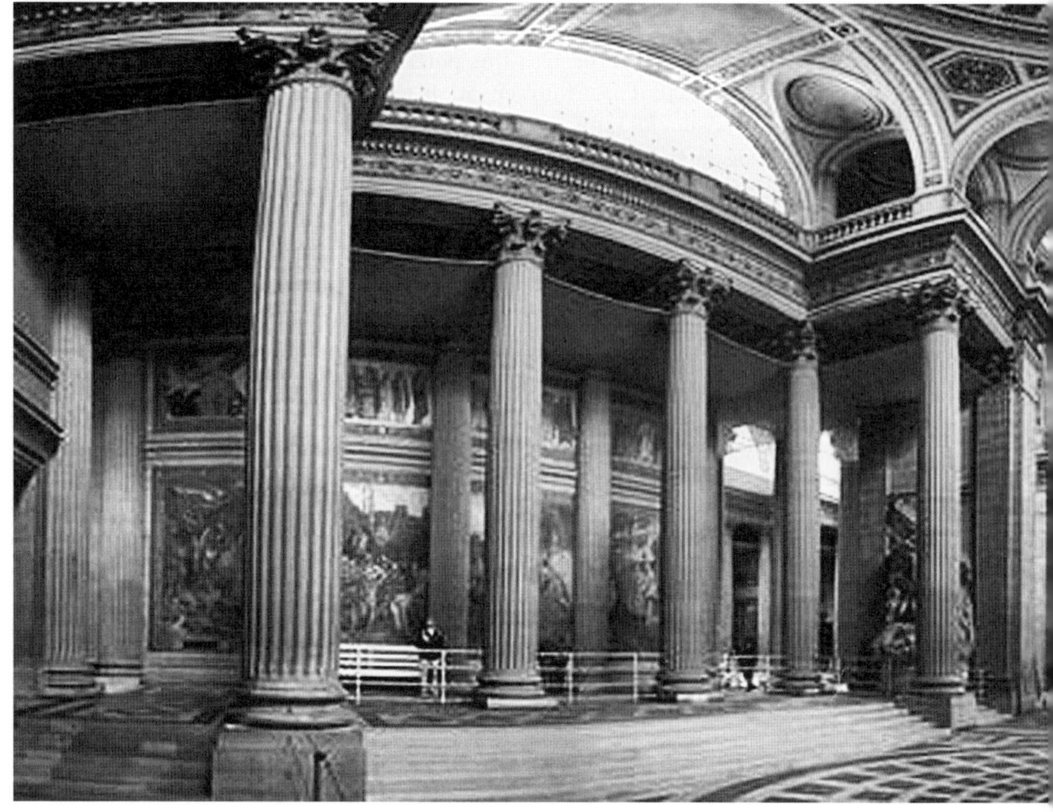

imaginary discursiveness), it must be relaunched on the body by investing the process of enunciation which animates the formation of statements, engaging metaphoricity itself and the matter-sense of statements in a semiotics of sensation. Signs here do not form signifying chains transported into the imaginary by 'metaphor', but half-coded, half-decoded chains. They form Markov chains, connecting elements of every kind (words, figures, fragments of the architecture or installation, a whole multi-sensoriality mixed with a world of analogons and schemas and affects) that are caught up directly in 'physical' effects in which every kind of real distinction between form of expression and form of content is abolished. This is because an *intensive machine of deterritorialisation bearing on fluxes of signs* belongs to the diagram, and, more precisely, to the diagrammatic regime of contemporary art when the latter yields to it and is invested as such. It confers on signs a new material power of decoding (deductions of fragments of heterogeneous codes, a-signifying and post-signifying connections in continuous variation, intensive local recoding of the global expressiveness, movement of traits of expression) that destratifies the space (physical, symbolic, discursive, institutional) in which it is inscribed by rendering sensible the trans-semiotic presence of insensible/anaesthetised forces.

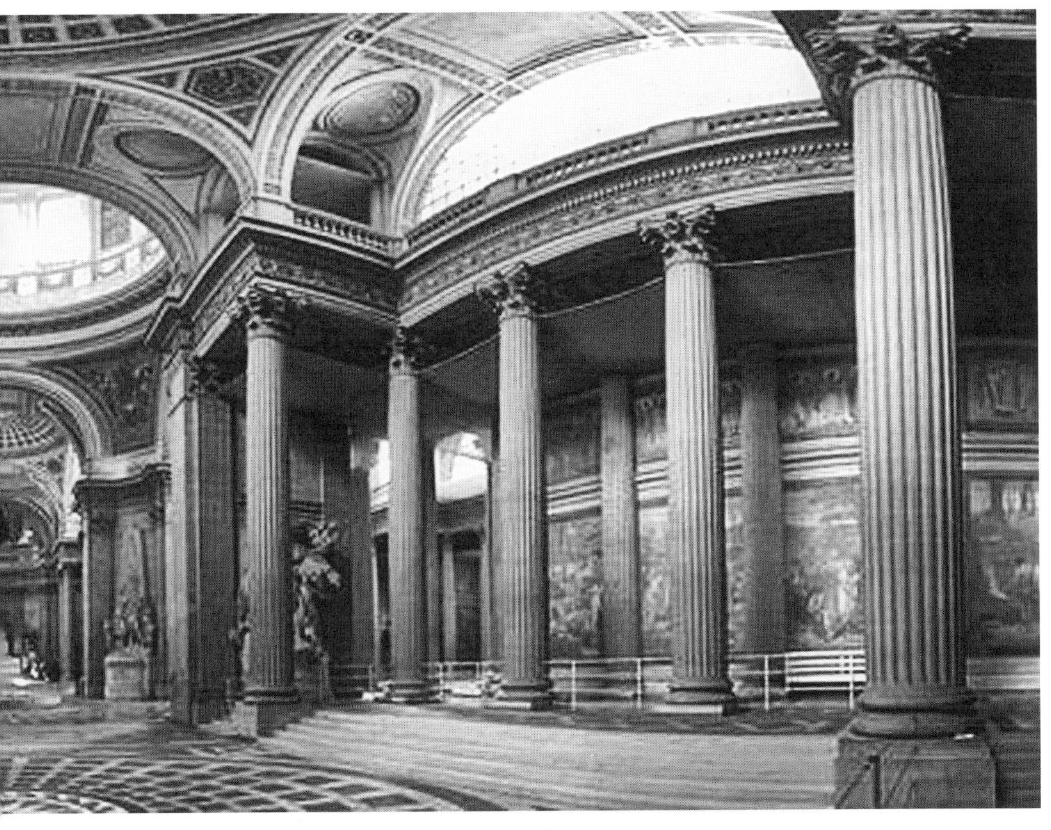

nterior of the Pantheon, Paris, 2005

In Neto's installation it would therefore be a matter of something completely different to an 'image', in the sense of an aesthetic *mise-en-scène*. Such a *mise-en-scène* would be charged with 'unveiling' an invisibility in a dialectic of hiding and showing internal to the image, or between images, or between the visible and the sayable. This invisible would be at one and the same time both the truth and the guarantee of the aesthetic operations of the *mise-en-scène,* even if this were at the cost of a permanent putting back into play of its operations (as it is with the sublime, for example). Rather, it is instead a matter of an *optically impenetrable* work which would in truth be better defined using two Brazilian passwords of the 1960s. It is a *coenesthetically 'penetrable' 'non-object'* (*Nao-objeto, Penetravel*). Lygia Clark and Helio Oiticica, in whose line of descent Neto's entire œuvre is situated, effectively made use of these expressions to think the 'total incorporation (in-corporation) of what one previously saw as *environmental*', according to a formula Oiticica used in his Notes on what he ends up calling the Ready Constructible (1978). He presents this as the 'proposition of a meta-sculpture or a *new perception* going from the sculptural to a sort of art simultaneously situated on the ground and in the air'.[8]

Leviathan Thot, Autumn Festival of Paris, 2006. Ernesto Neto's installation can be *penetrated* and *re-constructed* from everywhere and from all

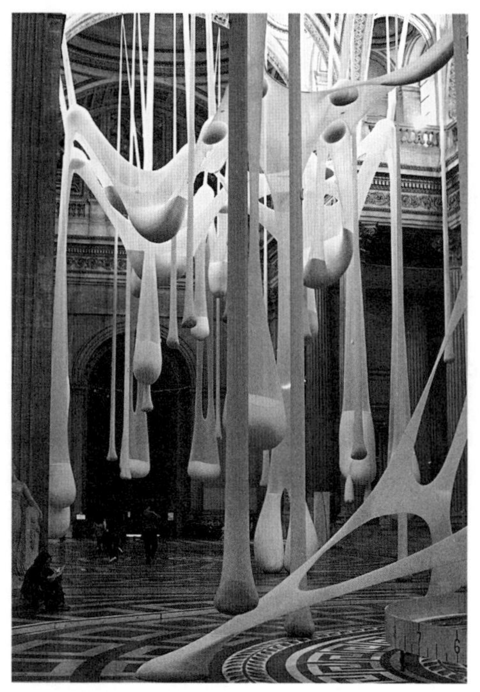

Ernesto Neto
Leviathan Thot, 2006

directions as it has neither beginning nor end. Certainly there is a centre, but of decentring and axes which derive from it only to be twisted out of joint. *Leviathan Thot* is a 'counter-installation' or an 'environmental appropriation' (in Oiticica's words). It doesn't seek to profit from the space of the Pantheon in order to *exhibit itself* (environmental art), or to exhibit its *heterogeneity*, in a symbolic or dialectical relationship to its environment. Rather, it is *in situ* that *Leviathan Thot* acts or agitates but so as to take on the *site-specificity* of the Republic's temple and locus of national memory, 'conceived ideally as the centre of the territory, the heart of the nation'.[9] (Unlike the temple of the Republic which, if one needed reminding, was – the usual sacred duty – *installed* comfortably and statically in St Genevieve de Soufflot following the much more visual than structural developments undertaken by Quatremere de Quincy on the orders of the constitutive Assembly in 1791.)

Consequently, Operation Neto modulates into a critical and clinical operation. Critically, *Leviathan Thot* confronts the building and its sheer size and grapples with it by placing all its physical and metaphysical coordinates into and under tension. The operation thus engages with nothing less than the *image of power* related to the *power of the image* which animates it and gives it a discursive existence – because the *architectural denunciation* of the Pantheon produced by Neto doesn't occur without the (Hobbesian) *metaphysical enunciation* that is projected onto it. This enunciation is de-posed in the title of the 'contra' installation in the manner of a '*d/enunciation*' reinforced by the mysterious *Thot* appended to it, and the no less strange orthography adopted by Neto for the Egyptian god Thoth.[10] Clinically, it sustains the claim to the affirmative dis-position of the operation: to the extent that this putting into tension is itself subtended by the fundamentally energetic nature of the process of environmental appropriation whose non-discursive seizing of being (*prise d'être*) liberates its effect as a 'counter-image' – from the labour of the negative within the image as much as with regard to a purely critical relation to its aesthetic forms – so as to introduce the intensive fact of a 'powerful non-organic life'.[11] Between the critical and the clinical, the pathology of the Body without Organs can thus awaken the anoptic quality of the Body without Image in a biopolitics of space which dismisses every metaphor of the invisible.

Political anatomy

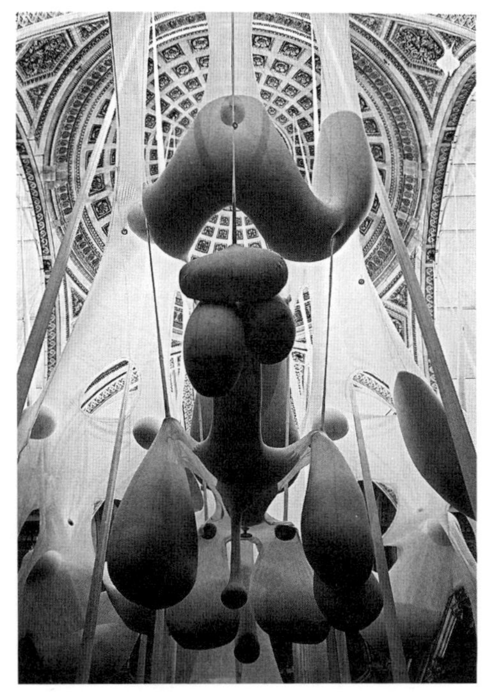

Ernesto Neto
Leviathan Thot, 2006

The decentring of the site is set in motion throughout the vertical elevation of the axis of the cupola-covered transept. For the monument, it is a manner of falling from its summit to be brought back down (but not thrown) to earth. *On the ground.* The epicentre of a slow turbulent fall from which one begins (but which one could reverse). The part of Neto's counter-installation occupying this space presents itself as a sort of tall, broad cylinder of fabric forming a vast, stretched-out and deformed reticulation, as if the reticular structure of the cupola was *torn apart.* It opens out towards the ground, where it is solidly anchored around the oscillations of Foucault's Pendulum. Under the impact of other forces, the catastrophe extends by contamination to the domes and vaults that develop geometrically around the central cupola.

This cupola is covered with octagonal panelling that converges towards the summit, the design implying a hemispheric anamorphosis of the gridwork of the panels. This type of composition is repeated in the other cupola and on the circular floor tiling corresponding to them. As to the properly orthogonal grid, it is visible in the many criss-crossing patterns and tiles on the ground, and it provides a subjacent order to the whole plan of the work as the principle of its rationalisation *more geometrico.*

One will notice straight away that the structure of the panelled cupola is not without analogy to the frontispiece of Hobbes's *Leviathan* as designed by Abraham Bosse, a major advocate of geometrically constructed perspective. The arrangement of the panelling in effect evokes that of the anonymous subjects presented from behind with their heads converging towards the sovereign, in an 'egalitarian' perspective, calculated in an egalitarian way. What is more, in the image, the sovereign associates the sword and the cross, in the same way as the Pantheon associates a secular temple with a church, one which is not consecrated but is still present symbolically, topped with a cross to sacralise the Republic. The analogy extends further since the eye of the cupola opens onto a second cupola occupied by a painting by Antoine Gros, *The Apotheosis of Saint Genevieve,* the base of which itself figures a corona of personae surrounding four sovereigns. The smallest eye of the cupola opens in turn onto a pure summit of light, which comes from the skylighting of the external dome, an ultimate supplementary dimension covering the system and the central void of Power to which all must equally submit.

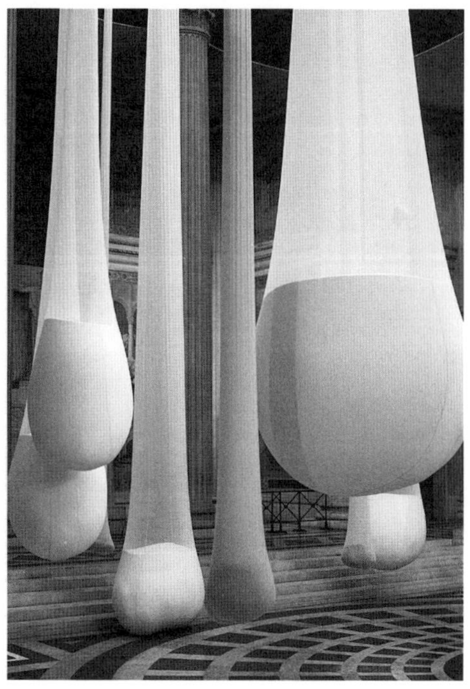

(Above and opposite): Ernesto Neto *Leviathan Thot*, 2006

It is *against* the ground and the aerial centre of this monument-image of power that Operation Neto works. The large and loose netting of the immense pseudo-cylindrical, spidery reticulation which descends from the central cupola is not the simple deployment in space of the patterning on the ground of large folded fabrics but the sensory diagram of forces which, by stretching, distend the grid and deform it, substituting for the geometric rigidity of a rigidly cellular world the perpetually changing dynamic of direct (immanent) relations between all the tensions. (One cannot but emphasise that here Operation Neto *naturally* incorporates, on the environmental plane, the dynamic-dynamiting operation produced by Clark and Oiticica with regard to the static, geometric and imagistic interpretation of the Mondrianesque reticulation of the plane of the tableau. Clark and Oiticica actualise the virtual energy of the tableau by beginning to *force* the tableau-form as much as the painting-form – before attacking, as their environmental explorations allow, the 'art-form' as such, according to Oiticica's expression.) Concerning the part of Leviathan we have just dealt with, Neto has said that it is the monster's head, 'the seat of fear ... the seat of the purification of sentiments' by the cold and calculating rationality of modernity. At its feet, Thoth, the Egyptian god of writing and calculus whom the Greeks associated with astronomy and 'politics', watches over Foucault's Pendulum, which hangs in the middle of this central piece. But this god is an ambivalent figure: the god of writing and of calculus, he is also the registrar of the dead; he counts down the days of the living and weighs up the heart–soul of death. He is thus qualified from every point of view to preside over the death of Leviathan, of which he is at the same time both the instrument of power and the first 'bureaucrat of death' (*un fonctionnaire de la mort*).

The extendable fabric which (dis)incarnates the head of Leviathan – a sort of stripped off epidermis – is nothing but a bare surface, where the grid, both sign and operator of rationality in the cupola, is submitted to the dynamicising and dynamiting of its geometry. The whole of the central apparatus is suspended at eight points from the eye of the cupola (by analogy with the octagonal structures of the edifice). Like everywhere else, it results from a system of equilibrium between the weights and counterweights of suspended masses, between the gravity to which they are submitted and the elasticity of the tissue which contains them. The disfigured cylindrical net, which constitutes a sort of 'dorsal fin' for the ensemble, comprises at its base four terminal prolongations in the form of weighted pockets, sinking to the ground, where they anchor it, divided up around the pendulum. The counterweight is assured by the hanging of four large pendentives that Neto calls 'drops', which descend halfway to the ground and whose weight overhead the visitor senses; while eight slim 'columns', on the contrary, run all the way to the ground which they are held just above or joined with (without settling on it). The body moving around the counter-installation experiences in a coenesthetic manner the work of muscles tautened by the tensions this skeletal Leviathan undergoes from both above and below. It *participates* in this politically informed sensation *in situ*.

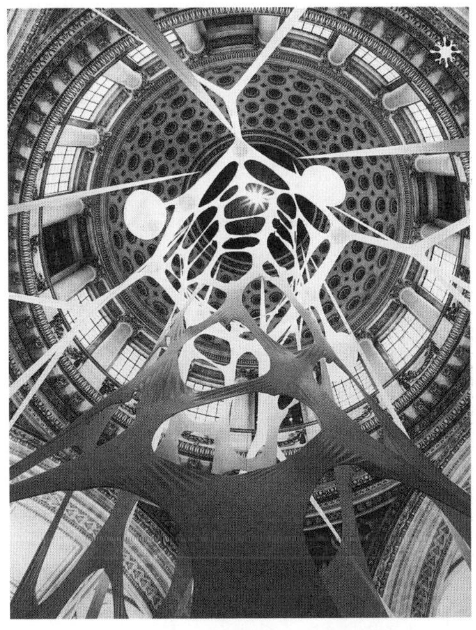

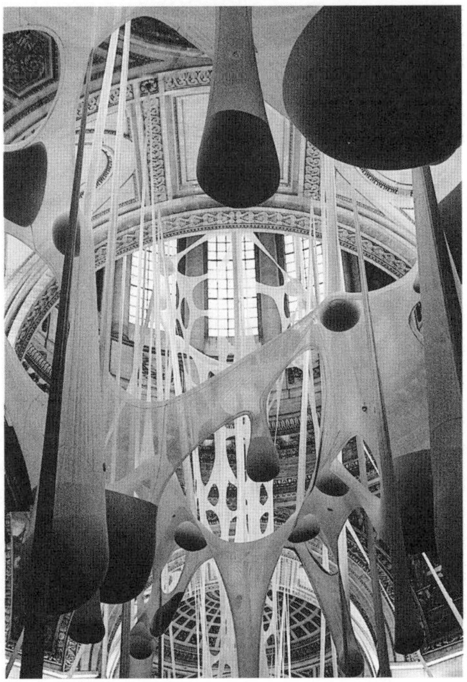

The decisive political stake of this apparatus is nothing less than the subversion of the art that Hobbes explicitly declares, in the introduction of his work, to 'create this great leviathan that is called Commonwealth or State (in Latin civitas)' ('Commonwealth', it will be recalled, is the English translation of *res publica*). In the optic of a constitutional reduction to the One, the art which stems from it bears the imperative of effectively producing a *public representation* of the body of the Republic, such that the multitude of subjects 'see' that they *constitute* its members, that the sovereign at its head is the bearer of the *most real image of Power*, capable of unifying the body of the people by representing all its members in a consenting organism, at peace with itself, which is nothing other than the 'State', the constitutional state. Such a representation can only *link or bind* its subjects together under the sovereign that they institute in a constitutive manner by defeating 'this other multitude which has no order, which is like a many-headed hydra' (*Leviathan*, VI, I).[12] Failing which, the Republican Contract which founds our democratic societies on Representation (nationally and in all the plasticity of the term) is unable to become effective. Magisterially analysed in all its visual strategies by Horst Bredekamp, this is what the frontispiece executed by Abraham Bosse for Leviathan teaches us.

> The gaze that men from everywhere direct towards the head of the colossus is directed back by its eyes to the observer, who embraces the ground-level view of the figures with back to us and is at the same time, at the level of the gaze of the sovereign, directly interpellated by it. The contradictory character of the body politic as the product of men subjected by the sovereign is already manifest in the exchange of looks between citizens, Leviathan and the observer.[13]

The common orientation of everyone towards the head of the sovereign proclaims the moment of contractual engagement of all, including the observer, who also *participates* in the apparatus, in this way verifying that representation is *tutela praesens*. 'It is only by its representative, that is to say, the sovereign, that the commonwealth is a person and has the capacity to do anything at all: the sovereign is the only legislator' (*Leviathan* XXVI). But again, as Bredekamp explains

> for conventions and laws to become controlled actions, words must be changed into bodies, and it is this mediating step that the image of Leviathan accomplishes ... It [thus] becomes a powerful machine for definitions, a 'sovereign definer'.[14]

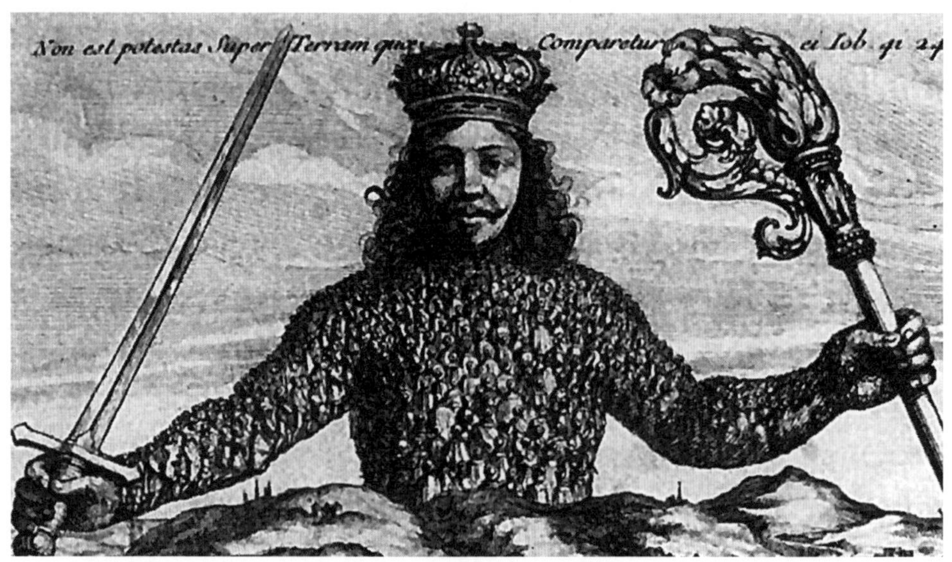

Detail from the title page of the first edition of Thomas Hobbes's *Leviathan*, 1651

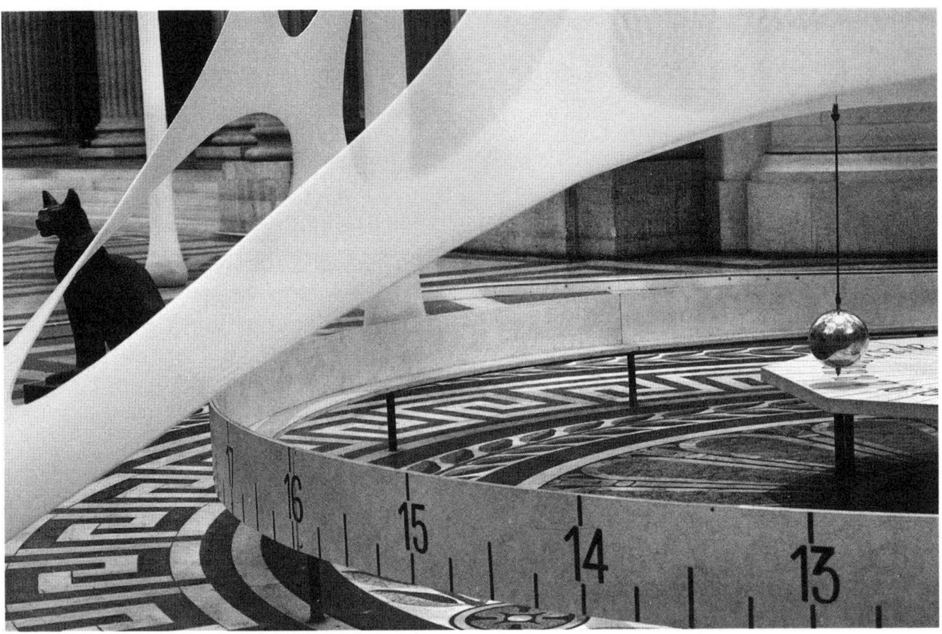

Ernesto Neto
Leviathan Thot, 2006

One must understand that the contractual basis of the state *formally* founded on an egalitarian definition of citizens so as to suppress the state of nature (the perpetual war of the multitude maintained through a relative equality of forces) calls for the control of words as much as for the monopoly of violence. Relayed and represented by images which incorporate their sovereign majesty, the control of words is oriented towards 'the fact that we can command and understand commands'; it is the 'greatest benefit of speech' (*De Homine* X, 3), the exercise of which requires 'perspicuous words, but by exact definitions first snuffed, and purged from ambiguity' (*Leviathan*, V).[15] Hence the *representation* of Leviathan on the frontispiece of Hobbes's book is the centre of gravity of images because it is the exclusive sign of the *sovereignty* of the state related to the *right of representation*. We have seen one avatar of this sign in the structure of the cupola of the Pantheon that Neto literally tears up, by opposing to its 'regime of representation' something quite other than an aesthetic regime of the image, in Jacques Rancière's sense.

In this process, Neto also attacks the political body of Leviathan understood as an *Artificial Man*, in its modern constitution. In theory it is indifferent whether the representative is a monarch or a representative assembly – because it is the *representative* character of the sovereign, depositary of the 'personality of the republic', which founds absolute sovereignty on an egalitarian 'republican' contract of all with all (*inter pares*). Hence sovereignty is in truth the axiomatic corollary of representation (the *pact of representation*). Leviathan is thus the symbol of a *homo artificialis, automaton* or *machine*, whose power can only obey the principled rationality which created it in the name of the people (*Rex est populus*), whilst each individual recognises him- or herself as the *author* of the acts and judgements of this *actor*, this sovereign representative that every individual institutes. In this way it is verified that the power of the legally represented 'subject' has no other condition of reality than the subjectivation of a power which finds here its first modern 'contractual' form, where right does not exist without *subjection* to a *possessive market society* (according to the expression proposed by Macpherson for the 'congruence of sovereignty and market society').[16] The legal-contractual representation which founds its own absolute political validity is in effect constitutive of this new notion which has the name POWER. Hobbes is, in this sense, both the 'founder of liberalism' and the 'Marx of the bourgeoisie' (Leo Strauss, for example, explains that Hobbes is the 'father of Modernity', whilst Tonnies reminds us of the importance of 'Hobbes's theorem', mediated by Rousseau, for the constitutional beginnings of the French Revolution). To speak like Hegel, it is that in Hobbes, the 'true idea is there'.

In *We Have Never Been Modern* – whose influence on his installation Neto acknowledged – Bruno Latour summarises the situation:

> Hobbes invents the naked calculating citizen, whose rights are limited to possessing and to being represented by the artificial construction of the Sovereign. He also creates the language according to which Power equals Knowledge, an equation which is at the root of the entire modern Realpolitik.[17]

This is announced by the first phrases of *Leviathan*, grounding in the theory of art the mechanical creation of a political, or artistico-technological, android – which presides over the birth of modern political philosophy as a *science of submission* rationally founded on a calculus of interests (*philosophia civilis*).[18] It is the Order that is so defined, by the universalisation of the calculus, and not Justice – if not the *market concept of justice*[19] – which makes the multitude a single body submitted to the will of one alone. The sovereign governs with unlimited power in the name of all those he represents, who in return *equally* authorise the 'public person' to decide and to act in its place. Failing this, there would only be an aggregate totality, a *multitudo dissoluta*, because it is via the head of the sovereign, who personifies the *common*-will thus represented, that the political Body lives and moves. In this way the civil 'unity' of the people, the people 'united in one person ... called a COMMONWEALTH' (*Leviathan* XVII), strictly correlated with the existence of the state, is substituted for the 'dissolute' multiplicity of the multitude, a sort of *Moby Dick* avant la lettre.[20] (It follows that: 'that men distinguish not enough between a People and a Multitude ... lead[s] to the dissolution of Government' *De Cive* XII 8.) Via this short circuit (which is also the shortest circuit) between aesthetics and politics, Operation Neto stages a sort of critical and clinical diagnosis of representation, in every sense of the term, aiming at an *expansive disorganisation* of the multitude living under the republican regime of contractual representation,a regime for which the Pantheon is the temple as much *ex nostro abritrio* as *more geometrico*.

The disorganisation that affects the centre of Leviathan extends out to the other members of its body so as to invest the *multitudo dissoluta* with a radical vital recomposition. If this is the more properly affirmative component of Operation Neto taking place alongside the critical moment that was necessitated by the political take on the Pantheon, both are part of the same lesson in political anatomy.

Hand–brain

It starts up again from the top of the reticulated cylindrical shape. The fabric of this volume, in a tension that runs counter to its vertical fall, is stretched towards the exterior in four long forking branches. At their extremities, these four forks are then fixed on to the two 'arms' forming extensions towards the centre of the members of Leviathan occupying the four lateral axes of the Pantheon. The ends of these forking branches fix these arms across the fabric which is stretched under the weight of their endings. They form a sort of suture between the heterogeneous parts of the body of Leviathan. Although there are similarities between them, and internal symmetries, each one of these developed branches of the 'installation' is different from the others and is assembled in a fashion that is both 'vital' and inorganic. Neto calls this heterogeneous body a 'humanoid monster' and adds that 'in this highly masculine building it is a work of highly feminine contrast'. Rather than this contrast – the polarities of which could be inverted or associated within the terms of the opposition – a new ambivalence may be pointed out, related to the figure of Thoth. The statue which is on guard at the foot of Foucault's Pendulum isn't really Thoth (figured with the head of an ibis or a dog or a cynocephalus) – and in any case, the identity of the gods of the Egyptians is no less variable than their names. Rather, it is a copy of Bastet (or Bast or Ubasti), the cat-goddess, the peaceful avatar of a lion-goddess. Bastet has been considered most notably as the protector of the home and of motherhood, and associated with the joy of music and dancing, those arts which Neto associates with the Brazilian life experience, the *vivência brasileira* of his work.

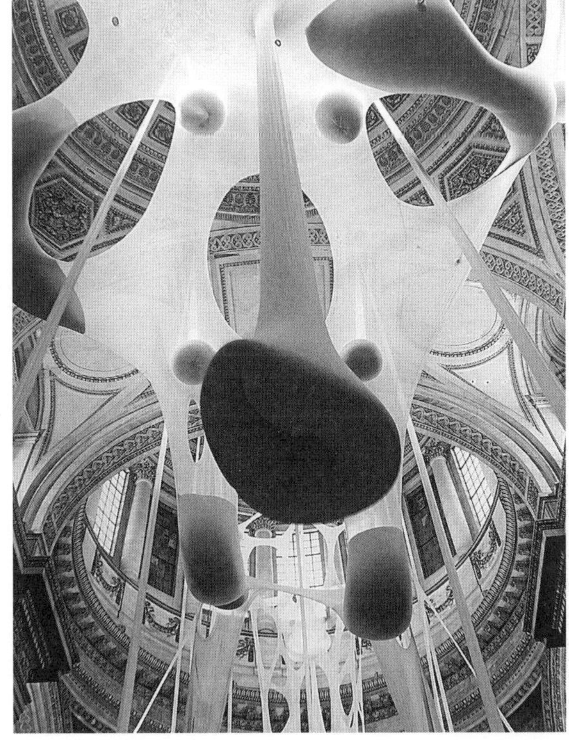

Ernesto Neto
Leviathan Thot, 2006

Nothing is positively figured outside of the 'representation' aimed at by the defection whose object it is and which is also that of the image whose aesthetic form is as if devoured by the omnipresent apparatus *which is the whole of what one perceives*. It is experienced corporeally, in a coenesthetic fashion, as a sensational bloc of forces put into continuous variation. Thus, in the watering of the fabric filtering the light, it is not the optical effect which matters for itself, but the degree of tension of the elastic tissue-skin that results from the reciprocal, quantitative-energetic play of all forces, linking up step by step. If something akin to 'organs' appears – Neto talks of a head, stomach, arms, fingers and even alludes to sexual organs – they only function as pure intensities which accumulate in pockets or flow in a 'jet of energy' playing on the 'fluid aspect of matter'.[21] Forms here don't assume any function: they are the contingent result of a static energy (i.e. one that is frozen, *suspended*). This static energy itself results from the technically highly complex process by which the fabric, cut out in inert forms on the ground, is raised and stretched in such a way as to distribute both matter and the tensions of which it is susceptible so as to balance out the weights. Things only move now by a gentle, accidental oscillation incorporating the gradient of freedom belonging to the system. This is not without producing a rhizome-effect in the intensive–extensive continuum thus projected.[22] Tensions here function directly in an unformed

Ernesto Neto
Leviathan Thot, 2006

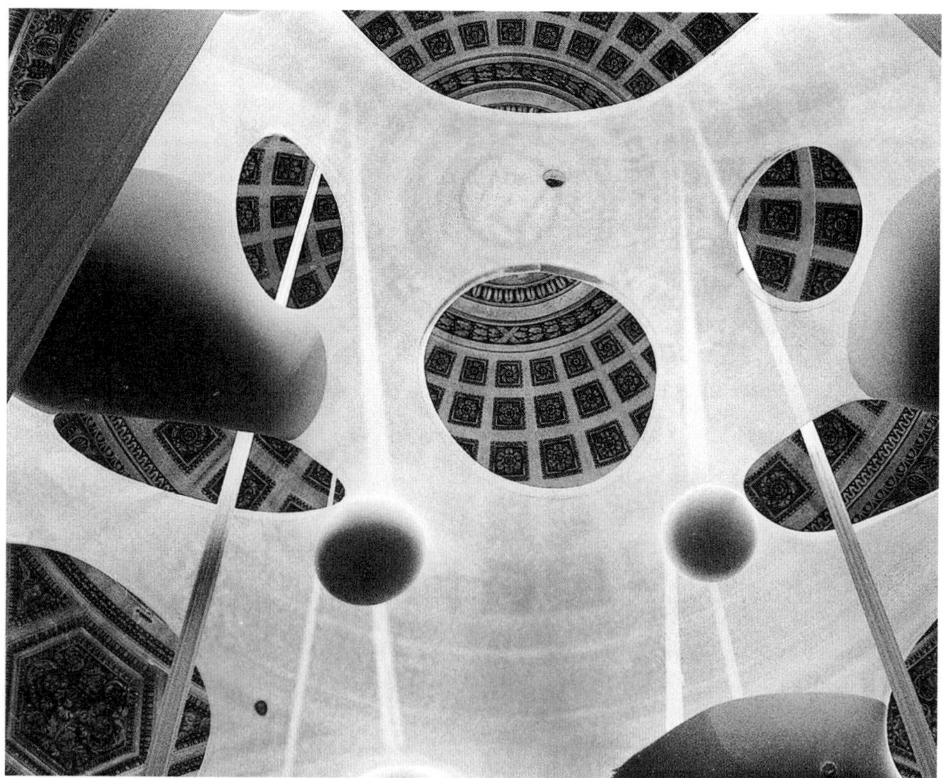

matter, a matter-flux only presenting degrees of intensity, resistance, conductivity and stretching which condition its extension in space and which the ambulant relaunches coenesthetically on his or her own body. Extension itself becomes the result of a fusional multiplicity whose 'quality' is the contraction, the *intension* of the quantity liberated by the *dissolution* of constant form as a *state function*, to the profit of dynamic differences which bring into relation the most diverse latitudes and longitudes, the most varied of speeds and slownesses. The organising form of matter is in this way *suspended* by the putting into tension of the materials-forces, whose local results mobilise the ensemble of 'trajects'. *To suspend* is to struggle *with* the universal gravity which *striates* homogeneous space through 'the verticals of gravity, the distribution of matter into parallel layers, the lamellar and laminar movement of flows' summarised by Deleuze and Guattari as 'the space of *pillars*'.[23] But to suspend is equally to stop the regulated exercise of the organs (as forms subjected by the head) of the Leviathan-Body, and the relation that every human organism is supposed to maintain, using its head, with metric space in general. The organism's machinic enslavement to the abstract form of space-measure is part of the domain of Thoth. In this way Operation Neto is as much the putting to work as it is the result of a confrontation between two types of science or two modes of scientific operation. On the one hand, a science of the state, originally founded on the hylomorphic articulation matter/form and Euclidian geometry (the Pantheon, in which Foucault's Pendulum was located, is an avatar of the generalised rationalisation of the world which stemmed from it). On the other hand, a nomad science, originally founded on Archimedean geometry and the physics of the ancient Greek atomists. It is the latter's turbulent and hydraulic models which are in a way revived by the materials-forces in heterogenesis resulting from the accidents which affect the members of *Leviathan Thot* submitted to gravity. For his part, Neto opposes Euclidian geometry to Riemannian geometry, the kind 'that addresses curves on minimal surfaces'.

But in the first place it will have been necessary to *skin* the Leviathan-Body *because organs stick to the skin before depending on 'this organic organisation of organs that is called the organism'*, from which the system of judgement of the Leviathan-God extracts a work that is useful 'to the *prosperity* and the *wealth* of all particular members' on which the whole 'force' of Leviathan rests (*Leviathan*, Introduction). The 'skin' here, which Neto specifies is neither the envelope nor the outgrowing of any 'flesh', is this *rising to the surface* of the organs liberated by the emptying out of the Corpus-Socius. This emptying out will have made a 'body without organs' surge up from and in the disaffected space of the Pantheon-Leviathan (the expression 'body without organs' may be found in Neto[24]), bearing with it an entirely different social physics to that of 'work'. The body of the spectator is forced to displace itself incessantly, to wander around so as to see and take in the excess of what it sees. The body is forced to *perceive* the space of the experiment within which it is caught and against which collision incessantly menaces, at the very moment that the 'hybrid element' is stretched out overhead like a skeletal star of skin. In this way, the spectator is subjected to the experience of the Body without Organs of Space itself, the intensive *Spatium* rather than *Extensio*, in the haptic destruction of the optic of power, resulting from the fluidification of space by mass. This itinerant geography, which decentres every point of view in the continuous variation of orientations of a generalised elasticity, puts us in movement, in 'becoming'. We ambulate in the smooth space of a *Nonument* (in the words of Gordon Matta-Clark) that only exists in the critical and clinical confrontation with the 'historical' striated space of the Monument, whose *sensible matter* has thus been awoken. This sensible matter propagates here like a counter-image liberating itself energetically from the task of *imaging* because it projects a new type of reality. An infra- and supra-organic reality, which draws its 'energy' as much from the space of virtualities liberated by the concrete physics of the power that acts with the forces internal to gravity as from the forces of the *multitudo dissoluta* caught up in and liberated from the monumental history of the Leviathan that it *invaginates*. It is by means of this body without organs, which is *in itself* a 'body without image',[25] that Neto can give body *for us*, in a certain *Delirium Ambulatorium*, to the (rhizomatic and bioenergetic) subversion of the image of the state-machine, the *state-form* such as it is inscribed on the pediment of the Pantheon sculpted by David d'Angers, where Nation appears between Liberty and History.

Although Neto could not have conceived as complex a work as this without the support of an overall plan superposed on the ground and elevation plan of the Pantheon, the very course of the operation made this plan itself undergo a heterogenesis such that the result doesn't correspond to any prior image. Guided by this plan, together with a rough sketch and the help of a thread of red velour, Neto sized up and marked out the openings and multiple sections of fabric on the folded layers of material destined to become the diverse members of this inorganic body. The fabric was then cut out following this thread and sewn together before being filled with various substances (polystyrene, sand, lavender). *Cut out/sew in*. Confronted with the work, the plan appears as a graphical formalisation, an optical blueprint of an operation which escapes it because it is of an entirely different nature. This supple line was drawn/weighed up/posed by what Neto calls a 'hand-brain'; it slipped between the fingers, was 'worked' by the displacement of the body, applied by gravity – all operations that transform an inert trace on paper into a living, fluid line, fluctuating according to the artist's intimate dance with all the parameters – both present and virtual. Because there is a 'pressure of virtuality which disquiets the image that is already available to make space for a new dimension' opened up by a gesture which 'is not a simple spatial displacement: it decides, liberates and proposes a new modality of "moving"' (as affirmed by Gilles Châtelet to explain how the *virtual requires the gesture*).[26] And the artist could only evaluate coenesthetically the degree of elasticity of the Lycra at the moment he laid down his visually static but virtually dynamic line. In this regard, nothing is more striking than the distance between the sketched plan on the ground – right and proper, with the 'fine' curves and symmetries of its biomorphic and pseudo-organic regularity – and the body which takes on a life of its own in suspension in space. It is a life which is elastic as much as rhizomatic, so much does the plasticity of mass affirm here its irreducible difference from extension (*Extensio*), in suspension in space submitted to resistance – that is to say, to speak like Leibniz, *action and passion*. No direct deduction from the plan to the body can be made at all.

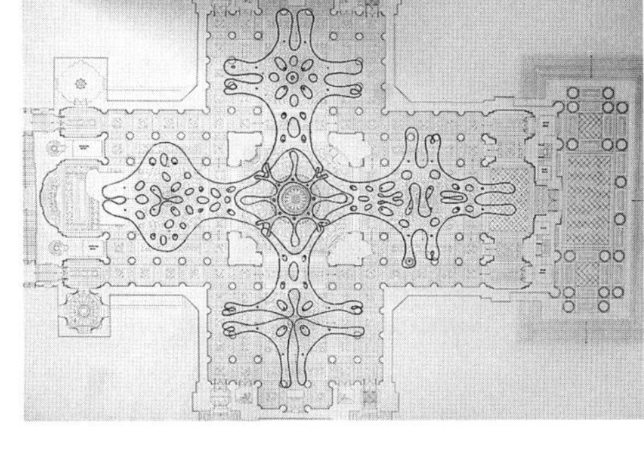

Ernesto Neto
Leviathan Thot, diagram, 2006

In the erection of the diverse members of the body ('the experience begins', says Neto),[27] gravity henceforth becomes the fundamental agent to which all the virtualities of both space and the volume of the cut and sewn material forms are subjected *by force*, giving rise to continuous processes of transformation. In the course of this operation, which is carried out slowly, the relationship between the different tensions and the equilibrium between weights and counterweights become the object of multiple adjustments, engendering highly sensible singularities that animate the energetic materiality thus put in motion. The *modulation* of fluid matter into 'pockets', 'tubes' or 'pipes' in and by this immense living abstract machine clearly marks here the rupture with a hylomorphic scheme. Simondon has shown that this hylomorphic scheme was in the first place and above all informed by a social representation of work where

> form corresponds to what the man in charge has himself thought and which he must express in a positive manner when he gives his orders ... to those who will manipulate matter; it is the very content of this order, that by which he governs ...; it is in the content of the order that the indication of matter is indeterminate whilst form is logical and expressible determination.

He concludes that it is through the same social conditioning that 'the mind is distinguished from the body in the same way as the citizen from the living human being'.[28] From the point of view of whoever accomplishes the material operation, the idea according to which 'modulating is moulding' a flowing matter that can only be *followed* 'in a continuous and perpetually variable manner' expresses a total de-conditioning which is as much physical as it is social. It is a *temporal modulation* at the heart of which what is produced becomes an *event*, the event of an active force which affects matter with a *baroque* expression (Deleuze's definition of mannerism is rediscovered in Simondon's modulation).[29] Or rather a matter of expression that is *neo-baroque* in its manner of raising its deformations to the state of tense fluxes which make classical-modern reason[30] radically diverge and whose operational machination appeals to an intuition in act as much as to an extension of its act, which redefines the artist as an *artisan* and the artisan as *the itinerant, the ambulant*.[31]

One may recall that the operation began well before the setting up of the installation, when Neto bundled up the Lycra in his workshop in Rio (the workshop of a couturier rather than the studio of an artist) before laying it out in the Pantheon, as he says, like 'a travelling salesman, a street vendor', a *camelot* carioca. These *camelots* are the 'natural' inhabitants of the favelas and champions of the 'informal' economy which informs and deforms the landscape of Rio, deployed in an 'unplanned order'. They are, Franck Leibovici summarises, 'the social equivalent of the favelas, which are themselves the urban equivalent of *bromeliae* growing all the way down the trunks of palm trees'.[32] It is also this 'tropical forest' that in a sort of environmental mutualism Neto makes grow (processually, not iconically) right in the middle of the Pantheon, as it grows all over Rio, with the favelas whose physical and human geography clings to hillsides. If *natural* or, more broadly – Foucault's Pendulum obliges – *cosmic* mutualism (as Brazilians also say, à la Deleuze) has some paradigmatic (or *cosmopolitical*) relevance here, Operation Neto evidently shows that it is on condition of understanding environmental mutualism in a strictly constructivist sense – in the words of Oiticica, 'anti-naturalist' and 'multi-transformable'. As Latour puts it definitively, between 'nature' and 'society', 'if we are constructivist in one instance, then we have to be constructivist for both'.[33]

As to the whiteness of the material Neto unpacks in the Pantheon before he cuts it up, this ready-made colour immanent to an industrial-synthetic material, which confronts us strangely with the 'white without form' denounced by Hegel in the Preface to *The Phenomenology of Spirit*, is directly incorporated into the environmental value of the installation. It works away haptically in the light under the effect of the tensions which the Lycra undergoes, but in the manner of *a bodily restraint* (*une contrainte par corps*) which violates and blinds the optical reception of light in the 'total activity of the eye'.[34] (Impenetrable, *white without form* is *a tangible white* forbidding any 'division of retinal activity', *gathered, crushed, forbidden, deranged* in the ready-made white.) It is worth recalling here that Oiticica conceived, even hallucinated, Malevich's *White on White* as 'a necessary step in which the "plastic arts" shed their privileges by whitening themselves so as to become skin/body/air'. It is exactly the 'monumental' components that Neto utilises which he comes back to in the text presenting *Leviathan Thot*,

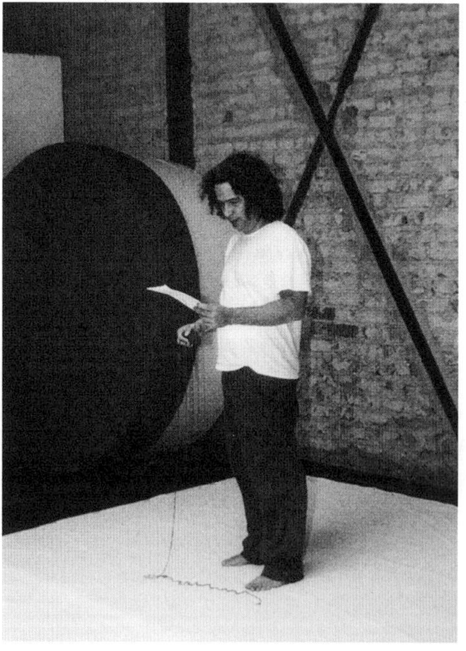

Ernesto Neto installing
Leviathon Thot, Pantheon, Paris, 2006

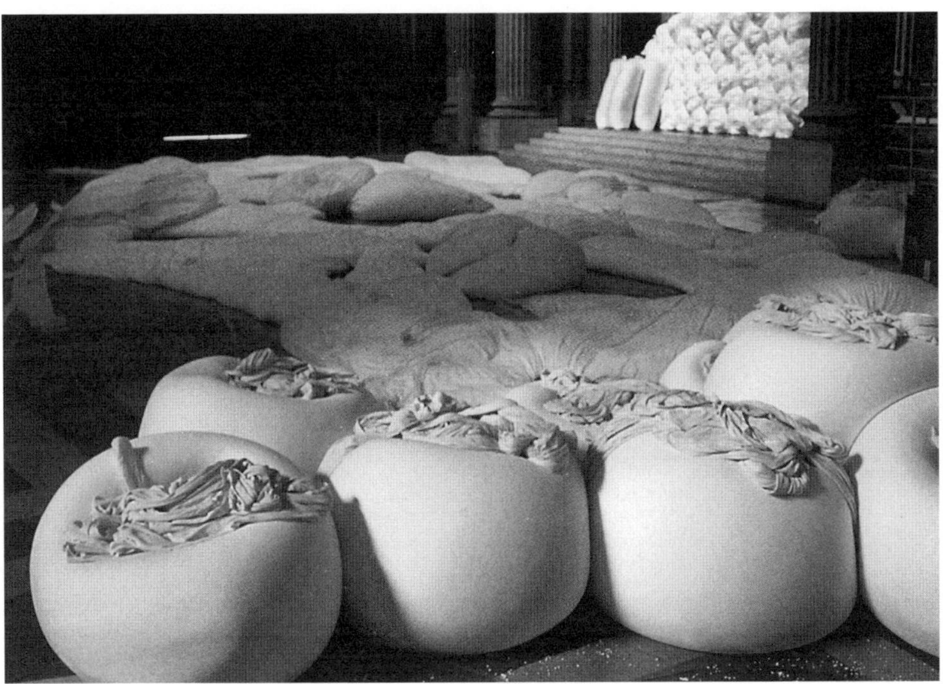

Ernesto Neto
Leviathan Thot, 2006

specifying their tensive or intensive values so as to define the mutualism of his apparatus – giving a meaning to what he calls the 'ethic of action' (*a ética da açào*).[35] There comes a moment when, as he writes,

> the touching, the intimate relation, the spatial limit between skin and matter, solid in its essence but liquid in its spherical envelope, which adjusts to every movement like the sand which flows through the neck of an hourglass, whose fluid mass defines the body of the work, are intensified in ascension ... Like mutualism ... in a tropical forest ..., everything is reorganised in this space of passage, of tensions, volume adapts and forms itself again here and there in a dance of calculations and chance.[36]

Translated by Andrew Goffey

1 Georges Didi-Huberman, *Confronting Images*, Penn State University Press, University Park PA 2004.
2 Jacques Rancière, *The Future of the Image*, Verso, London 2007.
3 The French *chaînage* has been variously rendered here as 'chaining together', 'chain' or 'linking' [*trans.*].
4 Gilles Deleuze, *Francis Bacon: The Logic of Sensation*, Continuum, London 2003, p.100.
5 Rancière 2007, p.82.
6 Félix Guattari, 'Échafaudages Sémiotiques', *Révolution Moléculaire*, Encres, Paris 1977.
7 The author prefers to render *agencement* as 'agency' wherever possible, in contrast to its standard rendering as 'assemblage' [*trans.*].

8 Helio Oiticica, 'Notes sur le ready constructible' 1978, in *Hélio Oiticica*, exh. cat., Galerie nationale du Jeu de Paume, Paris 1992, p.200.
9 Mona Ozouf, 'Le Panthéon: L'École normale des morts', in *Les lieux de la mémoire*, ed. P. Nora, Gallimard, Paris 1997, p.155.
10 Neto told me that he had wanted to introduce a principle of variation that accorded with his own 'operation' on Leviathan. I therefore respect the spelling *Thot* where it is a question of the title of the work and use the normal spelling for the figure of the Egyptian God.
11 On the 'powerful non-organic life' in its relation to the body without organs, see Deleuze 2003, pp.46–7.
12 The citation is from the Sorbières translation of Hobbes, *De Cive*.
13 Horst Bredekamp, *Stratégies visuelles de Thomas Hobbes*, Éditions de la Maison des sciences de l'homme, Paris 2003, p.9.
14 Ibid., pp.128–9.
15 From which it can be verified that an analytic definition of philosophy cannot work without its a priori being conditioned by political information. Hobbes appears here as the proto-founder of linguistically defined analytic philosophy.
16 C.B. MacPherson, *The Political Theory of Possessive Individualism: Hobbes to Locke*, Oxford University Press, Oxford 1962, p.95.
17 Bruno Latour, *We Have Never Been Modern*, Harvard University Press, Cambridge MA 2006, p.26.
18 *Philosophia civilis*, which, if we are to believe Hobbes in the epistle dedicatory of *De Corpore*, '[is] no older than [his] book *De Cive*'. Its modernity is thus inscribed in the wake of the scientific revolution of Copernicus and Galileo (to which Hobbes adds the name of Harvey, the principal physician to King James and King Charles).
19 MacPherson 1962, p.86.
20 Which one must take literally: Mob = the dangerous mass and Dick = the devil.
21 According to the declarations made by Neto in the video accompanying his installation.
22 'the final global result [is] synchronised without a central agency', Gilles Deleuze and Félix Guattari, *A Thousand Plateaus*, trans. Brian Massumi, Minnesota University Press, Minnesota 1987, p.19.
23 Ibid., p.408; emphasis added.
24 In the catalogue, Ernesto Neto, *Leviathan Thot, Festival d'Automne*, Éditions du Regard, Paris 2006, p.35.
25 Gilles Deleuze and Félix Guattari, *Anti-Oedipus*, trans. Robert Hurley et al., Athlone, London 1984, p.9.
26 Gilles Châtelet *Les enjeux du mobile*, Seuil, Paris 1993, pp.32–3.
27 *Leviathan Thot, Festival d'Automne*, p.35.
28 Gilbert Simondon, *L'individu et sa genèse physico-biologique*, PUF, Paris 1995, p.49.
29 Gilles Deleuze, *The Fold: Leibniz and the Baroque*, Athlone, London 1993, p.19.
30 Because the Baroque is 'the ultimate attempt to reconstitute a classical reason', ibid., p.81.
31 Deleuze and Guattari 1987, p.409.
32 Franck Leibovici in *Leviathan Thot, Festival d'Automne*, pp.29–30.
33 Latour 2006, p.95.
34 'The sensation of white or of light, that is to say the total activity of the eye', writes Schopenhauer in his letter to Goethe, 11 November 1815, when he tries to push his master's anti-Newtonism to its final physiological limit. Arthur Schopenhauer, *Textes sur la vue et sur les couleurs*, Vrin, Paris 1986, p.125.
35 In an interview given in the review *Artes & Ensaios*, 16 July 2008, UFRJ, Rio de Janeiro 2008, p.16.
36 Ibid., p.53.

4
This is Not My Body
Elisabeth Lebovici

> Indeed there are not two genders, there is only one, the feminine, the 'masculine' not being a gender. For the masculine is not the masculine but the general.[1]

These two sentences, written by Monique Wittig in 1983, pronounce a regime of visibility and invisibility for the feminine in language. They can also be applied to the image. They signal, to me, one of the major shifts, or even one of the major 'kicks', that women artists have delivered against the classical thinking of visibility and invisibility in the iconic image, even before second-wave feminism began to redefine the very notion of the 'canon'.[2] Women artists have been undoing the autonomy and the universality of the aesthetic image, by developing their art, not only for the production of effects in signification or communication, but as a form of agency.

Difference and the 'neighbourhood' of the sexes

Let's exchange, for a moment, visibility for invisibility. The French 1979 paperback edition of Roland Barthes's *Le degré zéro de l'écriture* features on the front an artwork which generally goes unnoticed. Inside one finds a caption which quite imprecisely says: 'Painted relief by Sophie Taeuber-Arp, 1938.' A woman artist is in the foreground but stays more or less invisible.

Yve-Alain Bois's essay 'Sophie Taeuber-Arp Against Greatness', discussing her depictions of white shapes in relief, which figure in the catalogue of the exhibition: *Inside the Visible (an elliptical traverse of 20th century art, in of and from the feminine)* notes the near invisibility of the artist, this 'maker of works as beautiful and intelligent as *Relief rectangulaire, Cercles Découpés* or *Cônes surgissants* with its cut out background and menacingly protruding elements.'[3] Yet Sophie Taeuber (1889–1943) went unnoticed for almost fifty years. This didn't happen to Hans Arp, an artist who always admitted he owed her much. They lived together. But there was more to this artistic couple. There was a common wish for anonymity, a refusal to be named as singular authors.

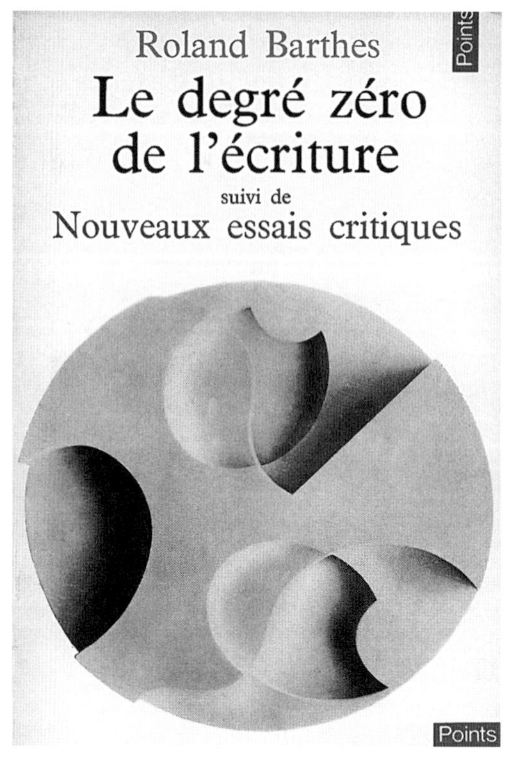

Book cover of Roland Barthes's *Le degré zéro de l'écriture suivi de Nouveaux essais critiques*, (with painted relief by Sophie Tauber-Arp, 1938) Paris 1972

Their work in common culminated in a threesome with producer Theo Van Doesburg in the painted decoration of L'Aubette in Strasbourg, which eventually added to the invisibility of this woman artist in art history.

Sophie Taeuber has a much more interesting œuvre than this account of her life as a victim of patriarchy suggests. She is one of the most compelling artists of the twentieth century, partly because she extended her production into multiple fields, encompassing dance and performance, puppet theatre, textile design – the so-called 'feminine' disciplines; although Hans made textiles and embroidery, too. She was commissioned to design for a gallery, an office, villas and apartments, and of course, for the entertainment complex of L'Aubette, but she also supervised the construction of the couple's home and studios in Clamart-Meudon. She involved herself in teaching, in arts counselling, in journalism as an editor of the magazine *Plastique*, and she was the first woman artist to be acknowledged at Black Mountain College. She also provided for cultural exchange between France and Poland and visited herself the avant-garde museum Sztuki in Łodź. The exchange of roles seems to have happened on many occasions in the activities of the couple.

In the *Tondo* relief on the cover of *Le degré zéro*, neither painting nor sculpture, which looks like a maquette as well as a finished work – a far more interesting ambiguity than with the first one – the questions go back and forth from contiguity to continuity: a paradox with which Sophie plays. She works with several layers, irregular portions of ellipses and discs, which suggest a life of their own, a rotation of their own, and a common displacement. As Yve-Alain Bois suggests, 'these works are highly compositional, but the composition itself is given as transient'.[4] This implies vocabularies other than formal ones. The pairs 'continuity/contiguity' and 'compositional/transient' are at work and play a role in undoing the paradigm of sexual difference.

The difference between the sexes was one of the most passionately discussed issues of the twentieth century. In the late 1990s, notably in France, with debates on gay marriage and homosexual kinship, it was made into a principle transcending all other dualism in Western thought. Even some non-religious 'experts' of the Left raised their voices in order to maintain the 'Symbolic Order', invoking Jacques Lacan as well as Claude Lévi-Strauss, as the Names of the Fathers. *The Elementary Structures of Kinship (de la parenté)* became dogma. The 'specialists' were to talk as social scientists, as anthropologists, like Françoise Héritier, as psychoanalysts, like Julia Kristeva, or as philosophers, like Sylviane Agacinski, when they raised their voices against what they would call a rupture with the Law. Françoise Héritier, for instance, as a (famous) anthropologist, asserted that sexual difference

> is at the ground of the creation of the fundamental opposition that enables us to think. For thinking is first to classify, to classify is first to discriminate, and the fundamental discrimination is based on the 'difference des sexes'. This is an irreducible fact: one cannot argue that these differences don't exist; they are impassable 'end stops' of thought, as day and night. Our modes of thinking and our social organisations are thus based on the principal observation of the difference between the sexes.[5]

This discourse was countered by feminist anthropologists and psychoanalysts, such as Sabine Prokhoris, who in her book *Le Sexe prescrit*, challenges the very notion of sexual difference as 'observed': 'a difference isn't some thing but a way within other possible manners, to interpret, to treat, the relation and thus the discrepancy between things observed'.[6] Therefore, she writes, why not observe it through the effects of resemblance or neighbourhood, for instance? That Sophie and Hans thrived collaboratively making or exchanging collages, textile designs, wood sculpture, or drawing 'with four hands', constitutes for me a good example of this *voisinage*; not in marital life, but in collaborative works. In the series of *Duo Collages*, for instance, they worked together towards dissolving the singular notion of a sexed subject.

This is not my body

Sophie Taeuber and Hans Arp were dancers, too. As artists, they exemplified an intriguing possibility that bounced back and forth during the twentieth century, weaving a strong relationship of *voisinage* between the body and abstraction. As Dadaist Richard Huelsenbeck put it: 'In that period as we danced, sang and recited night after night, abstract art was tantamount to absolute honour.'

Sophie Taeuber's work embodies this sense of neighbourhood: in 1916, in her hometown of Zurich, she enrolled in a course in artistic expressive dance with choreographer Rudolph Laban, who had arrived from Germany. There, she became friends with dancers such as Mary Wigman, who would perform at the Dadaist soirées of the Cabaret Voltaire (under the disgraceful sobriquet 'Labanese girls'). At the opening of the Galerie Dada in 1917, Sophie Taeuber performed with a rectangular mask which covered her face, and wore over her arms tubes of cardboard, which ended in mechanical pincers for fingers (overleaf). These determined a limited movement, rejecting mimetic gestures.

In the journal *Dada*, one reads: 'Miss Sophie Taeuber. Delirious bizarreness in the spider of a hand vibrates rhythm rapidly ascending to the paroxism of a beautiful capricious mocking dementia.' Her dances were driven by bodily reflex reactions, without preconceived scores, and stimulated by the noise of a gong, which motivates not only the muscles but also the nerves, not only movement but fragmentation. Hugo Ball recounts:

> It was a dance full of peaks and edges, full of a glare, of a body torn in pieces. Each gesture is broken in a hundred – sharp, bright, pointed. To the hypersensitive nervous system, the silliness of perspective, of lighting, of atmosphere opens the way to a spiritual fun, to an ironic gloss; her creations are full of the grotesque and ravishing spirit of fables. Her body has a feminine intelligence and enriches the world at each new dance.[7]

Here the body is described with more intensity than the figure: a kind of continuous discontinuity challenges binary divisions between mental and physical, poetry and performance, machine and human. But, on the other hand, Sophie also wears a mask, so that she isn't recognised as 'Ms Sophie Taeuber', the teacher at the Zurich School of Applied Arts. This tension between visibility and invisibility in the image is, therefore, also driven by her status as a woman, which constrains her public appearance.

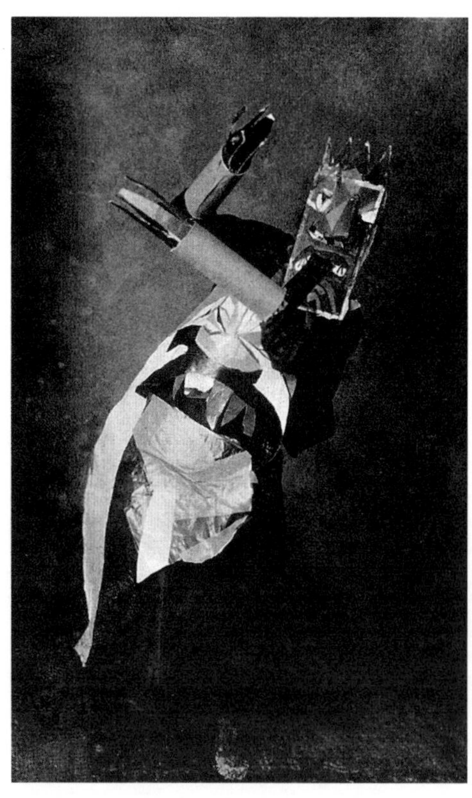

Sophie Taeuber dancing in mask and costume, 1917

This tension can also be recognised as a paradox, of the kind that Joan Wallach Scott has historicised under the title 'Only Paradoxes to Offer', in order to consider the relations between 'the feminine' and 'the general', between different feminisms and universalism, equality and difference. Each time that feminists argued for political rights in the context of liberal democracy, she argues, they have faced an impossible choice. On the one hand, they have insisted that the differences between men and women are irrelevant for citizenship. On the other hand, by the fact that they acted on behalf of women, they have reintroduced the very idea of difference they sought to eliminate. This paradox – the need both to accept and to refuse sexual difference in the public sphere – has been the constitutive condition of the long struggle by women to gain the right of citizenship. This paradox may equally be used in our reflections on the work of women artists.

As has repeatedly been written, the 'body' appears as a signifier for 'women' in Western discourse. Yet the shortcut taken by women artists in engaging their body – the bodies they have at hand – to make art never appears as essentialist. The shortcut of the body is used to activate and reactivate forces, to display what a body can do or where it can go, as well its alienation, its obstacles. The notion of a shortcut can also be used to handle the way women have quickly adapted to and adopted 'new technologies' in art making: photo, video, cyberfeminist ... These are media which you learn without having to go through the traditional master–apprentice relation, and many women have been passing on their knowledge to others. The current wave of 're-enactments' of so-called historical performances of the 1970s can also be understood in terms of embodiment, interweaving representation and materiality. And there is again a shortcut to be acknowledged here between activist use and aesthetic use, even if today all these means are absorbed into exhibition, museum or gallery spectacles.

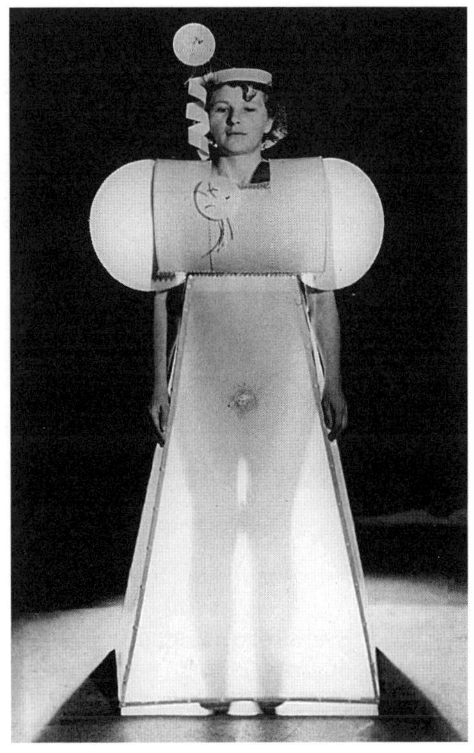

Marie Vassilieff, *Rhodoid Vowel Dress* for theatre company Art et Action at Exposition Universelle des Arts et Techniques de Paris, 1937

Although she only performed as a dancer for a few years, Sophie Taeuber imbued all of her work with dance: not only in the realisation of L'Aubette, the restaurant, cinema, bar, tearoom, nightclub leisure complex in Strasbourg (see over), but also in her *Line drawings* (1940–43), which are like performative trajectories. Like the *Dance Diagrams* (1962) by Andy Warhol, they are driven from the floor to the wall, still branding the work as horizontal choreographies that make concrete – or act as quotations of – the bodily gestures.

The irruption of gendered bodies by women artists who stepped into the world as art-activists has moved away from the social norms regarding sex. For since the 'female sex' does not imply a *reciprocal* 'male sex', and as sex can be understood as a political and cultural interpretation of the body, women become ontologically suffused with sex: they are their sex, and reciprocally, sex is necessarily feminine. So the use of the body by women artists reclaiming their own images raises issues in sexual politics that go way beyond images.

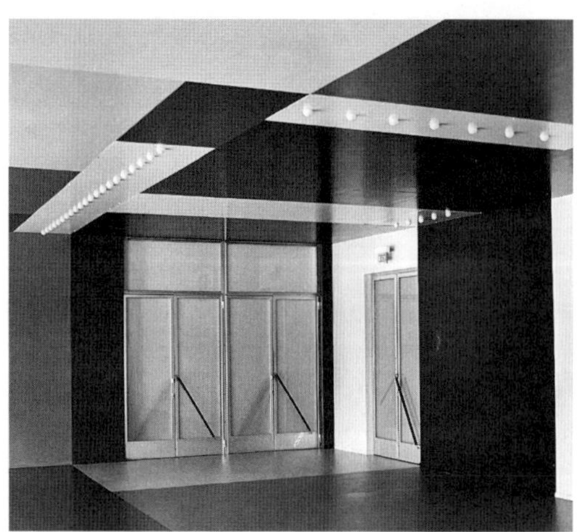

The Foyer-Bar from l'Aubette, Strasbourg, by Sophie Taeuber-Arp, 1928, as restituted in 2006

Smashing the glass bubble

In New York at the beginning of the 1960s, Louise Bourgeois short-circuited this concern by smashing 'the glass bubble that encapsulated sculpture in a world of illusion, representation, idealisation'[8] and also in the general language of art. In her work of the time, the encounter implied going face to face with the reality of the body, without metaphor – body as egg, body as cylinder. Breasts, anuses, mouths, penises, faeces appear as 'desiring machines' shaking the economy of visual representation.

Not very far away in place and time – New York, the 1960s – at the Judson Dance Theater, in a medium traditionally disdained as minor art, artists of all types used the body as a medium to affirm new intellectual possibilities, smashing the hegemony of mind over flesh. As Yvonne Rainer, one of the Theater's main protagonists, put it: *The Mind is a Muscle.*[9]

Before joining the workshops of the Judson Dance Theater, Carolee Schneemann had been close to the scene surrounding Happenings and Assemblage in New York. *Eye Body* (1963), one of her first actions (though only for the purpose of producing photographs), features her actual body combined in the work as 'integral material'. In the repertory of notes and pictures in which this was theorised in 1979, in *More Than Meat Joy*,[10] one can read how in 1962–3, she foresaw the development of her artwork into performance situations, which already struck her as 'too much'. This excess is not only in the situation but also in its duration and space, transferred to the audience, from the optical to the physical, from passivity to activity:

> In this way the audience is actually visually more passive than when confronting a work which requires projective vision ... During a theatre piece the audience may become more active physically than when viewing a painting or assemblage; their physical reactions will tend to manifest actual scale – relating to motions, mobilities the body does make in a specific environment. They enlarge their kinaesthetic field of participation; their attention is required by a varied span of actions, some of which may threaten to encroach on the integrity of their position in space. Before they can 'reason', they may find their bodies performing on the basis of immediate visual circumstances.[11]

Schneemann is looking here for something that has the capacity to undo the boundaries of the self in the face of an overwhelming sense of pleasure,

pleasure, indicating the presence of an experience that exceeds the limits of an individual's discursive position.

In its beginnings, as narrated by dance theorist Sally Banes, the strongest concern at the Judson Dance Theater was the notion of 'letting go', as in Yvonne Rainer and Charles Ross's *Room Service* 1963–4, an open-ended game of 'follow the leader'; or in Carolee Schneemann's *Lateral Splay* 1963, in which the dancers ran as hard and as fast they could until they collided with some obstacle, an 'explosive and linear refrain, a propulsive jet of movement cutting through the sequences of other works and materials of the environment'.[12] Special exercises were designed, such as performing blindfolded, keeping in constant contact by crawling 'over each other's arms, legs, bellies, back, in order to arrange a kind of organless, collective, body', as Lygia Clark too would propose in her experimental environments. But the other side of breaking with technique was the suppression of energy, and relaxation of the body, negating the physical tension of usual ballet dancing.

Reworking sexual imagery was at the core of Schneemann's *Meat Joy*, combining semi-nudity (wearing underwear), bodies and matter, various textures and flesh. This event was first staged in Paris in 1964 at the Festival de la Libre Expression, at the invitation of the artist Jean-Jacques Lebel (before going to Dennison Hall in London and then to the Judson Church in New York). To Nouveau Réalisme's use of the walls, the signs and the debris of the city as aesthetic substance, Schneemann added her own particular incorporation of self-produced, sexualised and erotic imagary. This celebration of flesh as material required raw fish, chickens, sausages, wet paint, transparent plastic, rope, brushes and paper scrap as physical equivalences. Performed as a 'psychic and imagistic stream in which the layered elements mesh and gain intensity by the energy complement of the audience', it included certain constant parameters – sequence, light, sound, materials – but other components varied, such as attitude, gesture, duration, and the relationships between performers, including 'several women whose gestures develop from tactile, bodily relationships to individual men and a mass of meat slices'.[13]

Schneemann breaks out of the categorisation by which her gender is reduced to an image. In directing every aspect of production – performing troupes and technicians, as well as lights, sound, props, electronic systems, costumes – and then physically moving in what she has created, Schneemann shifts from image-maker to creating her own self-images. Therein, perhaps, lies the 'obscenity' of which she has been accused. Acknowledging that Schneemann's performances and films are 'self-shot, without an external controlling eye', what is found most obscene in her work is the lack of an external gaze.[14]

This is even more controversial when the artist's body figures prominently as an erotic subject. Presented at the Cannes Film Festival in 1967, Schneemann's *Fuses*, a 22-minute film about sexual intimacy, explores sexuality from her perspective as both subject and film-maker. Combining photographic footage of sex between herself and her partner, with layers of paper, collages, painting and tinting applied directly to the celluloid frame, Schneemann provides a cinematic eroticism, challenging dominant representations of sex in cinema and proposing an alternative to patriarchal representations of sexuality. In her insistence that she is and can be both image and image maker, Schneemann is a forerunner both of performance art and new media installations, as well as of much contemporary feminist art as well.

In 1967, invited as a body that 'speaks louder than the word'[15] to the Roundhouse in London, for the 'Congress of the Dialectics of Liberation', organised by the Institute of Phenomenological Studies, with the participation of Gregory Bateson, David Cooper, Ronald Laing, Erving Goffmann, and Herbert Marcuse, among others, Schneemann encountered the hostility of the group, leading to the rejection and sabotage of her work. She would later identify the prejudice underlying this ostracism as resentment over the participation of a woman as 'a sort of unclassifiable physical extension'[16] which unleashed a profound somatophobia in philosophy's phallic economy. After all, what are these actions, performances and films, if not the reshaping of sculptural representation?

In the work of Carolee Schneemann, Yoko Ono, Ann Halprin, Yvonne Rainer, Meredith Monk, Atsuko Tanaka, Yayoi Kusama, Esther Ferrer, Jackie Raynal, Gina Pane, Valie Export or Lygia Clark (to refer only the works of the late 1960s) the body 'captures the image'. It will not appear again as a 'passive' medium – as inert matter, as Christian precedents have it – nor as mere 'facticity', anticipating some meaning, as if the body were alienated or indifferent to signification, and signification was disembodied consciousness. These women artists opened a field of visibilities that would be claimed by feminism, in its 'second' wave, as it expanded into the 1970s.[17]

Incorporating gender

In the late 1980s, when the photographic self-portraits of Claude Cahun begun to re-emerge, and as they started to circulate in the early 1990s, the time was perfect for them to engage in renewed discussions of sex and gender. It is as if they came into existence as 'readymades' for discussion. Producing multiple images of gender that seemed outside both feminine and masculine norms, these self-portraits seemed to embody Joan Rivière's 'Masquerade of Femininity' (1929).

Cahun's self-images have circulated under the rubric of 'queer' theatricality, with a strong appeal to emerging theories of gender performance. Many noticed coincidences between the photographic works and theoretical writings of the 1980s, so that it now takes more of an effort to reconsider Claude Cahun in her own space and time than it does to reconsider her work in a postmodern context.[18] It is only after this initial reception that new readings of these self-portraits (which appeared publicly around thirty-five years after Cahun's death) began to re-envision a specific time and space for them. Paris between the wars appeared then as the site for a construction of a visual culture in which a network of women were able to emancipate themselves from the constraints of gender, and recognise themselves as part of a lesbian culture.

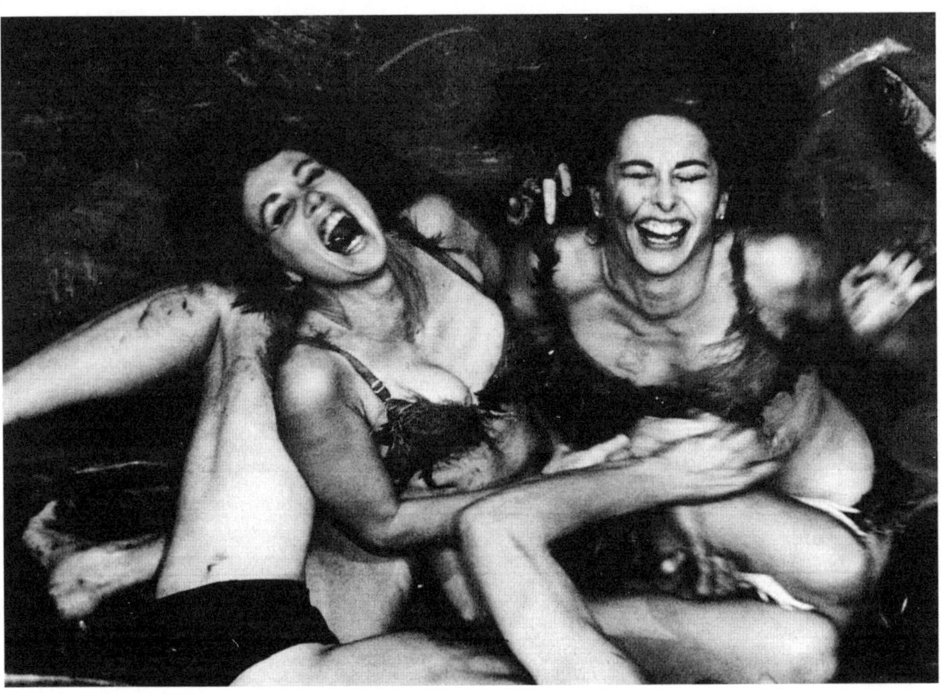

Carolee Schneemann, still from *Meat Joy*, 1964

In Wittig's terms, a lesbian is not a woman. If 'woman' only exists as a term that stabilises a binary opposition to 'man', and that relation is heterosexual, then refusing to appear as a woman is choosing to appear as lesbian.

So what is left, when the body, which had been 'rendered coherent through the category of sex, is disaggregated, rendered chaotic'?[18] Cahun's self-portraits do not just go against an inner truth of gender, they also scatter the very notion of self. A 'massacre' of the self is the object of both writing and image-making in the book *Aveux non Avenus* (*Avowals Unavowed*) produced in 1930 by Claude Cahun and Marcel Moore – the names being 'drag' identities for two women, lovers, partners, companions and co-authors. Cahun's text is intertwined with ten inserts by Marcel Moore, as cutouts, disassembled and reassembled fragments and quotations from the self-portraits. Each of these montages revolves around vision but mostly plays on the 'I', the subject, and its relation to the 'eye', the eye and the lens which regard this 'I'. The coded language for the couple thus plays with the formation or deformation of a body in process, a 'becoming lesbian' as a collective body.[19] The 'I' of autobiography has been doubled and replayed by a twofold, collaborative 'You'. It is not only by chance that the collaborative formation in the production of Cahun's self-portraiture was foregrounded in the late 1990s, precisely at the time when the experts of the 'Symbolic Order' made their case for sexual difference. In the case of Cahun and Moore, it was not the old story of an artist using assistants, but a lifelong game between two companions, so that Claude Cahun's name is

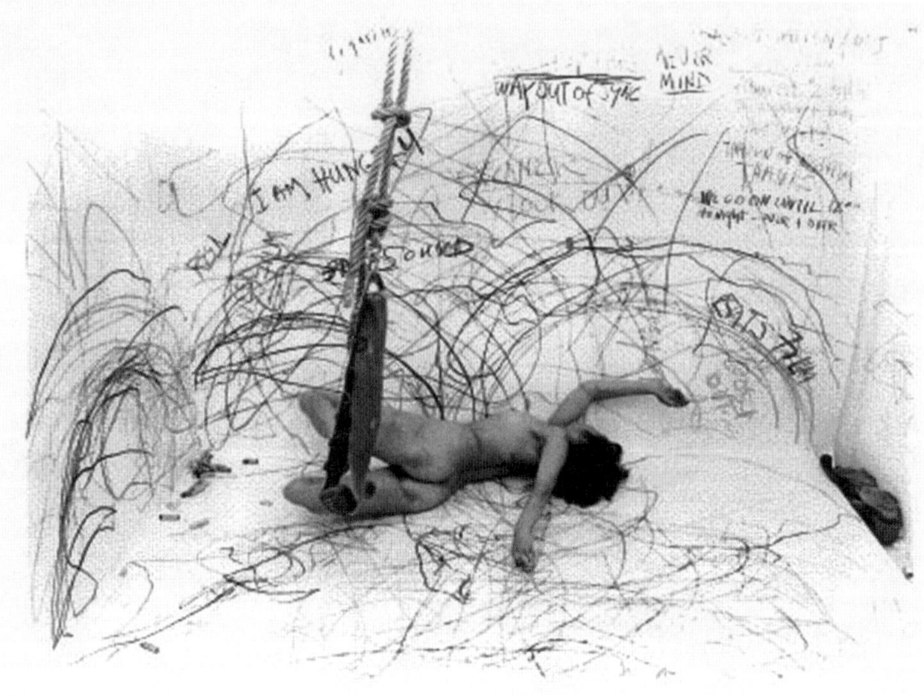

Carolee Schneemann, still from *Up To And Including Her Limits* (1973–6), Studiogalerie, Berlin, 1976

now put together with that of Marcel Moore, as a twofold artist. The success of today's cooperative or socially engaged artistic identities should thus be considered in the context of resistance and counteraction to the transcendent difference between the sexes (*difference des sexes*).

Display of gender/gender as display

As an activist, in 1992 Zoe Leonard made a poster of a woman's vagina which read: 'Read my lips before they are sealed'. At Documenta IX, the same year, Leonard chose to exhibit, without the traditional devices (framing, matting, protective glass, etc.), black-and-white photos of female genitalia. Each picture was a kind of cutout in the style of traditional museography, with its wallpaper decor and its framed pictures representing 'women', or rather an essentialised woman, painted more or less in the nude. By proposing a close-up shot of particular female genitalia, Zoe Leonard introduced a particular point of view into the universal language of the museum, by foregrounding its sexual politics and its politics of domination. In her earlier photographs taken in museums or galleries, Zoe Leonard had already shown the display of gender assignation, in dolls, in wigs, in fashion shows, in anatomical figures, as a norm that can't be fully internalised. In the Natural History Museum, the 'transition to upright walking' diagram charts the 'evolution of man'; but the subject is, as well, two little girls looking, trying to find their place in the patriarchal culture, which includes science as well as museography. One girl is absorbed in what she observes, the other is more sensitive to the presence of the photographer, recording the scene. For Leonard 'the conflict between the act of observation and the one of performance appears often in my work.'[20] Who is looking? What are they looking at? What are we looking at? Whose agency are we looking at? These questions about the order of seeing and its subversion are part of Leonard's case studies.

What exhibition of gender allows certain people to be identified as human, so that they have rights, to be cared for when they are sick, or to be mourned when they are dead? In Leonard's photographs or installations, there are numerous examples of gender presentation, displaying the various ways in which a body performs its cultural significance: whether a bearded woman as chopped head specimen in a glass bell, photographed from five different angles; a female anatomical model engaged in a defensive gesture as an indication of chastity; or a mustachioed doll in its transparent package. The unbearable violence of the apparatuses disciplining the body (*Beauty Calibrator, Gynecology Instruments, Chastity Belt*) sits alongside the triumphant flesh of the performer Jennifer Miller, photographed twelve times as a non-conformist bearded 'Pin-Up Calendar'. This way of including uncategorised genders, as well as showing the invisible violence inflicted by gender-based norms, has stretched to other forms of racial and sexual constructions (e.g. creating a fictional character through the archival function of photography, such as in Fae Richards Photo Archive), all of which encounter discrimination and erasure. Positing the body, not as an outside to representation, but as a site for rendering visible normative statements founded on the refusal of alternative possibilities, provides new perspectives on old questions about images.

Zoe Leonard, *Untitled* 1992, Installation in Neue Galerie, Documenta IX, Kassel

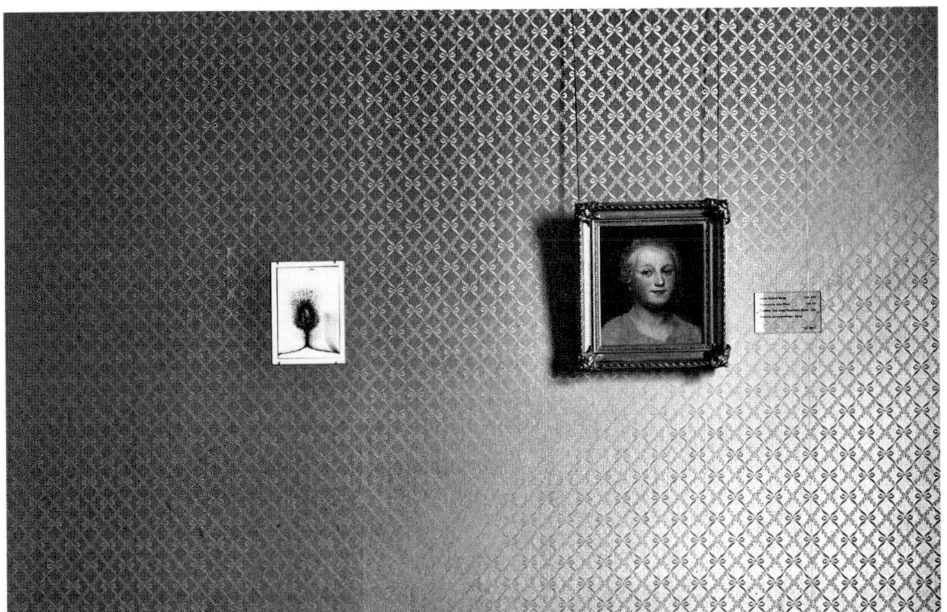

1 Monique Wittig, '"The Point of View": Universal or Particular', *Gender Issues*, vol.3, no.2, June 1983, pp.63–9; republished in M. Wittig, *The Straight Mind and Other Essays*, Beacon Press, Boston MA; 1992, p.60.
2 See Griselda Pollock, *Differencing the Canon: Feminist Desire and the Writing of Art's Histories*, Routledge, London 1999.
3 Yve-Alain Bois, 'Sophie Taeuber-Arp against Greatness', in *Inside the Visible (an elliptical traverse of 20th century art, in of and from the feminine)*, La Chambre, Courtrai 1994–5, p.413.
4 Ibid.
5 Françoise Héritier, interview in *La Croix*, November 1998.
6 Sabine Prokhoris, *Le Sexe Prescrit, la différence sexuelle en question*, Aubier, Paris 2000, pp.146–9.
7 Hugo Ball, 'Uber Occultismus, Hieratik und andere seltsame schöne Dinger', in *Berner Intelligenzblatt*, 15 November 1917.
8 See Rosalind Krauss, 'Louise Bourgeois: Portrait of the Artist as Fillette', in *Bachelors*, MIT Press, Cambridge MA 1999, p.54.
9 This was the title of a choreographed, multipart performance for seven dancers, interspersed with film and text, built upon a backbone of variations on Yvonne Rainer's former dance solo, Trio A.
10 Carolee Schneemann, *More than Meat Joy: Performance Works and Selected Writings*, Documentext/McPherson, Kingston and New York 1979.
11 Ibid., p.10.
12 Ibid., p.49.
13 Ibid., p.62.
14 See Shana MacDonald, 'Carolee Schneemann's Fuses as Erotic Self-portraiture', *CineAction*, Winter 2007.
15 Schneemann 1979, p.151.
16 Ibid.
17 Abigail Solomon-Godeau, 'The Equivocal: I', in Shelley Rice (ed.), *Inverted Odysseys*, MIT Press, Cambridge MA 1999, p.114.
18 Judith Butler, *Gender Trouble: Feminism and the Subversion of Identity*, Routledge, London and New York 1990, p.161.
19 Cf. Tirza Latimer, *Women Together/Women Apart: Portraits of Lesbian Paris*, Rutgers University Press, New Brunswick NJ and London, 2005.
20 Zoe Leonard in an interview with Anna Blume, in *Zoe Leonard*, exh. cat., Secession, Vienna 1997, p.23.

Art and Immaterial Labour

5
Metamorphoses
Antonio Negri

To begin with, let us try, from a materialist standpoint, to situate historically the concept of plastic and figurative art – in other words, the definition of its historically determinate link, if there is one, to the development and structure of modes of production. Can this be done? Obviously, once we're obliged to speak of art and immaterial labour, this is a useful thing to do; in fact, its 'immaterial' character does not strip 'labour' – not even in its relationship to artistic production – of its historical centrality, and does not drain labouring activity of that economic energy and ontological power which must indeed exist in order for labour to be exploited under capitalism. So is such a definition possible? I think so. In fact (notwithstanding the superficiality and flimsiness of art markets – that is, of artistic phenomena tied to the circulation of capital), we can outline a somewhat crude but nevertheless effective correspondence between the different epochs of artistic activity ('styles' and 'poetics'), on the one hand, and the forms of capitalist production and organisation of labour, on the other. In what follows, I would like to sketch out the figures taken by this relation.

Let us go back, then, to the period that witnessed the increasing centrality of working-class struggle to capitalist development. From 1848 to 1870, this centrality expresses itself with vigour in the massive growth and concentration of working-class labour in all its materiality. Does the 'realism' of artistic expression (between Courbet and Cézanne, for instance) display this new historical condition of work? I think it is possible to answer affirmatively if we consider the force with which the denaturalisation of the real and the structural materiality of the subject begin to appear in this realism, precisely in correspondence with the first great episodes of industrial and metropolitan centralisation in the exploitation of labour-power.

The period of 'impressionism', between 1871 and 1914, corresponds instead to policies on the side of the bosses that deepen the division of labour and its specialisation – policies to which there corresponds, on the workers' side, a subversive project aiming at the self-management of production.

We witness a first great episode in the 'emancipatory overdetermination' by the professional worker of the conditions for the accumulation of capitalist production. Labour becomes aware of the fact that its enemy, the capitalist world, may be dissolved and possibly reconstructed if one grasps (that is, if one reappropriates) the key to production: labour itself, within the 'mode of production'. It is in labour that the world is dissolved and reconstructed – and possibly the artworld too. This is the slogan of this first phase of artistic transformation in the history of the present: creation consists in dissolution.

Then comes the October Revolution. As the tsunami of revolutionary thought and subversive action spreads around the world; as capital, in order to respond to the challenge, finds itself obliged to enforce further proletarian growth and concentration in the productive base, to establish new norms of worker consumption (welfare), to push abstraction to the highest level, and to introduce 'scientific management' into the organisation of labour – well, it is then that, in the aesthetic field too, the 'abstract form' of artistic production prevails. This abstraction is at one and the same time the representation of the abstraction of labour and – from the workers' standpoint – the material for an alternative imagination. What, in fact, is socialism if not the project autonomously to organise the abstraction of labour?

From 1917 to 1929, from the storming of the Winter Palace to the Great Crisis, this is an 'expressionist' abstraction, in the sense that it heroically defies the real and current determinations of exploitation while violently anticipating, aggressively advancing and seeking to overturn its degree of abstraction. This abstraction traverses the figurative, destroys and reconstructs it, experiencing revolutionary passion and the desire for a constructive aesthetics in epic excess.

Then, having been led back to the market and the circulation of commodities, abstraction takes ever more analytical forms – forms that remain abstract, but are precisely analytical, multifarious, sometimes ephemeral, often open to experimentation and to each of the innovations that the crisis (and the ensuing renewal of the capitalist mode of production) makes possible, and which the development of proletarian struggle demands. After 1929, the only artistic production is the one expressed by the mass-artist, embodied in his constructive capacity, as though artistic production constituted the form of this capacity. And this is the story which, amid constant experimentation, leads us all the way to '68. This is the period in which abstraction and production are intertwined: the abstraction of the current mode of production and the representation of possible worlds; the abstraction of the image and the use of the most varied materials; the simplification of the artistic gesture and the geometric destructuring of the real, and so on and so forth. Picasso and Klee, Duchamp and Malevich, Beuys and Fontana, Rauschenberg and Christo: we recognise in them artists sharing the same creative experience. A new subject and an abstract object: a subject capable of demystifying the fetishised destiny imposed by capital.

And then? What can we draw from this? '68 comes and we reach a moment when contemporary art confronts new questions. How does the event arise? How can passion and the desire for transformation develop *here and now*? How is the revolution configured? How can man be remade? How can the abstract become subject? What world does man desire and how does he desire it? What are the forms of life taken by this extreme gesture of transformation?

Let's sum up. First, we have the phase of reappropriation and self-management (1848–1914), dominated by the development of the 'professional worker', his struggles, his utopia and his revolution. Following the Paris Commune, this phase splits, in what concerns artistic trends, into the two directions of 'realism' and 'impressionism'. Then comes the revolutionary phase beginning in 1917 and ending in 1968, all of it internal to the abstraction of labour-power, which in turn divides after 1929 into 'expressionism' and abstract experimentation; this is a period during which the mass worker comes forward as the hegemonic subject over/against the abstraction of labour and undertakes the project of its socialist management. We then arrive at a new period – the *constitutive* period of the 'social worker' and 'cognitive labour-power'. But constitutive of what, when, where?

Immaterial?

It is worth asking ourselves right away if the phrase 'immaterial labour' is apposite. Today, paradoxically, saying 'immateriality' no longer means saying abstraction, but rather concreteness; no longer vision and spirituality, but rather immersion into bodies, expression of the flesh. Immaterial labour constructs material products, commodities and communication. It is socially organised through (very material) linguistic, electronic and cooperative networks and through multitudinous movements and associations. This is a fleshy immateriality, that is to say a mobile and flexible materiality, an ensemble of bodies. Here, then, (from the artistic standpoint) is the final paradox of this story: artistic development transforms the abstraction of the social relations in which we are immersed into corporeal figures, releasing the vitality of the flesh into images that move and inflect themselves, in a process of continuous transformation. From Bacon through Warhol to Nam June Paik, the artist imagines a thick space, a molten turmoil, and looks fearlessly to a world freed from its internal architecture. Artistic development now takes place not so much in immaterial as in biopolitical terms. The attempt to traverse social communication, to catch one of its figures on the wing, is accompanied by an immersion into the chaotic and productive tumult of forms of life. Today's artistic paradox consists, intensively as well as extensively, in wanting to produce the world (as well as bodies and movements) otherwise, from within a world that refuses to recognise any worlds other than the existing one, and in knowing that this outside to be constructed must be the other of an absolute inside.

Obviously, what I've said up to now does not intend to be a new narration of the history of art. It suffices for us to establish the fact that *artistic activity* always takes place within the (existent) mode of production and reproduces it – that is, it either produces or challenges it, endures or destroys it. Artistic activity is a mode, a singular form of labour-power. Not by chance, every product of artistic activity can thus become a commodity, just as, conversely, the selfsame product can be elevated by presenting itself as an invention – or in any case as a *sui generis* production and an irreducible singularity. Like every object of production in the era of capital the artwork is two things: a commodity and an activity. It is on the basis of this twofold character of productive activity that we can grasp what I would like to identify here as the internal reality of the artistic relationship, current and/or contemporary: not only, therefore, that mode of producing art which comes under the production of commodities, but that mode of producing art which is nothing other than the figure, the power of being creative in the world. Labour-power as a free bird in the forest of life.

In this regard artistic labour gains the *ontological relevance* possessed by all forms of labour in their creative facet. This is all the more so to the extent that artistic labour, through the very evolution of modes of production, becomes indistinguishable from cognitive labour. Artistic labour takes on the characteristics of cognitive labour: leading the production of commodities back to the circulation of commodities, the linguistic analysis of reproduction, virtual valorisation, networks and cooperation, and so on and so forth. This ontological relevance has long been emphasised in studies on art. Particularly important in my view is the contribution of the 'Vienna School', at the end of the nineteenth and beginning of the twentieth century, when, analysing along with Alois Riegl late Roman and/or Byzantine artistic *industry*, its authors delineated the set of forces and social models involved in artistic doing, and were thus able to grasp its ontological over-determination: *Kunstwollen*; that is the singular will of art-making, the turning of every technique back on the one who uses it, as well as the blurring – through production – of subject and object in the historical process. In other words, we are dealing with an overdetermination of labour: *Kunstwollen* animates industry and industry breathes in *Kunstwollen*. Now, in every one of the eras we've mentioned what was experienced in the late-romantic period lives again. It is also worth underlining that the *Kunstwollen* is, on the one hand, of comprehensive significance for the era it describes and, on the other, singular in terms of the form through which it combines materials, the modes of production it employs, and the needs and tastes it mobilises. *Kunstwollen* is an intentionality which in its realisation does not lose its spatio-temporal impact, but instead renews it. It develops it, here and now, in a cognitive manner, showing work to be the 'formative form' of the living. The technical medium is spiritual, and vice versa.

Let's take two more references from the history of art criticism, from the works of Wilhelm Dilthey and Michel Foucault, respectively. The uses of this discussion will become clear as we proceed. Now, in Dilthey the relationship between the mode of production and artistic experience initially seems to be articulated in a very different manner from the Vienna School: the artwork is the product of an individual *Erlebnis* and artistic experience has strong psychological connotations. Little by little, however, Dilthey's aesthetics – or, better, his analyses of the singular 'poetics' of romantic and post-romantic authors – develops the concepts of historical structure, expressive technique and the singularity of artistic perception, concepts which issue into a vision that is very close to that of the Vienna School. But Dilthey goes further: in artistic production, the exchange between the agent and what is acted upon becomes ever deeper and serves as the motor behind the ontological transformation of agents.

As for Foucault, he offers the *episteme* as the linchpin of the interpretation of an era, but at the same time he exposes the development of the era itself to the edge of innovation and the rhythm of discontinuity. He insists especially on the hybridisation and interface processes within which the transformations of the *episteme* take place. To the question, 'What is an author?', Foucault already replied in 1969: *qui importe qui parle!* ('who cares who's speaking!'). In 1971, with reference to Manet, Foucault sets down the forms taken by the metamorphosis of the artistic gesture: Manet – *tableauobjet* – 'the fundamental precondition in order one day to be freed from representation itself and to allow for the play of space with its pure and simple properties, its own material properties'.

Why, then, are these authors, Dilthey and Foucault – who represent a before and after vis-à-vis the shift that introduces us to postmodernity and the hegemony of immaterial labour over the artistic scene – so important? Because here ontology and history are intimately tied together. The biopolitical is announced at this crossroads.

Biopolitical labour

Let's return to where we began this reflection; that is, at the point where we stopped tracking the course of art history, around 1968, in terms of that turn which we identified in the end of the era of the mass-worker. Let's now enter the new phase that opens up here. Dominated as they are by globalisation and the saturation of the experience of life under capitalism, both art and labour, as we saw, have become abstract; nevertheless, subject and object refer back to one another in the play of production, where every 'outside' has vanished. But how can we identify the emergence of the beautiful in the passage from modern to postmodern? How can the will to make art allow us to traverse its abstraction? In order to reopen the discussion we will need to underline that a mutation has already taken place, perhaps even an anthropological *metamorphosis*. In this existence of ours, creating has likely lost all links to any kind of nature, and leaving all 'preconceptions' aside it is no longer even a sublimation: rather, it is something *beyond measure*, an *excess* that discovers forms for a surplus of productivity. When labour-power is cognitive, the desire for artistic expression is to be found everywhere; when the mass of workers is transformed into a *multitude* of *singular* producers, artistic activity affects the forms of life and these forms become the flesh of the world.

Bernard Stiegler, following in the footsteps of André Leroi-Gourhan and Gilbert Simondon, has depicted this shift very effectively. He captures the tendency towards a unification of anthropogenesis and technogenesis, as the world exposes itself to a veritable machinic turn. Cognitive labour produces objects that modify the subject. No longer in metaphysical (Heideggerian) terms but in critical (Kantian) ones, cognitive labour illuminates or 'unveils' through technology that 'secret of truth' which subjects produce through constant interrelation. 'Depth' is discovered when it is introduced into the circle of inside and outside, constitutive and constituted. Ultimately, the Kantian schematism – the definitive impasse of modern philosophy around which the 'death of man' ferments and is eventually recognised – does not issue into the sublime but rather into the circle of constitution. It is played out between the subject and the technical object, and the latter also posits itself as subject. Following Stiegler, human becoming, through man's prostheses, constitutes the ultimate fate outlined by cognitive labour. Metamorphosis is a figure for the ontological relevance of artistic action. But we need to introduce a further element. We have begun to perceive the efficacy of immateriality and cognitive labour with regard to art. We identified this shift in the postmodern turn, and in its unification of anthropogenesis and technogenesis. But (for a number of reasons which we won't go into here) today the situation has been stabilised. We are no longer moving towards the postmodern, or rather, we have already moved beyond every post-. We exist in contemporaneity and this contemporaneity has further intensified the transformation of labour. From being immaterial, cognitive, affective, it is becoming ever more *bios*: it is *biopolitical labour*, an activity that reproduces forms of life. Labour is thereby infused with a series of new attributes.

First, it presents itself as *event* – that is as a vital excess beyond measure. The event detaches itself from the continuity of life's customary horizon, but it is simultaneously internal to it, dwelling at its centre. It exists in that artificial depth which characterises every immersion into the world of immanence; that is, in a thoroughly constructed world where nothing natural exists any longer. The event is not an 'outside', but an explosion in the 'inside', where the impossibility-of-an-exit announces a creative excess.

Second, biopolitical labour presents itself as a *multitudinous* event. We have already spoken of the ontological relevance of artistic labour and of how this ontological relevance was always marked by the *Kunstwollen*, overdetermined by an *episteme*. But the event that we identify and interpret in the production of biopolitical labour has the same collective and cultural characteristics within contemporary industry. The multitudinous character of cognitive labour is thus reconfirmed. However, this multitudinous character does not simply express a concept of interactive cooperation. The various hermeneutic schools (from Gadamer to Jauss, passing through Eco) have insisted on this effect; Simondon's interindividual or transindividual approach described its figure and movements in the very constitution of 'technical objects'. But all of this does not suffice to understand and grasp the peculiar consistency of the artistic phenomenon produced by cognitive labour. In effect, it reveals itself to be something that goes beyond itself, which transcends (in this world that knows no 'outside') the independence and autonomy of its own production. In other words, it is given as a *multitudinous excess.*

So, third, still seeking that ontological relevance which the Vienna School had already so powerfully presented as the interpretive mark of the artistic phenomenon, we find ourselves specifying the *multitudinous event* as an excess open onto the *common.* Artistic production traverses industry and constitutes common languages. Therefore, every production is an event of communication, and the common is constructed through multitudinous events. Consequently, this is how the capacity to renew the regimes of knowledge and action that – in the era of cognitive labour – we call artistic is determined.

There's a final point that is worth dwelling on. By insisting on the biopolitical we are reminded, retracing the history of ancient 'poetics', of Ovid's *Metamorphoses*. I suggest rereading them: you will find yourselves immersed in a mythical configuration of life which destroys all of its parameters of necessity; you will be lost in a labyrinth of animal figures, of human and divine vicissitudes, of natural and technical prostheses that fill every space in the narrative. That is what cognitive labour (and every mode of production linked to it) manages to do. Every mythical resonance that this doing had in Ovid has vanished. Consequently, in this disenchanted world in which we find ourselves we frequently come up against things which are, as it were, too real: this world of ours sometimes fills up with monsters, and we end up trembling. We would like this not to be true, but it is: that is the contemporary. We recognise this each and every time we deal with the monsters that our action and work produce and that relations of domination cause to proliferate. And the monster – as we saw when we reflected on the 'reversibility' which is always created in the relation between machinic subjects and objects – the monster lives inside us, or is one of our prostheses, and it can turn back on us and partake in our metamorphosis. This is all the more reason for us to recognise the danger, every time we highlight the physical character of immaterial labour, the flesh of cognitive labour – in brief, the common of life, the biopolitical, which constitutes us. Yet another paradox? Of course. In effect, moving within abstraction and immateriality, confronted by monsters, we are increasingly required to determine testing criteria that will have a bearing on corporeality – that is, on the vital modalities of *existential critique*.

Artistic production today

The discovery that contemporaneity, and the mode of production that prevails within it, unfolds in danger, in contact with the monster, makes a reflection on the common obligatory: a *decision on the sense of being* – that is, on the direction that the event and the multitude must take in order to give meaning to the common. The aesthetic gesture (when it is interpreted in the form that we have done here) finds *ethical decision* on its path. We live in the midst of transformation, of the metamorphosis of space and time determined by the contemporary accumulation of work and civilisation. Bodies are at stake within the process of transformation. Crises constantly break out which allow of no external solution. That is where we are, and we cannot go elsewhere. But we have this astonishing speech that we are capable of expressing, this creative capacity that we can put forward. By recapitulating the productive and the ontological, the event and the common, art thus could (perhaps it simply must) give ethical meaning to this predicament, helping us to construct that multiple paradigm in which being for the other, being in the common, triumphs.

Can we draft prescriptions for a *style* that would be infused by an ethics? Asking oneself this is like asking oneself if it is once again possible to have access to a grand narrative on being. Or, better, whether it is possible to get close to a concrete utopia. I think so. And I would like to propose, coherently with what we have critically constructed up to this point, a three-stage approach, through which a style of artistic production may be defined today.

The first stage consists in the *immersion* into the infinite movement of the bodies and events that surround us, from images of life to expressions of knowledge; or, better, to undertake that work of *deconstruction* of the real that immersion as such demands, when it is driven by a critical desire. Bare life and clothed life, poverty and wealth, critical desire and construction of the real – this always constitutes the section of the diagram of immersion into true reality. We find ourselves partaking in the composition of the *swarm* of singularities. These singularities want to converge in the common while keeping their freedom.

The second stage is reflexive. It presents itself as the moment of the *recognition* of the common. Here we act as a reconstituted swarm, not merely as a multitude but as a swarm that organises the figures of flight and movement, the manner in which it is delineated as a viable and/or volatile direction, the materialist *telos* that surges up from below, from each and every one of its singularities. Thus the impoverished immersion (of the lone singularity) into the multiplicity of the swarm finds here the direction and cohesion of love. Through love – that is, through that force which Spinoza saw as forming itself out *conatus* and *cupiditas* – the solidarity of bodies and decisions of the spirit is constructed. A veritable *metamorphosis* thus takes place within the complex multiplicity that constructs the swarm. Immaterial labour has finally found an ethical legitimacy that is structurally bound to the way it reinvents itself as form of life. Art defines itself as form of life, characterised by poverty at its base, and by revolutionary will at the apex of the becoming-swarm.

We have now reached the third stage of this movement. Some time ago, Paolo Virno, anticipating many of the insights and concepts that were later expressed with respect to immaterial labour, defined the performances of this labour in terms of the *masterwork* (*capolavoro*). This hermeneutic anticipation by Virno should be given its due. But it should be developed further, once the homology between the formation of the multitudinous swarm and the operationality of immaterial labour (as well as cognitive and affective labour) is recognised. The common that has developed within artistic forms must now be embodied in a collective decision, in a common government. Or, better, it should be organised by a governance of/on/in the forms of life that have been constructed. The highpoint is to be found in this construction of the ethico-political limit of the common, in this internal government of agency; that is, when the experience of the common – in opposition to any illusion of community – expresses free and rich forms of life.

To take up again the image of the beautiful which, as we recalled above, the Kantian schematism began to formulate, we could say that beyond a sublime that organises itself at the limit of the mathematical infinite and a second model of the sublime that is elevated by the immensity of nature, there is a third model which hinges on ethical action, on the constitution of the multitudinous *telos*. This third model of the sublime takes shape at the limit constructed by *amor* (in Spinoza) as it completes the movement of *cupiditas*. The common as ethical sublime, the common as aesthetic sublime: against every spiritualist mystification there stands here that intersection of anthropogenesis and technogenesis identified by Stiegler and which we had considered with reference to the constitution and disclosure of the common.

Translated by Alberto Toscano

6
Art, Work and Politics in Disciplinary Societies and Societies of Security
Maurizio Lazzarato

According to Michel Foucault, for some time we have been leaving disciplinary societies in order to enter into societies of security that, unlike the former, '*tolerate* a whole host of behaviours that are *different, varied, or even deviant and antagonistic* toward one another'.[1]

These societies lead us beyond disciplines, because they put in place policies regarding the government of conducts that are exercised through the management of heterogeneities and the 'optimisation of systems of differences' – that is, through the differential administration of inequalities (disparities in situation, income, status, knowledge, and so on).

Again according to Foucault, in societies of security the function of liberal policies regarding the government of conducts is 'to produce, instigate and enhance freedoms', 'to introduce a surplus of freedom', but to do so 'through a surplus of control and intervention'. The government of conducts, Foucault says, 'produces freedom, but, in the same gesture, implies that limitations, controls, and coercions are set in place'.

Following Félix Guattari, we can make these statements more precise. While contemporary capitalism produces a 'generalised control, it is nevertheless forced to preserve a minimum of degrees of freedom, creativity, and inventiveness in the domain of the sciences, technologies and the arts, without which the system would collapse in a kind of entropic inertia'.[2] Just like the production of disparities or inequalities, the production of freedom is differential. Depending on the situations, activities, social groups and balance of forces at stake, there will be what Guattari defines as absolutely heterogeneous 'coefficients of freedom'. The government of conducts will then be exercised through a modulation of coefficients of heterogeneity and coefficients of freedom.

In order to grasp these modalities of the government of contemporary capitalism, it is perhaps useful to analyse what modernity regarded as the very paradigm of freedom, heterogeneity, difference and deviance: art and the artist. To the passage from disciplinary societies to societies of security there corresponds a transformation in artistic practices and techniques, in the conception and function of art, artists and publics, in the relationship that the latter entertain with society, the economy and politics. In order to analyse this passage we will make use of Jacques Rancière's 'aesthetic regime of the arts' – which in my view makes perfectly explicit what we no longer are – alongside the work of Marcel Duchamp, and freely interpret a novella by Kafka, which will allow us to grasp what we are in the process of becoming.

The practice and anti-dialectical thought of an anartist

In Rancière's 'aesthetic regime of the arts', art is a specific activity that suspends the customary connections and spatio-temporal coordinates of sensory experience, which is marked by the dualisms of activity and passivity, form and matter, sensibility and understanding. These dualisms, which Rancière defines as a 'partition of the sensible', are political in the sense that they separate and hierarchise society according to relations of domination that organise the power of men of 'refined culture' (activity) over men of 'simple nature' (passivity), the power of men of leisure (freedom) over men of work (necessity), the power of the class of intellectual labour (autonomy) over the class of manual labour (subordination).

This conception of art as a heterogeneous and 'specific sensorium', opposed to the sensorium of work qua domination, harbours the promise of the abolition of the separation between 'play' and 'work', between activity and passivity, between autonomy and subordination, in accordance with two different modalities which are in effect two politics of aesthetics. According to Rancière, these two modalities inform the politics of art to this very day. The first (the becoming life of art) does politics by suppressing the separation between art and life, and therefore by suppressing itself qua separate activity. The second (resistant art) does politics by jealously safeguarding this very separation, as a guarantee of autonomy from the world of commodities, markets and capitalist valorisation.[3]

This partition of the sensible that distributes places and functions in society, the economy and politics, as well as in art, is one we have been in the process of leaving behind ever since the end of World War II. Under the conditions of contemporary capitalism, all these dialectical oppositions no longer represent alternatives. They have become mere options for capital.

Play – which Rancière, following Schiller, treats as the prerogative of humanity, since it consists in a gratuitous and non-finalised activity, grounding both 'the autonomy of a proper domain of art and the construction of the forms of a new collective life'[4] – no longer constitutes an alternative to work as domination. The dialectical opposition between play and work has been transformed into a continuum, of which play and work are only the two extremes. Between the two, it is possible to arrange in a thousand different ways the coefficients of work and play, autonomy and subordination, activity and passivity, intellectual and manual labour, which nourish capitalist valorisation.

Marcel Duchamp invites us to insert into the intervals of dialectical oppositions a third term which acts neither as a mediation nor as an agent of overcoming, but as an operator of disjunction that dispels the oppositions which structure not only our aesthetic principles and tastes but, more generally, our ways of saying and doing. The spread of this artistic practice and thought, which in the main came together at the beginning of our century, is strictly tied to the growing power and consolidation of that government of conducts which was deployed starting at the end of World War II and which experienced a strong acceleration from the 1960s onwards. In the interval between the artwork and the industrial object, Duchamp inserts his best-known invention, the readymade. The readymade instigates the flight of the use-value both of the industrial object (its utility and functionality) and of the artwork (a non-utility which has its function, a non-finality which has its place in capitalist society and valorisation).

The readymade short-circuits and problematises the worker's manufacture, but also the talent and virtuosity of the artist. It comes after Rimbaud's 'century of hands' – the hands of the artist's craftwork as well as of the worker's manual labour. The readymade does not involve any virtuosity, technique or particular know-how, so it 'desacralises' and deprofessionalises the artist's function, making it possible 'to lower his social status'. Anyone can become an artist, anything can become a work, all that is needed is for each to find its public (and the institution's visibility and statements).

In the interval between play and work, we can introduce choice. The readymade is not fabricated, but chosen. 'The difficulty for me was to choose.' But for Duchamp this choice is neither intentional nor conscious; it expresses neither the interiority nor the taste of the artist. He chooses to choose, instead of fabricating something with his own hands. Duchamp will even say that 'one doesn't choose a readymade, one is chosen by it', so that the choice dispels the opposition between determinism and free will. In the interval between activity and passivity, we can insert the 'doing nothing', which is the refusal to accomplish what is asked of you, whether it be the passivity of the worker or the activity of the artist (or the immaterial labourer). 'Acting at the minimum', rather than allowing oneself to be trapped by the alternative between artistic creation and waged labour. For Duchamp both are functions, occupations to which one is assigned. On the one hand, 'now artists are integrated, commercialised, too commercialised'. Ever since there has been a market for painting, painters 'no longer make painting, but cheques'. On the other, 'to be forced to work in order to exist is a kind of infamy'. 'Doing nothing', 'acting at the minimum', means subtracting oneself from the distribution of competencies in contemporary capitalism.

We could continue having fun exploding dialectical oppositions. For reasons of time, I will just mention another one, without developing it further: in the interval of the opposition between the sensible and the intelligible we can, following Duchamp, introduce 'belief'.

Duchamp explains himself very clearly concerning the false heterogeneity represented by dialectical oppositional couples. In fact, if two things are opposed to one another, it is in favour of their very homogeneity.

> If I am against the word 'anti', it's because it's a little like 'atheist' as compared to 'believer'. An atheist is almost as religious as a believer, and an anti-artist is almost as artistic as an artist ... 'An-artist' would be a lot better, if I could change the term, than 'anti-artist'.[5]

With his customary humour, Duchamp uses a readymade to undermine the dialectical logic of exclusive disjunction of the type 'either/or', and to allow the logic of inclusive disjunctions of the 'and' to function.

> I lived in Paris in a tiny apartment. In order to use this meagre space to the utmost, I decided to use a single door panel which shut alternately on two frames. I showed it to some friends, telling them that the proverb according to which 'A door must be either shut or open' was thereby caught in a flagrant crime of inexactitude.

The door at rue Larrey, simultaneously open *and* shut, is an example of the 'co-intelligence of contraries' whose closest counterpart in the domain of philosophy seems to me to be the disjunctive synthesis.

The readymade does not testify to the dialectical passage from the prosaic world of commodities to the proper world of art, nor to the blurred boundary between art and non-art; nor indeed does it constitute a simple amalgam (or clash) between heterogeneous elements. In Rancière's dialectical logic, modern and contemporary art is this very passage, this blurring, this clash. With the readymade, the manufactured or fabricated industrial object does not move into the aesthetic domain but, on the contrary, introduces us to a 'completely empty domain, if you will, empty of everything to the point that I have spoken of complete anaesthesia'. This empty region 'where neither time nor space reigns' is the place from which simultaneously to problematise the modes of constitution of the artwork and of the commodity, interrogating the forces, principles and *dispositifs* that institute them and consolidate them into values.

Art does not represent a promise of the overcoming of domination, as in Rancière's aesthetic regime of the arts, because Duchamp's gesture not only suspends the preconditions for the exercise of this regime, but also suspends aesthetic values and tastes as such. What interests Duchamp in the 'creative act' is not so much the artwork as such, but 'the subjective mechanism that produces an artwork'; that is, the process of social production that institutes art, the artist, the work and the public. Duchamp's techniques are not exclusively artistic techniques, but rather 'mental techniques' (Jean Philippe Antoine) or 'techniques of subjectivation' (Félix Guattari). Duchamp's techniques amount to a method for extricating oneself from all established values, not just aesthetic ones. Given a thing, a word and the relation between the two, how can we be rid of the social clichés borne by this relation?

> We are confounded by an accumulation of principles and anti-principles which generally cloud our minds with their terminology.

The void, the 'freedom of indifference', and complete anaesthesia are not the bearers of some kind of post-modern nihilism, but rather techniques to suspend the prefabricated sensations, habits, judgements (or prejudices) which are crystallised in tastes as well as in words.

> Taste confers a sensual feeling, not an aesthetic emotion. Taste presupposes an authoritarian spectator who imposes what he loves or does not love, and translates into 'beautiful' and 'ugly' what he finds pleasant or unpleasant [a translation of the unknown into the known, the already-there – ML]. In a completely different way, the 'victim' of the aesthetic echo [who is forced to think and feel despite himself – ML] is in a comparable position to that of a man in love, or a believer, who spontaneously rejects the demands of his ego and who, now deprived of supports, subjects himself to a pleasing and mysterious constraint. By exercising his taste, he adopts an attitude of authority, whilst when he's touched by aesthetic revelation, the same man, in a quasi-ecstatic mode, becomes receptive and humble.

The dissociation of art and taste leads to the openness of the 'idiot' who falls in love, to the innocence of the idiot who believes in God, of which the Dadaist idiot is but one embodiment. By rejecting prejudices, conventions and established values – among which we must include the self – the idiot returns to this 'point of emergence of the production of subjectivity', which for Guattari constitutes the specific task of the artist.

'Shock has been one of the principal themes of modern art, its material.' But in Duchamp shock does not simply have the 'critical' function of uncovering the world of commodities, and it does not represent the occasion for a possible gain in awareness. The suspension of established values which shock is capable of producing is the precondition for mobilising, in the 'creative act', not the consciousness of the author and the public, but their affects (as might be done by a medium or shaman), non-verbal semiotics (the inert materials which become expressive), and non-sense (the a-signifying, non-discursive and asocial 'existential function' which sets in motion a process that will produce sense, discourse, significations, sociality). Shock is the precondition for openness to a process of transformation of subjectivity.

The plays on words that accompany all of Duchamp's works and *dispositifs* express the modalities of rupture of discursive formations. In order to express oneself artistically and in general within societies of security it is necessary to interrupt communication, to neutralise the signifying power of language. Words are wielded as weapons to open breaches in consensus and in the semiotic pollution that besets us. By short-circuiting dialectical oppositions, Duchamp opens up an 'undecidable' process. Duchamp's practical artistic propositions are undecidable because – to translate this concept from Deleuze and Guattari into Rancière's dialectical categories – autonomy and heteronomy, activity and passivity, freedom and domination are not already assigned to specific and different sensoria (those of art and of work as domination), but are distributed across a continuum in which the coefficients of freedom and domination, activity and passivity, traverse art as well as work.

Shock in Duchamp, like conflict for us today, issues into undecidable propositions, since neither the philosophy of history nor the dialectic of class struggle can serve as a standard and guide for action, or serve as guarantor for its evolution. These propositions are undecidable because their fate depends entirely on their immanent becoming. This is a situation of absolute immanence, for there is no model – either positive ('play' in art) or negative (domination in work) – to which we can refer in order to combat it or realise it.

The aim of these practices and techniques which it would be difficult to define as exclusively aesthetic, of these undecidable propositions, is the production of subjectivity, the production of a modus vivendi. They are ethico-politico-aesthetic techniques, as in Félix Guattari's aesthetic paradigm or Foucault's production of subjectivity. Art does not entirely pass into life, nor does it hold itself in splendid autonomy, as the avant-gardes dreamed, because between art and life there is always a gap that cannot be filled. But it is on the basis of this gap, by installing oneself in its interval, that a production of subjectivity may take place.

> I wanted to make use of painting, make use of art as a tool to establish a modus vivendi, some way of understanding life, that is probably to try and make my life itself into an artwork, instead of spending my life making artworks in the forms of paintings ... The important thing is to live and have a conduct. This conduct governs my painting, my plays on words and everything I've made, from the public point of view, at least.

To reduce these techniques of subjectivation to the individualism of Max Stirner, whom Duchamp read assiduously, would be as reductive as equating Foucault's practical and theoretical ethos with dandyism. It is more interesting to see in these modi vivendi a political problem which the failure of the relationship between the political and aesthetic avant-gardes has bequeathed to us: the impossibility of separating political revolution from the revolution of the sensible, macro-political revolution from micro-political revolution, the question of politics from that of ethics.

Kafka, art, the work, the artist and the public

During the 1990s and since in the struggles of the *intermittents du spectacle* (precarious media and entertainment workers in France) an out-and-out contest was unleashed among the forces of the Left (political parties, unions, intellectuals, artists) to find out who best conformed to the disciplinary attribution which defines the functions and the roles of art, the artist and the work – whose pitiless dissection at Duchamp's hands we have just examined.

A 'holy alliance' was formed to defend the neo-archaism of art as exception (a French cultural exception) and of the artist as the professional of the profession (in terms of a defence of full-time artistic employment).

To interpret the deep transformations in artistic and cultural practices under the sign of 'great art', in order to condemn it for anti-proletarian elitism, like Boltanski & Chiapello or Bourdieu, or to celebrate its 'revolutionary' force as Badiou (another defender of dialectical thought) envisages, is a testament to the impotence of critical thought. Badiou's advocacy of a 'great art' for the workers and the people is just as reactionary as the separations between 'artistic critique' and 'social critique' made by the sociologists who authored *The New Spirit of Capitalism*.

In order to grasp our current predicament it is better to turn to Kafka, who in his very last story, from 1924, engages in a dialogue at a distance with Duchamp. In 'Josephine the Singer, or the Mouse Folk'[6] we encounter two poles of art-production. If, with Duchamp, we had witnessed the point of view of the artist confronted with the impact of industrialisation, the birth of the art market and the transformations of the public, with Josephine and the mouse people it is the latter that is at stake: a public that coincides with the people.

The mouse folk are a 'people of workers', endowed with a 'certain practical cunning', fearing neither adversities nor 'work'. Josephine the singer, as the narrator informs us, belongs to this people; that is, she works to earn her living like every other 'worker' and sings to enchant the mouse folk. In other words, she exercises two professions. The race of mice does not love music and is not musically talented. The mice, busy with their everyday worries, cannot 'rise to anything so high and remote from our usual routine as music'. Only Josephine knows how to elicit the love of music in the people. Where does this power of her singing to deeply affect its listeners come from? Where does the passion for this art originate? And, as the narrator asks himself, what kind of art are we dealing with, since the people do not love music?

Evidently, we are not dealing with the classical principles of aesthetics, since Josephine's art is not 'so great that even the most insensitive cannot be deaf to it; her singing does not 'give one an immediate and lasting feeling of being something out of the ordinary', and what the people hear is not 'something that Josephine alone and no one else can enable us to hear'. 'Among intimates we admit freely to one another that Josephine's singing, as singing, is nothing out of the ordinary. Is it in fact singing at all?', the narrator asks. Josephine's singing 'hardly rises above that of our usual piping – yet perhaps her strength is not even equal to our usual piping, whereas an ordinary farm hand can keep it up effortlessly all day long'. Piping is the 'real talent of the people' of mice. 'We all pipe, but of course no one dreams of making out that our piping is an art.' So there's nothing exceptional, no genius, no sublimity, no technique and no talent in Josephine's art, since the capacity to pipe is shared by all, and requires no virtuosity. It is not just the 'anyone' (even the vulgar farm hand pipes whilst working) and the 'anything' (a piping so feeble that it is difficult to tell it apart from the silence surrounding it) which seem to define her art, but also the 'anywhere'. Josephine's 'concerts' are prey to the fortuitousness of circumstances, as well as her whim. 'She can do this where she likes, it need not be a place visible a long way off, any secluded corner pitched on in a moment's caprice will serve as well.'

Were this true it would certainly deny Josephine her claim to the status of artist. The fact that her status 'has never been quite defined' is indeed what makes her nervous and uneasy. To resolve the enigma of this 'mediocre' art the narrator multiplies the questions and suggest several avenues. All these questions will be left unanswered, which leaves the public of readers – as well as Duchamp's 'posterity, that pretty bitch' – with a total freedom of interpretation.

The first avenue we encounter in the story is given by the readymade. The effects of Josephine on the public are perhaps due to a new 'form of singularity', the fact that someone makes 'a ceremonial performance out doing the usual thing', 'usual workaday piping'. Here the narrator provides an extraordinary definition of the readymade – whose existence Kafka himself almost certainly ignored – by inventing a form that Duchamp had not envisaged: readymade quotidian action, an action that, like that of piping, everyone is able to reproduce.

> To crack a nut is truly no feat, so no one would ever dare to collect an audience in order to entertain it with nut-cracking. But if all the same one does do that and succeeds in entertaining the public, then it cannot be a matter of simple nut-cracking. Or it is a matter of nut-cracking, but it turns out that we have overlooked the art of cracking nuts because we were too skilled in it and that this newcomer to it first shows us its real nature, even finding it useful in making his effects to be rather less expert in nut-cracking than most of us.

As in Duchamp, the readymade is a mental technique that forces one to think, that obliges one to interrogate the 'real', since, after having experienced this strange piping, the mice can affirm that 'we admire in her what we do not at all admire in ourselves'.

But there are numerous avenues available in order to try and grasp the sources of Josephine's art. The mouse folk is a people of workers which, because of their practical spirit, basically have no childhood, since they become adults very rapidly, precisely in order to work. By suspending the space–time of everyday banality by means of techniques that are neither beautiful, nor extraordinary, nor sublime, Josephine's art opens onto the innocence of childhood, onto its pre-linguistic and pre-cognitive world, before the latter is fixed into words, tastes, opinions and judgements.

> Piping is our people's daily speech, only many a one pipes his whole life long and does not know it, where here piping is set free from the fetters of daily life and it sets us free too for a little while. We certainly should not want to do without these performances ... [since, into the people's dreams] Josephine's piping drops note by note ... [and] something of our poor brief childhood is in it.

But perhaps the effects produced by Josephine's art are also due to the specific techniques she employs. Josephine's singing, 'a mere nothing in voice, a mere nothing in execution', is not the product of any technique. Were she to use techniques of musical virtuosity, she would not exercise any fascination over the mouse folk: 'A really trained singer, if ever such a one should be found among us, we could certainly not endure at such a time and we should unanimously turn away from the senselessness of any such performance.'

The effects that she produces are thus perhaps due to the fact that 'her means are so inadequate'. Non-virtuosity and the weakness of materials are 'democratic' techniques to neutralise the authority of tradition, the author and the work over the public. But perhaps the force of her singing comes from something else. Josephine does not measure herself up to the history of art and its traditions, but she plugs into the outside, into what happens. She makes art as much with small events as with large ones.

Among the mouse folk, 'a certain tradition of music is preserved, yet without making the slightest demand upon us'. On the contrary, 'every trifle, every casual incident, every nuisance, a creaking in the parquet, a grinding of teeth, a failure in the lighting incites her to heighten the effectiveness of her song ... So all disturbance is welcome to her; whatever intervenes from outside to hinder the purity of her song' contributes to 'awaken the masses'. But Josephine 'likes best to sing just when things are most upset', in the midst of great contemporary events, and it is here that a different politics is opened up between Josephine's art and the people.

The relationship between Josephine and the people (the community of mice is coextensive with the public) is a problematic one, since it involves the relation between individual and people, community and singularity, freedom and equality (one of the main themes that also preoccupy Duchamp's oeuvre).

> No single individual could do what in this respect the people as a whole are capable of doing. To be sure, the difference in strength between the people and the individual is so enormous that it is enough for the nursling to be drawn into the warmth of their nearness and he is sufficiently protected. To Josephine, certainly, one does not dare mention such ideas. 'Your protection isn't worth an old song,' she says then ... she believes it is she who protects the people.

When she rebels against the people's communal grip, when she tries to evade its 'stable mass', its collective 'protection', Josephine is equated with an infant and the people with a father. (For Foucault, patriarchy is the aspect of the regime of sovereignty which reproduces itself within the disciplinary regime, and without which the latter could not function.)

It is true that 'whenever we get bad news ... she rises up at once' and sings, but it is not she who saves the people, 'who have always somehow managed to save themselves'. Boltanski and Chiapello might well share the narrator's viewpoint, since 'social critique' does not need 'artistic critique' in order to save itself. The events of '68, as they say, are an 'exception'. The workers' movement has always saved itself. It doesn't need Josephine. Nevertheless,

> in emergencies we hearken better than at other times to Josephine's voice ... It is not so much a performance of songs as an assembly of the people ... yet to be only an incidental, unnoticed performer in a corner of the assembly of the people ... she would certainly not make the sacrifice of her singing.

The singer nurses other *différends* with the people-public, and the main one concerns the economic status of her activity. She exercises two professions (working and singing) and she wages a veritable fight for recognition – even of an economic kind – of her singing-piping.

> Josephine has been fighting for exemption from all daily work on account of her singing; she should be relieved of all responsibility for earning her daily bread ... which – apparently – should be transferred on her behalf to the people as a whole.

She lays claim to something like a guaranteed income, or at least she would like to be assured of some continuity of income since what she demands is not a direct wage, but an income drawn from the sum of the incomes of the mice. Josephine seems to be soliciting here what she refused earlier, namely the (social) 'protection' of the people, of the community. But perhaps we should not view this as a contradiction, but rather as the need to establish a new relationship between (social) 'protection' and 'individual freedom', community and singularity, freedom and equality.

On the basis of the singer's claim, it is the very status of work that becomes undecidable, since according to Josephine the strain produced by singing is greater than that of the work necessary to earn her daily bread:

> Josephine argues, for instance, that the strain of working is bad for her voice, that the strain of working is of course nothing to the strain of singing, but it prevents her from being able to rest sufficiently after singing and to recuperate for more singing ...

We can understand, then, why Josephine's status is never clarified. If art in disciplinary societies is defined in opposition work, when Josephine struggles, in various guises, for the 'recognition' of the strain of her singing, it is this very opposition that no longer makes sense. It is the status of both art and work that must be clarified. This would lead to the invention of a new system – at once economic, political and aesthetic – whose conditions cannot even be envisaged within the theoretical framework of the present-day Left.

It is striking that the questioning of the category of work comes – as it does in France today with the *intermittents du spectacle* – from artists.

The labouring mouse-folk are not ready, like the reformist and revolutionary Left, to ask what work has become today. The caricatural version of this attitude can be found in the self-styled 'new radicalism' of Alain Badiou, who wants to advocate both 'great art' and the 'revalorisation' of the figure of the worker and the factory as a political place, while three-quarters of the workforce today (90 per cent in the USA) will never cross the threshold of the factory gates. We are still within the art–work opposition, great art and workers – that is, within a world that has been completely turned upside down both on the side of art and on that of work.

In Kafka's story, Josephine's stubborn struggle and the working people's utter refusal of her claims will lead to her disappearance: 'The people listen to her arguments and pay no attention. Our people, so easily moved, sometimes cannot be moved at all. Their refusal is sometimes so decided that even Josephine is taken aback.' In an entirely arbitrary way, these pages of Kafka evoke for me the relationship between political and artistic avant-gardes in the Soviet Union. Josephine has come up against the 'authoritatively sovereign' people, just as the futurists and constructivists hit up against the 'stable mass' and 'sovereignty' of the working class-turned-state. This evocation in turn makes me think of a remark by Duchamp, according to which he does not believe in the universal and eternal 'essential aspect' of art. For Duchamp, 'one could create a society that would refuse art, the Russians got close. It's not funny, after all, but it's something that can be considered.' For the narrator 'Josephine's road ... must go downhill', she will be 'forgotten', while the 'authoritatively sovereign' people 'continue on their way'.

Prolonging our interpretation, we could affirm that the refusal of the people/class to integrate these new aesthetic practices and their new economic and political conditions in turn leads at first to the decline and then to the disappearance of the people/class.

To conclude: there is no politics of art as such, just as, moreover, there is no politics of politics as such. The transformations of aesthetic, political and economic practices are the elements of a single assemblage traversed by a single problem, of which work, art and politics constitute the different facets or viewpoints. A politics capable of confronting the capitalist government and management of differences implies not only a strategy that articulates political revolution with the revolution of the sensible, the macro with the micro, but also a politics transversal to the separate orders of the economic, the political, the social and the cultural artistic – a politics whose outlines are sketched in Kafka's story.

Translated by Alberto Toscano

1 Michel Foucault, 'La sécurité et l'état', in *Dits et écrits*, vol. 2, Gallimard, Paris 2001, p.386.
2 Félix Guattari, *Chimère*, no.28, p.18.
3 Jacques Rancière, *Le partage du sensible: Esthétique et politique*, Le Fabrique-Éditions, Paris 2000; translated by Gabriel Rockhill as *The Politics of Aesthetics: The Distribution of the Sensible*, Continuum, London and New York 2004.
4 Jacques Rancière, *Malaise dans l'esthétique*, Galilée, Paris 2004.
5 All Duchamp quotations are from Bernard Marcadé, *Marcel Duchamp, la vie à crédit*, Flammarion, Paris 2007.
6 All quotations are taken from Franz Kafka, 'Josephine the Singer, or the Mouse Folk', trans. Willa & Edwin Muir, in *The Complete Stories*, Schocken Books, New York 1971, pp.360–76.

7

The Materiality of the Immaterial: Foucault, Against the Return of Idealisms and New Vitalisms

Judith Revel

For some years, philosophical thinking has seemed to revolve around themes and terms whose centrality merits consideration – so much more so, probably, in that this debate has been formulated from positions and questions that are moreover very heterogeneous. I am especially thinking of a whole series of considerations found at the crossroads of two fields of enquiry that the tradition of the history of philosophy has nevertheless sought to oppose: on the one hand, an extraordinary renewal of problematics arising not so much from aesthetics as from artists and art critics themselves; and, on the other, paths opened up by a reformulation of categories of political economy and the sociology of work. At the intersection of these two spaces of reflection are to be found a certain number of notions – 'art', 'creation', 'invention', production', 'technique', 'work', 'materiality' and 'immateriality' – which undoubtedly merit attention. To participate in this day devoted to 'Art and Immaterial Labour' is in this sense to seek to problematise something which cannot be taken for granted and which represents for so many among us the heart of our own thinking and practice.

I would like to begin with the different meanings Michel Foucault successively gave to the notion of 'art' in order to try to show the extent to which the concepts of creation, innovation, production and work can be seen as linked together and how far they also imply, in their way, a relation to both the powers and the strategies of resistance. I will equally try to show an essential element of Foucauldian analysis, namely that what is produced – the production of value or the production of subjectivity, the production of forms or languages or the production of political action – totally deconstructs the old metaphysical opposition between the 'material' and the 'immaterial', or more exactly that it displaces and reformulates their criteria. For Foucault, as we know, the challenge is to describe 'a history of systems of thought', to recall the title of his chair at the Collège de France; but it is also, in an immediate and inseparable way, the will to say and put into practice possible resistances to historically determined systems of knowledge/power.

There is a strong temptation to imagine that the only conceivable resistance would be from an *outside* of powers, forms of knowledge or history itself. This is what I will call the new metaphysical 'temptation', which is precisely that: the idea that an 'outside' is possible, that there are at least margins in which to take refuge. In the end, it is the idea that materiality – that of bodies and signs, of work and suffering, of conflict and desires, in sum of the life of men and women in history – is the sign of our confinement and subjection. Against this, I will try to show that for Foucault it is from within the materiality of life – as a historical production, within the very meshes of power – that resistance is possible. Freedom is not a ghostly *outside* but the material concretising of 'inside', reconstituted as weapon of war – in other words, as a creative, incommensurable, excessive (*excédante*) matrix.

Consequently, it will be a question of avoiding the dangers of a fascination for 'archaeological' materiality – for example that of the old Fordist paradigm of work, or that of a direct opposition between technique and art – just as it will also be a question (and here there is no doubt a polemical element which I absolutely maintain) of avoiding, due to new theorisations of 'immateriality', being reduced to recycling a certain 'idealist temptation', residues of metaphysics or that vitalist irrationalism, which as we know was so historically powerful a century ago on the intellectual scene; or, more generally, a whole series of theories which would forget that nothing escapes history and its material, social, economic and epistemological determinations. It will then be necessary to ask in what manner it is today possible to think at once of creation and historical determination, immateriality and materiality, resistance and powers, resistance and capitalism, art and labour, the production of value and the production of the self; and in what ways this stake probably represents the essential element of all political and aesthetic thought.

The problematisation of art

In thirty years of research, Foucault developed three different formulations of the question of art. The first, which is important even if not greatly thematised, corresponds to the omnipresence (in particular in the texts of the 1960s) of references to literature and painting, as well as, to a minor extent, music. Depending on the case, the reference to art can be used in a strategic way, either as the example of an act of resistance against the devices (*dispositifs*) of established power – by accentuating the critical dimension of the creative act, as is generally the case in the analysis of the 'speech' (*parole*) of certain authors, a sort of war-machine flung against notions of the work and the author, of which Raymond Roussel is the clearest example – or, on the contrary, in order to show how the *épistémè* of an age is concentrated and rendered tangible (and by that fact made readable) in it – as for example is the case of the analysis of *Las Meninas* 1656 by Velásquez which opens *Les Mots et les choses*[1] or, later, by way of Manet's *Bar des Folies-Bergères* 1882, during a memorable conference, given in Tunisia in 1971.[2] Let's call this first formulation 'linguistic' in the widest sense, to the extent to which it works on expressive forms – in other words, those which reveal signs and produce meanings.

What is immediately striking, when one looks at these texts, is the omnipresence of materiality. There is in Foucault a reflection about art as, at once, a registration of instituted signs and forms and a resistant counter-production of signs, or rather a counter-signifying or hetero-signifying production (I am here borrowing the beautiful expression Gilles Deleuze and Félix Guattari use in *Mille Plateaux*[3]). It is thus really a question for Foucault of describing the spaces of dominant representation and intelligibility characteristic of a given period (for example, the painting by Velásquez as a representation of the space of intelligibility of the classical age; or that of Manet as a figuration of the emergence of a new epistemic space in the nineteenth century); but there is *also, still*, a question of imagining the forms that 'regimes of counter-signifying signs' could take; in other words, of posing the question of the conditions of the possibility and modalities of a resistance which would choose as its battlefield heterodox expression, what Foucault still sometimes called 'structural esotericism'. What is fascinating is that Foucault considered this resistance only because it was given as a strategy of displacement in the direction of the materiality of signs.

I will give only one example, in the literary field, since it was there that, at the beginning of the 1960s, Foucauldian discourse found its most resonant formulations. In Raymond Roussel, as well as (to various extents and with some differences) in Louis Wolfson or Jean-Pierre Brisset, literary production and resistance to the instituted order of language were assessed in accordance with the extraordinary capacity to invent, from the very interior of language, an innovating language. I stress: not another language outside of that which is ours, but rather a distortion of the existing language, a bending, an unveiling, an endless return of language. This twisting, which turns the reassuring stability of language inside out, like a glove, is possible only because Roussel, Brisset and Wolfson (and before them, Foucault said, were Nerval, Baudelaire, Mallarmé and so many others) displaced the privilege of meaning towards the very substance of the sign. They reconstituted the linguistic link (the account arising from it) beginning with the homophones, assonances, wonders of echoes and sonorous mimesis, the rhythms and acoustic mirrors, and from this 'speech' (*parole*) rendered in its pure materiality, brought to life the most powerful of war-machines against the old idea of language as signifying representation of (and, if possible, truth to) the existent. Here, then, literature and poetry paradoxically found their creative impetus their possibility for invention, for divergence, for difference: in short an exit from the institution of signs to the extent that they chose to play matter against the hegemony of meaning. And it produced meaning only because they unpacked the exorbitant privilege beforehand. I would refer you to another image: one of the collages of Matisse – directly cutting into the blue of the matter so as not to have to trace (in other words, to divide) the signs from what precedes their signification. This is another way of saying that matter does not always flow into categories of meaning – as though the materiality of the world should always be overdetermined by the immateriality of the mind – but that, at times, it produces exactly the opposite effect. It is matter, how we work it and bend it to our desire, to our imagination and to our power of creation, which innovates the meaning of the world. It can thus be seen, from Foucault's work in the 1960s, how strongly the direct opposition between materiality and immateriality is at once at the centre of Foucauldian thinking and at the same time entirely rearticulated, in order to allow resistance to be thought as a creative difference.

The second problematisation of the notion of 'art' concerns, from the time of *La volonté de savoir*, the first volume of *The History of Sexuality* (1976),[4] the opposition Foucault effected between *ars erotica* and *scientia sexualis* as two different modalities of organising the relations between power, truth and pleasure. As Foucault introduces it,

> two principal regimes can be distinguished. One is that of art érotique. Its truth is extracted from pleasure itself gathered as experience, analysed according to its quality ... and this refined knowledge is, under the seal of the secret, transmitted by magisterial initiation to those who have demonstrated that they are worthy of it ... Western civilisation, for centuries in any case, has barely understood art érotique: it has entered into relations of power, pleasure and truth, in a completely different way: that of a 'science of sex'.[5]

The opposition, structured at the start from what was placed between the Greek world and pastoral Christianity, interests us because it does not simply involve a division into periods. Or, rather, behind such a division there is, on the one hand, an art, in other words, as Foucault tells us, at once a practice (in the case of *l'ars erotica*, a practice of the body), an experience (of pleasures) and a relation to truth; and, on the other hand, knowledge, codes and conduct. In the first case, it is really a question of an aesthetic, and one that is inseparable from an ethic (since I take it to myself, or decide to follow rules of behaviour). In the second case, it is a system of forms of knowledge that are inseparable from a prescriptive morality – in other words, also from a codification of the fair and the unfair, the licit and the illicit, of good and bad, whose source must not only be external to the individuals over which it legislates but transcendent and immaterial.

I do not want to return here to the detail of Foucault's analysis. Let us limit ourselves to mentioning that the fundamental difference between *ars* and *scientia*, between art and knowledge, holds to the fact that if knowledge is a 'thing', an 'object', art in contrast is a practice, an experience, an action in movement. And where knowledge is an established discourse, experience implies on the contrary a transformation – of this 'self' that Foucault began at the time to think of as an unceasingly revived production, as experimentation of ways of life (*modes de vie*) and as subjectivation. If there is resistance, then, it is in the disproportion which appears between the institution and the movement, between morality and ethics, between objectivation and subjectivation, between reproduction and invention, and between the transition to the outside and the enfolding of the inside.

The third problematisation arises out of the analysis Foucault developed in the second half of the 1970s, in particular with the course at the Collège de France in 1977–8, of the 'arts of government': the way in which the pure transcendent singularity of power – that of Machiavelli's *The Prince*, for example – is transformed into a complex economy of forms of government, which, in its turn, was the object of reformulations between the sixteenth and seventeenth centuries. That could perhaps appear to be far from what we are concerned with, were it not the occasion in which Foucault stressed two points born of his two preceding explorations, to which we would like in our turn to return.

The first point is that there exists no 'outside' if this is understood as something external to history, or to the epistemic, economic and social determinations which cause us to be what we are, or to the relations of power in which we are entangled and engaged, no matter what we do. There is no exteriority to the powers, just as there is no exteriority to history: this might be a dreadful statement of impotence and despair, but on the contrary for Foucault it is the occasion to redefine completely what can be understood by resistance. The 'arts of government' and the possibilities of resistance to new strategies of government are given together, in a connected way: some relate to others that are themselves echoes of the first. To pose the question of knowledge, power or resistance, what comes first is really of no significance: the question of origin and foundation is a metaphysic which does not in fact interest us very much. On the other hand, it seems to us rather more important to underline that the 'arts' *also* play a role among the relations of power and the techniques of government.

The second point is that the appearances of the 'arts of government' correspond to the passage from an idea of power defined by its transcendence and uniqueness to one of multiple and immanent relations and defined by their mastery and efficacy over the material conditions of people's lives, or over those, also completely material, of the production and accumulation of wealth. What counts from then on is no longer so much the foundation of authority as the manner in which it is used.

I insist on these two points because they seem to me essential both to rethinking completely what an artistic act can be and to restore content to the very idea of resistance. In the first case, if there is also an 'art' (in other words, skill, shrewdness and innovation) at the side of power, it is necessary to ask ourselves what distinguishes the arts of government from an ethical and aesthetic relation to the self: what is the difference between the arts of government and the project of producing oneself in relation to oneself and others, as the Greeks sought to do? To create oneself as subject – what, with reference to both Baudelaire and Walter Benjamin, Foucault sometimes called 'dandyism' – is 'to make one's own life a work of art', in other words to delineate the space of a subjectivation, an invention of the self by the self and a freedom, within the systems of knowledge, methods of subjection and relations of power. But, inversely, to apply oneself to developing the arts of government is to include the management of these processes of subjection in the new economy of powers, seeking not to deny or prohibit them but to control and guide them. This is what Foucault called 'governmentality': at once the idea of a subjectivation defined as an action of creation (of the subject by itself), and that of a new rationality allowing the governing of this process. Far from directly opposing it, intransitive freedom (of subjectivation extended as creation and as *ars*) and the determinations of knowledges/ powers thereby intersect in a complex and intimate way.

If it is not, then, possible to oppose power to resistance in the name of another, more profound, opposition, between transcendence and materiality; if power has become material, effective and multiple, and is deployed in an infinity of ways, how can it be imagined that something like a resistance, a torsion, can emerge at the heart of this very material, in the very meshes of power? In short, how can materiality and creativity be taken into account if they have in their turn become the ground for the deployment of power?

The vitalist temptation

On this point, thinking in both political economy and the sociology of work can be useful for us. In descriptions of how the production of the value and organisation of work have changed during the past twenty-five years, or in the passage from 'Fordism' to 'post-Fordism' that some describe, we find the same questions. To say today that the production of value is no longer founded so much (as was the case in the past) in the value of trade goods – in other words, on a logic which sought to augment the number of goods produced while reducing their costs of production – but in the innovative and creative character of this production, or to say that what had been excluded by the process of economic development – the subjectivity of the worker, his life – is rediscovered, not just included in the process but at its very centre, is, in a certain way, to pose the question of difference, of the dissymmetry between art and production, or, if you like, between subjective resistance and its inveiglement by capital. I intentionally leave aside, for the moment, the question of materiality on which I would like to end my account.

What is the dissymmetry between art and capital, between the subjectivation of matter, and the way in which capital itself today uses this subjectivation to produce value, between resistance and the relations of power, between the ethical invention of ways of life and forms instituted and constrained by the dominant morality? This is, I believe, the question that haunted the final years of Michel Foucault's research. It is also, to a great extent, the question that traverses the work of many of us today. The response is undoubtedly not easy: in proportion that the relations of power have invested in what used to be unimportant and external for them (subjectivity, life, desires, languages, art); in proportion that they have finally integrated and 'devoured' what, for centuries, represented an area of recess, refuge and resistance, then the question of the space of possible resistance has recurrently been raised in more forceful ways. Today, if powers have become bio-powers and the economy a bio-economy – in other words, if the paradigm of work is henceforth founded on the inveiglement of processes of subjectivation and the innovation of life itself to produce value – what space remains for resistance?

What difference can resistance still offer?

It is in response to this question, I believe, that some people have given way to a kind of neo-metaphysical idealist or vitalist temptation. It was necessary to find a difference. They thought they could locate it in a return to something that would mark its divergence in relation to the materiality and historicity of relations of power. I will take a couple of examples, among many others, in a very cursory way.

My first example is the way Giorgio Agamben uses the concept of 'bare life'. 'Bare life' is never clearly defined by Agamben, except as what remains once power has totally invested, subjected and destroyed the lives of individuals. And the context in which Agamben places himself is then a 'saturated' context, that of the Nazi concentration and/or extermination (the point is quite ambiguous in Agamben's thought) camps. What remains is not a surplus, not an affirmative and positive difference in relation to power, but a remainder. And again: if power seeks to destroy our subjective singularity, then, Agamben tells us, what remains and resists is necessarily what is most impersonal and inappropriate within us, in other words paradoxically what carries in itself a universal value, what renders universal resistance for all people. And, as it is only with great difficulty that this impersonal universality can be defined, and good that Agamben carefully distinguished at the beginning *Bios* and *Zoè*, political life and biological life, and that he chose from the beginning to place his own thinking in the field of Bios (*bio*-politique), he ends by defining what resists in its impropriety as natural life, biological life. *Bare* life. Resistance is no longer a political and social construction of strategies of struggle, but a withdrawal into naturalness, life delivered up to its own improper universal and biological nature. It is a process without subjects or subjectivation, without conflict or antagonism. It is what remains: the remains of a process of subtraction. It is in some way 'human nature', the foundation, the essence and quintessence, the substratum of a desingularised humanity. And when one has at hand the tremendous pages Foucault devoted to the way in which power in the nineteenth century entirely reinvested the field of pseudo-naturalness to make it an instrument in the management of populations, one feels one's blood run cold on reading the pages of Agamben ... The resistance of life cannot be the naturalness of life. Resistance is always already political because life is always already within history, because it is the product of determinations which make it what it is. Bare life does not exist.

In my second example, the illusion consists in saying that it will be possible to resist power to the extent that we would be capable of finding a way out of its range. It is then necessary to seek an 'outside' of power and, if this 'outside' cannot be found, to be content with the margins. Theories of the margins, of marginality, of the remainder, moreover ignore precisely what is most characteristic of the bio-political configuration: the relations of power have from that point invested the whole field of existence. Ideas of 'outside' or 'margins' are fantasies, at least unless, once again, a way out of history is found. I have an immense admiration for – and a fundamental debt to – the work of Jacques Derrida. But I also believe that his entire thought is made possible by the exclusion of history – a refusal of history which he not only does not conceal but openly demands. To come out of history in order to find a way out of power, this is what all thought of the margins is founded upon. This is as true for Derrida as it was in the past for Maurice Blanchot – the former having become a metaphysician even while trying to destroy metaphysics; the latter as the reactionary he was, the aesthetic providing him with a flight outside politics, something undoubtedly also the case today for Agamben, who is good at thinking about the time to come and the breathtaking messianism of Walter Benjamin, but who does so only because it paradoxically allows him not to think about history – in other words, about the materiality of the relations of power.

Against this, how can we remain in history and in the political field in order to define resistance? The dissymmetry we seek must be played out elsewhere, and otherwise than has been suggested by Agamben and Derrida. And I believe Foucault himself has supplied the response. In Foucault, there exists a very simple definition of what relations of power are. A relation of power is, Foucault says, 'an action over the action of people', which means that the relations of power are the inveiglement, the management and the directing of people's free activity. This means at least two essential things. The first is that power is the management and exploitation of freedom. It is not opposed to freedom, since it has a need for it, but exploits it. As Foucault quite rightly commented, when the relations of power are glutted, there is no longer power but domination. There is thus no power without freedom. This is the first element of dissymmetry.

Second, power is *action over action*: thus it always comes second – logically, ontologically and chronologically. Freedom is intransitive but power is not. The transitivity of power is the necessity for it to apply itself to something that is, from the beginning, heterogeneous. In this sense, power nourishes itself on its other, upon which it is dependent. Power does not invent anything but applies itself. It does not create but manages. It does not produce but reproduces. From this double finding, the dissymmetry we seek undoubtedly begins to take shape. If resistance is possible, it is precisely through the intransitivity of freedom, from its capacity to create, invent and produce, from its *potentia* (English possesses only one word for the two distinct terms of *potentia* and *potestas*. I will therefore use the Latin terms). *Potentia* supports the innovation of the world, not its reproduction. It supports a political ethic conceived as an aesthetic of existence: remember the beautiful incitement Foucault underlined on many occasions, 'To make oneself a work of art', in other words literally to make one's life the ground of one's own resistance. It thus supports subjectivation, desires, languages and ways of life, quality and not forced objectivation, claims to universality, the order of discourse, quantity and economic moderation. Resistance is a creative development of life, art understood as a political paradigm as it puts its stake on the invention of existence against the reproduction of goods, the intransitive affirmation of freedom against the transitive management of subjection and exploitation. Resistance is an ontology.

The immaterial

There remains the question of the immaterial, and I would like to close on this point. Remember the three fields in which Foucault successively deployed his own use of the notion of art: invention of languages of resistance (the counter-signifying semantics), the invention of the self (the aesthetic of existence), and the invention of modalities of resistance within the meshes of that other art which is the art of government (biopolitics). In all three cases, it is a matter of inventing what is at once extraordinarily impalpable and concrete, immaterial and material: signs, structures and expressive forms; singular and common subjectivity; desires, pleasures and ways of life; strategies of struggle, of conflictuality and antagonism. In all three cases, nothing can resist without *potentia*, without an innovation, without an opening up of being (*ouverture de l'être*); in other words, without an affirmation of the ontological dimension of political acts of resistance. And yet this ontology is completely material: it is *in* history and is the product of a history in which it sinks its own incommensurability; it works bodies and relations, desires and actions, life understood as social and political life, struggle and institutions, practices and discourses. This immateriality is that of matter itself. Inversely, the very matter of resistance is its immaterial capacity to produce: an ontological creation of new being. In this respect, no doubt, art has opened the way to philosophical and political reflection: plunging its hands into the world to knead its flesh, because only materiality paradoxically allows the invention of new horizons on the edge of being – what Antonio Negri described some years ago both as *kairòs* and as *désutopie*: political resistance as the only possible ontology for our present, and the will of better worlds, here and now.

Translated by Michael Richardson

1 Michel Foucault, *The Order of Things: An Archeology of the Human Sciences* (1966), Tavistock, London 1970.
2 Michel Foucault, *La peinture de Manet*, Seuil, Paris 2004.
3 Gilles Deleuze and Félix Guattari, *A Thousand Plateaus: Capitalism and Schizophrenia* (1980), trans. Brian Massumi, University of Minnesota Press, Minneapolis 1987, ch.5.
4 Michel Foucault, *The History of Sexuality: An Introduction*, Pantheon, New York 1978.
5 'L'Occident et la vérité du sexe', *Le Monde*, 5 November 1976, p.24; reprinted in M. Foucault, *Dits et Écrits*, vol.3, text 181, Gallimard, Paris 1994, p.104.

8
(T)error and Poetry
Franco Berardi

1. The century of the future

Ninety-nine years ago Filippo Tommaso Marinetti published the first *Manifesto of Futurism*; the same year, Henry Ford opened his first automobile factory in Detroit. It was the beginning of the century that believed in the future. The Manifesto asserted the aesthetic value of the machine – that is, the 'external machine', not to be confused with the internalised and recombining machine of the bio-info era. Futurism exalted the machine as an external object, visible in the city landscape, but now the machine is inside us: we are no longer obsessed with the external machine. Instead, the 'info-machine' now intersects with the social nervous system, the 'bio-machine' interacts with the genetic becoming of the human organism.

The *Futurist Manifesto* declared the aesthetic value of speed. The myth of speed sustained the whole edifice of the imaginary of modernity, and acceleration played a crucial role in the history of capital – that is, the history of the acceleration of labour time. Productivity is the growth factor of the accretion of relative surplus value determined by the speed of the productive gesture and the intensification of its rhythm.

Ninety-nine years on, speed has been transferred from the realm of external machines to the information domain. In this process speed became internalised and transformed into a psycho-cognitive automatism. In the century of the future, the machine of speed accomplished the colonisation of global space; this was followed by its colonisation of the domain of time, lived experience, the mind and perception, which thus sanctioned the beginning of the century with no future.

The question of the relationship between an unlimited expansion of cyberspace and the limits of cybertime, of the time of the mind, and of social attention opens up here. At the point of the virtual intersection of the projections generated by countless issuers, cyberspace is unlimited and in a process of continuous expansion. On the contrary, cybertime, that is, the ability of the mind to process information in time – is anything but unlimited:

its limits are those of the human mind and are thus organic, emotional and cultural.

Subjected to the infinite acceleration of the info-stimuli, the mind reacts with either panic or desensitisation. Sensibility is the faculty that makes empathic understanding possible, the ability to comprehend what words cannot say, the power to interpret a continuum of non-discrete elements, non-verbal signs and the flows of empathy. This faculty, which enabled humans to understand ambiguous messages in the context of relationships, might now be disappearing. We are witness to the development of a generation of human beings lacking competence in sensibility, the ability to understand the other empathically and decode signs that are not codified in a binary system.

2. Deregulation

Futurism and the avant-garde set themselves the task of violating rules. *Dérèglement* was the legacy left by Rimbaud to the experimentation of the 1900s. *Deregulation* was also the rallying cry of the hyper-capitalism of late modernity, paving the way for the development of semio-capital. In the totalitarian period of the external machine and mechanical speed, having previously used the state form to impose its rule on society, capitalism decided to do without state mediation as the techniques of recombination and the absolute speed of electronics made it possible for control to be interiorised.

In the classical form of manufacturing capitalism, price, wages and profit fluctuations were based on the relationship between necessary labour time and the determination of value. Following the introduction of microelectronic technologies and the resulting intellectualisation of productive labour, the relationship between different magnitudes and different productive forces entered a period of indeterminacy. *Deregulation*, as launched by Margaret Thatcher and Ronald Reagan, marked the end of the law of value and turned its demise into a political economy. In his main work, *Symbolic Exchange and Death*, Jean Baudrillard intuitively infers the overall direction of the development of the end of the millennium.

> The principle of reality coincided with a certain stage of the law of value. Today, the whole system has precipitated into indeterminacy and reality has been absorbed by the hyper-reality of the code of simulation.[1]

The whole system precipitates into indeterminacy as all correspondences between symbol and referent, simulation and event, value and labour time no longer hold. But isn't this also what the avant-garde aspired to? Doesn't experimental art wish to sever the link between symbol and referent? In saying this, I am not accusing the avant-garde of being the cause of neoliberal economic deregulation. Rather, I am suggesting that the anarchic utopia of the avant-garde was actualised and turned into its opposite the moment society internalised rules and capital was able to abdicate both juridical law and political rationality to abandon itself to the seeming anarchy of internalised automatisms, which is actually the most rigid form of totalitarianism.

As industrial discipline dwindled, individuals found themselves in a state of ostensible freedom. No law forced them to put up with duties and dependence. Obligations became internalised and social control was exercised through a voluntary albeit inevitable subjugation to chains of automatisms. In a regime of aleatory and fluctuating values, precariousness became the generalised form of social relations, which deeply affected the social composition and the psychic, relational and linguistic characters of a new generation as it entered the labour market. Rather than a particular form of productive relations, precariousness is the dark soul of the productive process. An uninterrupted flow of fractal and recombining info-labour circulates in the global web as the agent of universal valorisation, yet its value is indeterminable. Connectivity and precariousness are two sides of the same coin: the flow of semio-capitalist production captures and connects cellularised fragments of depersonalised time; capital purchases fractals of human time and recombines them in the web. From the standpoint of capitalist valorisation, this flow is uninterrupted and finds its unity in the object produced; however, from the standpoint of cognitive workers the supply of labour is fragmented: fractals of time and pulsating cells of labour are switched on and off in the large control room of global production. Therefore the supply of labour time can be disconnected from the physical and juridical person of the worker. Social labour time becomes an ocean of valorising cells that can be summoned and recombined in accordance with the needs of capital.

3. Activism

Let us return to the Futurist Manifesto: war and the contempt for women are the essential features of mobilisation, which traverses the whole parable of historical vanguards. The Futurist ambition really consisted in mobilising social energies towards the acceleration of the productivity of the social machine. Art alimented the discourse of advertising as the latter fed into mobilisation. When industrial capitalism transposed into the new form of semio-capitalism, it first and foremost mobilised the psychic energy of society to bend it to the drive of competition and cognitive productivity. The *new economy* of the 1990s was essentially a *Prozac economy*, both neuro-mobilisation and compulsory creativity.

Paul Virilio has produced important works that show the connection between war and speed: in the modern forms of domination, the imposition of war onto the whole of social life is an implicit one precisely because economic competitiveness is war, and war and the economy share common ground in speed. As Walter Benjamin wrote: 'all efforts to render politics aesthetic culminate in one thing: war.' The becoming aesthetic of life is one aspect of this mobilisation of social energies. The aestheticisation of war is functional to the subjugation of everyday life to the rule of history. War forces the global masses to partake in the process of self-realisation of the Hegelian spirit, or, perhaps more realistically, to become part of capitalist global accumulation. Captured in the dynamics of war, everyday life is ready to be subjected to the unlimited rule of the commodity. From this standpoint, there is no difference between fascism, communism and democracy: art functions as the element of aestheticisation and mobilisation of everyday life. Total mobilisation is terror, and terror is the ideal condition for a full realisation of the capitalist plan to mobilise psychic energy. The close relation between Futurism and advertising is an integral part of this process.

In his *Art and Revolution* (Semiotext(e), 2007), Gerald Raunig writes of the relationship between the artistic avant-garde and activism. His work provides a useful phenomenological account of the relation between art and political mobilisation in the twentieth century, but it fails to grasp the absolute specificity of the current situation – that is, the crisis and exhaustion of all activism.

The term 'activism' largely became influential as a result of the anti-globalisation movement, which used it to describe its political communication and the connection between art and communicative action. However, this definition is a mark of its attachment to the past and its inability to free itself from the conceptual frame of reference it inherited from the twentieth century. Should we not free ourselves from the thirst for activism that fed the twentieth century to the point of catastrophe and war? Should we not set ourselves free from the repeated and failed attempt to act for the liberation of human energies from the rule of capital? Isn't the path towards the autonomy of the social from economic and military mobilisation only possible through a withdrawal into inactivity, silence and passive sabotage?

4. Lenin's depression

I believe that there is a profound relationship between the drive to activism and the male depression of late modernity, which is most evident in the voluntaristic and subjectivist organisation of Leninism.

Both from the standpoint of the history of the workers' movement in the 1900s and from that of the strategic autonomy of society from capital, I am convinced that the twentieth century would have been a better century had Lenin not existed. Lenin's vision interprets a deep trend in the configuration of the psyche of modern masculinity. Male narcissism was confronted with the infinite power of capital and emerged from it frustrated, humiliated and depressed. It seems to me that Lenin's depression is a crucial element for understanding the role his thought played in the development of the politics of late modernity.

I have read Hélène Carrère d'Encausse's biography, *Lenin*. The author is a researcher of Georgian descent, who in the 1980s also published *L'empire en miettes*, where she foresaw the collapse of the Soviet empire as an effect of the insurgence of Islamic fundamentalism. What interests me in Carrère d'Encausse's biography of Lenin, more than the history of Lenin's political activity, is his personal life, his fragile psyche, and his affectionate and intellectual relationships with the women close to him: his mother, his sister, Krupskaya, comrade and wife, who looked after him at times of acute psychological crisis, and, finally, Ines Armand, the perturbing, the *Unheimlich*, the lover whom Lenin decided to neutralise and remove, like music, apparently.

The framework of the psyche described in this biography is depression, and Lenin's most acute crises coincided with important political shifts in the revolutionary movement. As Carrère d'Encausse writes:

> Lenin used to invest everything he did with perseverance, tenaciousness and an exceptional concentration: such consistency, which he thought necessary in each of his efforts, put him in a position of great superiority over the people around him ... This feature of his character often had negative effects. Exceedingly intensive efforts would tire him and wear down his already fragile nervous system. The first crisis dates back to 1902.[2]

These were the years of the Bolshevik turn, of *What Is To Be Done?* Krupskaya played a fundamental role in the crisis of her comrade: she intervened to filter his relations with the outside world, paid for his therapy and isolation in clinics in Switzerland and Finland. Lenin emerged from the 1902 crisis by writing *What Is To Be Done?* and engaging in the construction of a 'nucleus of steel', a block of will capable of breaking the weakest link in the imperialist chain. The second crisis arrived in 1914 at the height of the break-up of the Second International and the split of the Communists. The third crisis, as you might guess, occurred in the spring of 1917. Krupskaia found a safe resort in Finland, where Lenin conceived *The April Theses* and the decision to impose will on intelligence: a rupture that disregarded the deep dynamics of class struggle and forced upon them an external design. Intelligence is depressive, therefore will is the only cure to the abyss, to ignore it without removing it. The abyss remains and the following years uncovered it, as the century precipitated into it.

I do not intend to discuss the politics of Lenin's fundamental choices. I am interested in pointing out a relationship between Bolshevik voluntarism and the male inability to accept depression and develop it from within. Here lies the root of the subjectivist voluntarism that produced the setback of social autonomy in the 1900s. The intellectual decisions of Leninism were so powerful because they were capable of interpreting the male obsession with voluntarism as it faced depression.

5. The next wave

By the beginning of the twenty-first century the long history of the artistic avant-garde was over. Beginning with Wagner's *Gesamtkunstwerk* and resulting in the Dadaist cry to 'Abolish art, abolish everyday life, abolish the separation between art and everyday life', the history of the avant-garde culminates in the gesture of 9/11. Stockhausen had the courage to say this, whilst many of us were thinking the same: terrorising suicide is the total work of art of the century with no future. The fusion of art and life (or death – what difference does it make?) is clearly visible in the form of action that we might call 'terrorising suicide'. Let us take Pekka Auvinen as an example. The Finnish youngster turned up to his class at school with a machine gun, killing eight people, himself included. Printed on his T-shirt was the sentence 'Humanity is overrated'. Wasn't his gesture pregnant with signs typical of the communicative action of the arts?

Let me explain: I am not inviting the young readers of this article to go to a crowded place with an explosive belt. I am trying to say, pay attention: a gigantic wave of desperation could soon turn into a suicidal epidemic that will turn the first connective generation into a devastating psychic bomb. I do not think that this wave of suicides can be explained in terms of morality, family values and the weak discourse used by conservative thought to account for the ethical drift produced by capitalism. To understand the contemporary form of ethical shipwreck we need to reflect on the transformations of activity and labour, the subsumption of the time of the mind under the competitive realm of productivity; we have to understand the mutation of the cognitive and psycho-social system.

6. Conjunction/connection

The context of my understanding of the present historical and cultural dynamics is the transition from a realm of conjunction to one of connection, with a special focus on the emergence of the first connective generation, those who learn more words from a machine than from a mother. In this transition, a mutation of the conscious organism is taking place: to render this organism compatible with a connective environment, our cognitive system needs to be reformatted. This appears to generate a dulling of the faculties of conjunction that had hitherto characterised the human condition. The realm of sensibility is involved in this ongoing process of cognitive reformatting; we see aesthetic thought as being inserted at a juncture. Ethical and political thought is also reshaping its observational standpoint and framework around the passage from a conjunctive to a connective form of human concatenation.

Conjunction is becoming-other. In contrast, in connection each element remains distinct and interacts only functionally. Singularities change when they conjoin; they become something other than they were before their conjunction. Love changes the lover and a combination of a-signifying signs gives rise to the emergence of a meaning that does not exist prior to it. Rather than a fusion of segments, connection entails a simple effect of machinic functionality. In order to connect, segments must be compatible and open to interfacing and inter-operability. Connection requires these segments to be linguistically compatible. In fact the digital web spreads and expands by progressively reducing more and more elements to a format, a standard and a code that make different segments compatible. The segments that enter this rhizome belong to different realms of nature: they are electronic, semiotic, machinic, biological and psychic; optic fibre circuits, mathematical abstractions, electromagnetic waves, human eyes, neurons and synapses. The process whereby they become compatible traverses heterogeneous fields of being and folds them onto a principle of connectivity.

The present mutation occurs in this transition from conjunction to connection, a paradigm of exchange between conscious organisms.

Central to this mutation is the insertion of the electronic into the organic, the proliferation of artificial devices in the organic universe, in the body, in communication and in society. Therefore, the relationship between consciousness and sensibility is transformed and the exchange of signs undergoes a process of increasing desensitisation. Conjunction is the meeting and fusion of rounded and irregular forms that infuse in a manner that is imprecise, unrepeatable, imperfect and continuous. Connection is the punctual and repeatable interaction of algorithmic functions, straight lines and points that juxtapose perfectly and are inserted and removed in discrete modes of interaction. These discrete modes make different parts compatible to predetermined standards.

The digitisation of communication processes leads, on the one hand, to a sort of desensitisation, to the curve and to the continuous flows of slow becoming, and, on the other, to a becoming sensitive to the code, to sudden changes of states and to the sequence of discrete signs. Interpretation follows semantic criteria in the realm of conjunction: the meaning of the signs sent by the other as she enters in conjunction with you needs to be understood by tracing the intention, the context, the nuances and the unsaid, if necessary. The interpretative criteria of the realm of connection, on the other hand, are purely syntactic. In connection, the interpreter must recognise a sequence and be able to perform the operation required by general syntax or the operating system; there is no room for margins of ambiguity in the exchange of messages, nor can the intention be shown by means of nuances.

This mutation produces painful effects in the conscious organism and we read them through the categories of psychopathology: dyslexia, anxiety and apathy, panic, depression and a sort of epidemic of suicide are spreading. However, a purely psychopathological account fails to capture the question in its depth, because we are in fact confronted with the effort of the conscious organism to adapt to a changed environment and a readjustment of the cognitive system to the techno-communicative environment. This generates pathologies of the psychic sphere and in social relations.

Aesthetic perception – here properly conceived as the realm of sensibility and aesthesia – is directly involved in this transformation: in its attempt to interface efficiently with the connective environment, the conscious organism appears increasingly to inhibit what we call sensibility. By sensibility, we mean the faculty that enables human beings to interpret signs that are not verbal nor can be made so, the ability to understand what cannot be expressed in forms that have a finite syntax. This faculty reveals itself to be useless and even damaging in an integrated connective system. Sensibility slows down processes of interpretation and renders them aleatory and ambiguous, thus reducing the competitive efficiency of the semiotic agent.

The ethical realm where voluntary action is possible also plays an essential role in the reformatting of the cognitive system. Religious sociologists and journalists lament a sort of ethical lack of sensitivity and a general indifference in the behaviour of the new generations. In many cases, they lament the decline of ideological values or community links. However, in order to understand the discomfort that invests the ethical and political realms, the emphasis needs to be placed on aesthetics. Ethical paralysis and the inability to ethically govern individual and collective life seem to stem from a discomfort in aesthesia – the perception of the other and of the self.

7. Dystopian poetry

The arts of the 1900s favoured the register of utopia in two forms: the radical utopia of Mayakovsky and the functional utopia of the Bauhaus. The dystopian thread remained hidden in the folds of the artistic and literary imagination, in Fritz Lang, expressionism, and a kind of bitter surrealism that underlies the field of vision that connects Salvador Dalí to Philip K. Dick. In the second half of the twentieth century the literary dystopia of Orwell, Burroughs and DeLillo flourished. Only today, at the beginning of the twenty-first century, does dystopia take centre stage and conquer the whole field of the artistic imagination, thus drawing the narrative horizon of the century with no future. In the expression of contemporary poetry, in cinema, video art and novels, the marks of an epidemic of psychopathology proliferate.

In her videos, Eija-Liisa Ahtila (*Wind* 2002, *If 6 was 9* 1995, *Anne Aki and God* 1998) narrates the psychopathology of relations, the inability to touch and to be touched. In the film *Me and You and Everyone We Know* (2005), Miranda July tells the story of a video artist who falls in love with a young man and of the difficulty of translating emotion into words and words into touch. Language is severed from affectivity. Language and sex diverge in everyday life. Sex is talked about everywhere, but sex never speaks. Pills accelerate erection because the time for caresses is limited.

A film by Jia Zhang-Ke, entitled *Still Life* (*Sanxia haoren*) and produced in Hong Kong in 2006, shows an unfolding devastation. This film is extraordinarily beautiful and tells a simple story, with the background of a sad, desolate and devastated China, as both the scenery and its soul. The predominant colour is a rotten, greyish, violet green. Huo Sanming returns to his place of birth in the hope of finding his wife and daughter, whom he had left years earlier to go and find work in a distant northern mine. His village, along the riverbank of the Yangtze, no longer exists. The construction of the Three Gorges Dam had erased many villages. Houses, people and streets were covered by water. The building of the dam proceeds, the destruction of villages continues and the water is going to keep rising. Huo Sanming arrives in this scenario of devastation and rising water and is unable to find his wife and daughter; so his search begins. He looks for them as groups of workers armed with their picks take walls down, as explosives demolish buildings in the urban centre.

After long searches he finally finds his wife; she has aged and been sold by her brother to another man. They meet in the rooms of a building as it is being demolished and talk about their daughter in whispers, with their heads down, against a dark green spaceship background of bricks and iron spattering onto a shitcoloured sky. In the last scene, a tightrope walker walks on a rope from the roofs of a house towards nothingness, against a background that recalls the dark surrealism of Dalí's bitter canvas. *Still Life* is a lyrical account of Chinese capitalism, acted inside out, from the standpoint of submerged life.

The Corrections, a novel by Jonathan Franzen published in 2001, speaks of psychopharmacological adjustments as the corrections used by a humanity devastated by depression and anxiety to adjust to an existence that must pretend to be happy. Corrections are the adjustment to a volatile stock market to avoid losing the money invested in private pension funds that might suddenly disappear. Franzen recounts the old age of a father and mother, a couple of oldies from the Midwest who have gone nuts as a result of decades of hyper-labour and conformism. Corrections are the small and unstoppable slides towards the point of turn-off, the horror of old age in the civilisation of competition, the horror of sexuality in the world of puritan efficiency.

Franzen digs deep into the American psyche and describes in minute details the pulpifaction of the American brain, the depression and dementia resulting from a prolonged exposure to the psychic bombardment of stress from work, the apathy, paranoia, puritan hypocrisy and the pharmaceuticals industry around them, the psychic unmaking of men who are encapsulated in the claustrophobic shell of economic hyper-protection, the infantilism of a people which pretends to believe, or perhaps really believes in the fulsome Christmas fairy tale of compassionately liberalist cruelty. By the end of the long-awaited Christmas dinner, as the psychopathic family happily gathers together, the father tries to commit suicide by shooting himself in the mouth. He is not successful.

Yakizakana no Uta, an animated film of 2004 by Yusuke Sakamoto, starts with a fish in cellophane wrapping on a supermarket shelf. A boy grabs it and takes it to the till; he pays, leaves, puts it in the bicycle basket and cycles home. 'Good morning Mr Student, I'm very happy to be with you. Do not worry, I'm not a fish who complains,' the fish says whilst the student briskly pedals home. 'It's nice to make the acquaintance of a human being. You are extraordinary beings; you are almost the masters of the universe. Unfortunately you are not always peaceful; I would like to live in a peaceful world where everyone loves one another and even fish and humans shake hands. Oh it's so nice to see the sunset, I like it ever so much.' The fish becomes emotional and jumps in the cellophane bag inside the basket. 'I can hear the sound of a stream ... I love the sound of streams, it reminds me something from my childhood.' When they get home the boy unpacks the fish and puts it on a plate, throws a little salt on it. As the fish gets excited and says 'Ah! I like salt very much, it reminds me of something ...' the boy puts it on the grill in the oven and turns the knob. The fish keeps chatting: 'Oh Mr Student, it's nice here, I can see a light down there ... I feel hot ... hot ...' until its voice becomes hesitant. It starts singing a song, more and more feebly and unconnectedly, like Hal in *2001: Space Odyssey* as his wires are unplugged.

Yakizakana no Uta was perhaps the most harrowing animation I saw in June 2006 at the Caixa Forum of Barcelona, during the *Historias Animadas* festival. Yet I perceived a common tone running through all of the works presented at the festival, one of ironic cynicism. *Place in Time* by Miguel Soares recounts millions of years from the standpoint of an improbable bug, an organic insect, as the world changes around it. *Animales de compania* by Ruth Gomes uses ferocious images to tell the story of a generation of well-dressed anthropophagi, young beasts in ties; they run and run to avoid being caught by fellows, colleagues, friends and lovers who wound, kill and eat them as soon as they fall into their grip, with terrorised smiles and dilated eyes.

This art is no denunciation. The terms 'denunciation' and 'engagement' no longer have meaning when you are a fish getting ready to be cooked. The art of the twenty-first century no longer has that kind of energy, even though it keeps using expressions from the 1900s, perhaps out of modesty, perhaps because it is scared of its own truth. Artists no longer search the way to a rupture, and how could they? They seek a path that leads to a state of equilibrium between irony and cynicism that allows them to suspend the execution, at least for a moment.

Is art the postponement of the holocaust?

All energy has moved to the war front.

Artistic sensibility registers this shift and is incapable of opposing it.

Translated by Arianna Bove

1 Jean Baudrillard, *L'échange symbolique et la mort*, Gallimard, Paris 1976, p.12; *Symbolic Exchange and Death*, trans. Ian Hamilton Grant, Sage, London 1993.

2 Hélène Carrère d'Encausse, *Lenin*, Fayard, Paris 1998, p.78; *Lenin*, trans. George Holoch, Holmes & Meier, Teaneck NJ 2002.

Art, War, Avant-Garde

9

War on Latency: On Some Relations between Surrealism and Terror

Peter Sloterdijk

Of all offensive gestures of aesthetic modernity, surrealism, more than any other, strengthened the insight that the main interest of the present time must focus on the explication of culture – provided we understand culture as the quintessence of symbol-forming mechanisms and art creation processes. Surrealism follows the command that demands occupation of the symbolic dimensions in the crusade towards modernisation. Its articulated and unarticulated aim is to make creative processes explicit and elucidate their sources as much as possible. For this purpose and without ceremony it brings forward the fetish of the epoch: the concept of 'revolution', legitimisation of all things. However, as in political spheres (where it de facto has never been a question of an actual 'turning' in the sense of a reversal from top to bottom, but of proliferation of top positions and their reappointment by representatives of the offensive middle classes, which indeed would not be possible without a partial transparency of the mechanisms of power – that is, democratisation – and seldom without an initial phase of open force from below), the misnomer of events is also evident in the field of culture. Here, too, there was never a reversal or *Umwälzung* in the precise sense of the word, but, rather, solely a redistribution of symbolic hegemony – which demanded a certain revelation of artistic processes and called for a phase of barbarisms and *Bilderstürme*. In the field of culture, 'revolution' is a pseudonym for 'legitimate' force against latent tendencies. It causes the new performers, who act with a clear conscience, to break from the holisms and comforts of bourgeois art settings. The recollection of one of the best-known scenes from the surrealistic offensive may well explain the parallelism between the atmo-terrorist explications of the atmosphere and the culturally revolutionary blows to the mentality of a bourgeois art audience.

On 1 July 1936, Salvador Dalí, who was at the start of his career as a self-proclaimed ambassador from the kingdom of the surreal, gave a performance at London's New Burlington Galleries on the occasion of the International Surrealist Exhibition, in which he intended to explain the principles of the 'paranoiac critical method' he had developed, with reference to his own exhibit. In order to make quite clear to his audience by his appearance that he was speaking to them as a representative of a radical Elsewhere and in the name of the Other, Dalí chose to wear a diving suit for his lecture. According to the report in the *London Star* on 2 July, a car radiator was attached to the top of the helmet; the artist was also holding a billiard cue in his hand and was accompanied by two large dogs.[1] In his self-portrayal, *Comment on devient Dalí*, the artist retells a version of the incident that resulted from this idea:

> I had decided to make a speech on the occasion of the exhibition, but wearing a diving suit, in order to allegorise the subconscious. Hence I was dressed in my armour and even put on shoes with lead soles, thus preventing me from moving my legs. I had to be carried onto the podium. Then the helmet was placed on my head and screwed tight. I started my speech behind the glass of the helmet – in front of a microphone that was obviously not able to pick up anything. My facial expression however fascinated the audience. Soon I was gasping for breath with my mouth wide open, my face turned red at first and then blue and my eyes started to roll. Apparently one (sic) had forgotten to connect me to an air supply system, and I was close to suffocation. The expert who had fitted me had disappeared. By gesticulating I made my friends aware that my situation was becoming critical. One fetched a pair of scissors and tried in vain to pierce the suit, another wanted to unscrew the helmet. As his attempt failed, he started to hit the screws with a hammer ... two men tried to tear off the helmet, a third continued to hit the metal, so that I almost lost consciousness. There was now a wild scuffle on the podium, during which I surfaced now and again like a jumping jack with dislocated limbs, and my copper helmet resounding like a gong. The audience then applauded this successful Dalí mimo-drama, which, in their eyes, no doubt showed how the conscious tried to seize the unconscious. This triumph was, however, almost the death of me. When they finally pulled off the helmet, I was as pale as Jesus on his return from forty days fasting in the desert.[2]

This scene illustrates two things: surrealism is a dilettantism, where technical objects are not employed on their own terms, but as symbolic draperies; nevertheless, it is part of the explicit-making movement of modern art, as it unmistakably presents itself as a process that breaks latent tendencies and dissolves backgrounds.

An important aspect of dissolving backgrounds in the cultural field is the attempt to destroy the consensus between the producing and the receiving side in artistic activity, in order to set free the radical intrinsic value of the showing-event and uncover the absoluteness of the production and the intrinsic value of receptivity. Such interventions are valuable as elucidation measures against provincialism and cultural narcissism. It was not without reason that the surrealists, in the early phase of their wave of attacks, developed the art of astounding the bourgeois as a form of action *sui generis*, since this helped the innovators distinguish between in-group and out-group, and also allowed the public protest to be considered a sign of the successful dismantling of a handed-down system. Whoever scandalises the public admits to progressive iconoclasm. He or she uses terror against symbols to burst mystified latent positions and achieve a breakthrough with more explicit techniques. The legitimate premise of symbolic aggression lies in the belief that cultures have too many skeletons in the closet and it is time to burst the interrelations between armament and edification that are protected by latency. When the early avant-gardes nevertheless came to an erroneous conclusion, this could be seen in the fact that the populace they intended to frighten always learned its lesson faster than any one of the aesthetic bogeymen ever anticipated. After only a few rounds of the game between the provocateurs and the provoked, a situation arose in which the bourgeoisie enticed by mass culture took over the explication of art, culture and significance through marketing, design and auto-hypnosis, whilst the artists often continued to astound only formally, without noticing that the time for this method had passed. Others underwent a neo-romantic turn and once again came to terms with profundity. Soon, many modernists seemed to have forgotten the basic principle of modern philosophy defined by Hegel that applies analogously to aesthetic production: the depth of a thought can only be measured by the power of its comprehensiveness – otherwise it remains an empty symbol for unconquered latent elements.

These results can be measured by Dalí's failed and hence informative performance. It proves, on the one hand, that the destruction of consensus between the artist and the public cannot succeed once the latter has understood the new rule through which the extension of the work to the environment of the work becomes itself the form of work. The enthusiastic applause that Dalí received at the New Burlington Galleries illustrated how consistently the educated audience adhered to the new terms of art perception. On the other hand, the scene showed the artist as latency-breaker, conveying to the profane people a message from the kingdom of Otherness. Dalí's function in this game was distinguished by its ambiguity, which tells us a great deal about his vacillation between romanticism and objectivity. On the one hand, he commends himself as a technician of the Other, since in the lecture he never held, but which can easily be anticipated by its title, 'Authentic Paranoiac Fantasies', he intended to deal with a precise method that would make access to the 'subconscious' controllable – that paranoiac critical method with which Dalí formulated formal instructions for the 'Conquest of the Irrational.'[3]

He confessed to a kind of photo-realism with regard to irrational inner pictures: he intended to objectify with masterly precision what had become apparent in dreams, delirium and inner visions. At this time he already understood his work as an artistic parallel to the so-called 'discovery of the unconscious through psychoanalysis' – a scientific myth adopted wholesale by the aesthetic avant-gardes and the educated audiences of the 1920s and 1930s (and brought to esteem once again by Lacan between the 1950s and 1970s when he reanimated the surrealistic form of lecture for a 'return to Freud').

From this perspective, surrealism takes its place in the manifestations of the operational 'revolution', which carries on the continuous advancement of modernisation. On the other hand, Dalí adhered, decidedly countercritically, to the romantic conception of the artist-ambassador who among the unenlightened transforms into a delegate of the Beyond, pregnant with sense. This attitude reveals him as a domineering amateur, surrendering to the illusion that he is capable of employing complicated technical devices to articulate metaphysical kitsch. The user attitude is typical in this case, childishly leaving the technical side of his own performance to experts of whose competence he had not convinced himself. Also the fact that the scene was not rehearsed shows the artist's poor, literary treatment of technical structures. Nevertheless, Dalí's choice of outfits has an illuminating aspect; his accident is prophetic – not only in terms of the reaction of the spectators, who proclaimed applause for what they failed to understand as a new cultural bearing. The fact that the artist chose a diving suit equipped with an artificial air supply for his appearance as ambassador from the deep leaves no doubt about his connection with the development of atmospheric consciousness, which, as we attempt to show here, is central to the self-explication of culture in the twentieth century. Even if the surrealist achieves only a semi-technical interpretation of the global and cultural background as the 'sea of the subconscious', he or she already postulates a competence to navigate in this space with formally expanded procedures. His performance makes it obvious that, in the present age, conscious existence must be lived as an explicit dive into context. Those who venture out of their own camps in multimilieu society must be sure of their 'diving equipment' – that is, of their physical and mental immune systems. The accident cannot be accounted to dilettantism alone; it also discloses the systematic risks of technical atmospheric explication and technically forced access to an other element – precisely in the way that the risk of poisoning the home troops was inseparable from the actions of military atmoterrorism in gas warfare.[4] If Dalí's portrayal of the incident is accurate, then he was not far from going down in history as a martyr of dives in the symbolic sense.

Under the given circumstances, the accident proved to be a form of production, in that it triggered panic in the artist, which had always been inherent as impetus for his work.

Permanent revolution, permanent fear

In the unsuccessful attempt to present the 'subconscious' as a navigable zone, the very fear of annihilation came to the fore, which the aesthetic explication process was activated to conquer and expel. To put it in general terms: the contraphobic experiment of modernisation is never really able to emancipate itself from its background of fear, as this would not be capable of appearing until fear could be allowed to enter into existence as fear itself – which, by the nature of things, presents an impossible hypothesis. Modernity as a background explication therefore remains caught in the circle of victory over fear through technology that causes fear. Primary as well as secondary fear always provides a fresh boost for the continuation of the process; its urgency justifies the use of further latency-breaking and background-controlling force at every stage of modernisation – or, according to prevailing phraseology, it demands permanent basic research and innovation.

Aesthetic modernity is a process of using force not against persons or objects, but against non-clarified cultural relations. It organises a wave of attacks against the holistic attitudes of the types belief, love and honesty and against pseudo-evident categories such as shape, content, image, works and art. Its modus operandi is live experimentation on the users of these definitions. Aggressive modernism consequently breaks away from the respect for classicists, in which, as it remarks with great aversion, at least vague holism is manifested – combined with a tendency to continue to follow a 'totem', retained in its undefined and undeveloped state. As a result of its keen wish for explicitness, surrealism declares war on mediocrity: it sees in it the opportune hideout for antimodern lethargies, which oppose the operative development and reconstructive revelation of integrated rules. As normality rates as a crime in this war of mentality, art as a medium of combating crime can build on unusual combat orders. When Isaac Babel declared 'banality is the counterrevolution', he indirectly expressed the principle of 'revolution'. The use of fear as a force against normality bursts aesthetic and social latency and raises to the surface laws according to which societies and works of art are construed.

Permanent 'revolution' calls for permanent fear. It postulates a society that proves itself repeatedly as readily frightened and controllable. New art is saturated with the excitement of the very newest, as it appears terror-mimetic and warlike – often without being able to define whether it declares war on the war of societies or wages war on its own behalf. The artist permanently faces the decision of whether to advance against the public as saviour of differences or as warlord of innovation. In view of this ambivalence in modernistic aggression, so-called postmodernism was not entirely wrong when it defined itself as an anti-explicit and anti-extremist reaction to the aesthetic and analytic terror of modern art. Like all forms of terrorism, the aesthetic falls back on the unmarked background in front of which works of art articulate and makes it appear on the forestage as an intrinsic phenomenon. The prototype of modern painting of this trend, Kasimir Malevich's *Black Square* of 1913, owes its inexhaustible interpretability to the artist's decision to evacuate the image space in favour of the pure, dark surface. Thereby its squareness itself becomes the figure, which in other pictorial situations appears as the carrier in the background.

The scandal of the work lies in, among other things, the fact that it still stands its ground as a painting in its own right and by no means presents merely an empty canvas as object of interest, as would have been conceivable in the context of Dadaistic campaigns to deride art. It may well be that the picture can be regarded as a minimally irregular platonic icon of the equilateral rectangle, deserving tribute due to its sensuousness. It is, however, simultaneously the icon of the aniconic or pre-iconic – of the

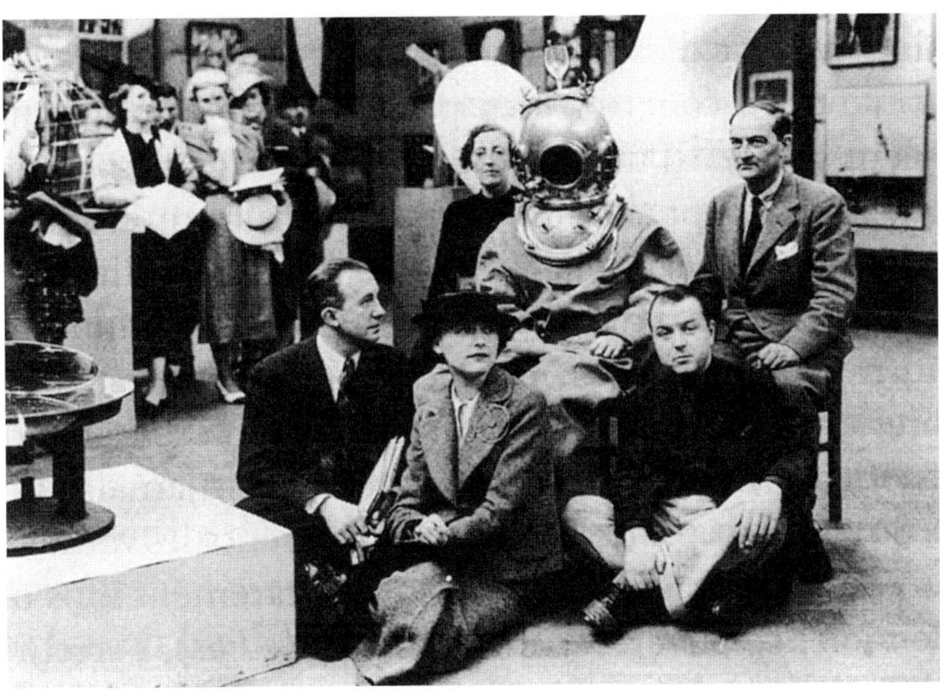

Salvador Dalí in a diving suit, Burlington Galleries, London, 1 July 1936

normally invisible picture background. The black square therefore stands before a white background, which surrounds it, almost as a frame. In the *White Square* painted in 1914 even this difference is almost effaced.

The basic gesture of such formal representations is the raising of the non-thematic to the thematic. Not only are the possibly varied picture contents, which could appear in the foreground, reduced to a background which always appears the same, but, far more, the background as such is painted with the greatest care and thus made explicit as figure of the figure-bearer. The terror of purification can be unambiguously seen in the desire for the 'supremacy of pure feeling'. The work of art demands the unconditional capitulation of the beholders' perception before its real presence. Although suprematism, with its anti-naturalism and its anti-phenomenonalism, makes itself clearly known as an offensive movement on the aesthetic flank of explication, it remains bound to the idealistic belief that to make explicit means the return of what is sensually present to what is spiritually absent. It is bound to old European and Platonic rules, in so far as it explains things upwards and simplifies the empirical forms to pure, primary forms. In this respect, surrealism operated differently by following more closely the materialistic, downward manner of explication – without going so far as to be named *sous* realism. Yet, whilst the material trend remained coquetry for the surrealist movement, its alliance with depth psychologies, in particular the psychoanalytic trend, revealed its own characteristic trait. The surrealistic reception of Viennese psychoanalysis is one of numerous cases illustrating that the initial success of Freudianism among the educated audience and numerous artists was not achieved as a therapeutic method, which naturally only a very small number of persons experienced first hand, but as a strategy for the interpretation of symbols and background manipulation, leaving every interested party open to the choice of application to suit individual requirements. Is not indeed the analysis one did not undergo always the most appealing?

Freud's approach led to the unfolding of a realm of a special kind of latency and came to be known by an expression adopted from idealistic philosophy – namely from F.W.J. von Schelling, Franz Schubert, Paul Carus and the nineteenth-century philosophies of life, especially Schopenhauer and Nicolai Hartmann – as 'the unconscious'. This defined a subjective dimension of security, of inner latencies and of the invisibly overlapped preconditions for an ego-ish state. According to the Freudian formulation, the meaning of the expression had narrowed radically and become so specialised that it could be put to clinical use. It no longer signified the reservoir of dark, integrating forces in a preconscious nature that possesses healing power and creates pictures, nor the underground of blindly, self affirming streams of will below the 'subject'. It defined a small, inner container that becomes filled with repressed emotions and is subjected to neurotogenic tension through the buoyancy of the repressed.[5]

The surrealists' enthusiasm for psychoanalysis was due to the fact that they confused the Freudian definition of the unconscious with Romantic metaphysics. From creative misinterpretation arose declarations such as Dalí's *Declaration of Independence of Fantasy and Declaration of Human Rights to Madness* in 1939, in which sentences are found such as:

> A man has the right to love women with ecstatic fishheads. A man has the right to find lukewarm telephones repulsive and to demand telephones as cold, green and aphrodisiac as the sleep of a Spanish fly when haunted by faces.[6]

The surrealistic allusion to the right to be mad warns individuals of their tendency to submission to normalising therapies; it wishes to make monarchists out of the usually unhappy patients who pursue their own return from an exile, neurotic with reason, to the kingdom of their very personal madness.

Total war, environmental war

We should not forget that what is today called the consumer society was invented in a hothouse – in those glass-covered arcades of the early nineteenth century, in which a first generation of adventure-customers came to breathe the intoxicating perfume of a closed inside world of consumer goods. The arcades represent an early stage of urban atmospheric explication – an objective turning out of the 'home addicted' disposition, which, according to Walter Benjamin, seized the nineteenth century. Home addiction, says Benjamin, is the irresistible urge 'to found a home' in all surroundings.[7]

In Benjamin's theory of the interior, the 'supertemporal' need for uterus simulation, expressly with the forms of a concrete historic situation, has already been conceived. Indeed, the twentieth century with its large buildings has shown how far the erection of 'living space' can be extended beyond the boundaries of the need to search for a comfortable interior. The year 1936 is enrolled in the chronicle of aesthetic and cultural theoretic atmospheric explication not only through Salvador Dalí's accident in London in a diving suit. On 1 November of the same year, the thirty-one-year-old author Elias Canetti gave a speech on the occasion of Hermann Broch's fiftieth birthday, a speech which was unusual in content and tone, in which he not only drew a detailed portrait of the author he was honouring, but at the same time shaped a new genre of laudation. The originality of Canetti's speech was that it raised the question of a connection between an author and his time in a manner previously unknown. Canetti defined the artist's stay in time as a breath-connection – as a special way of diving into the concrete atmospheric conditions of the epoch. Canetti sees in Broch the first grand master of a 'Poetry of the Atmospheric as a Static' – meaning, of an art which would be capable of illustrating 'static breathing space', expressed in a manner: making visible the climatic design of persons and groups in their typical spaces. '[His] involvement is always with the entire space in which he is present, with a kind of atmospheric unity.'[8]

Canetti praises Broch's ability to grasp every person he attempts to portray, also in an ecological sense: he recognises the singular existence of every person in his or her own breathing air, surrounded by an unmistakable climatic membrane, embodied in a personal 'breathing household'. He compares the poet to a curious bird with the freedom to creep into every possible cage and take 'air samples' from them. Thus he knows, bestowed with a mysteriously keen 'memory for air and breath', how it feels to be in this or that atmospheric habitat. As Broch turns to his characters more as a poet than a philosopher, he does not describe them as abstract ego-points in a universal ether; he portrays them as personified figures, each one living in its characteristic air membrane and moving between a variety of atmospheric constellations. The question of a possibility of poetry 'drawn from breathing experience' leads only to fruitful information in light of this multiplicity:

> Above all, the answer would need to be that the diversity of our world consists, for the main part, of the variety of our breathing spaces. The space in which you are now sitting in a certain order, almost completely closed in from the environment, the manner in which your breath blends to an air common to all ... all this is, from the point of view of the person breathing, a unique ... situation. Yet, go a few steps further and you will find a completely different situation in another breathing space ... The city is full of such breathing spaces, as full as it is of individual human beings; and in the same way as the split up of these people, of whom no one is the same as the other, a kind of every man's cul-de-sac constitutes the main excitement and main misery of life, one could also lament the split up of the atmosphere.[9]

According to this characterisation, Broch's art of narrative is based on the discovery of atmospheric multiplicity through which the modern novel reaches beyond the representation of individual destiny. Its theme is no longer individuals in their limited activities and experiments, far more the extended unity of individual and breathing space. The actions are no longer carried out between persons, but between breathing households and their respective occupants. Through this ecological viewpoint, the alienation-critical motive of modernity is given new basic principles: the atmospheric separation of people among themselves accomplished by their own respective 'households'; the difficulty for those with different outlooks, different membranes, different climates to reach them appears more justified than ever. The division of the social world into individual spaces of obstinacy, inaccessible to one another, is the moral analogue to the microclimatic 'split up of the atmosphere' (which for its part corresponds to a split up of 'world values'). As Broch, after his advance onto the individually climatic and personally ecological plane, had quasi-systematically grasped the depth of isolation in modern individuals, the question of the conditions of their unison in a common ether beyond the atmospheric separation must have occurred to him with a clearness and urgency unequalled in his own time or at a later point in time in the history of sociological examinations on the elements of social connection – with the possible exception of Canetti's related attempt in *Crowds and Power*.

In his speech in 1936 Canetti recognised in Hermann Broch the prophetic warner of an unprecedented danger to humanity, that in the metaphoric as in the physical sense was an atmospheric threat:

> Yet the greatest danger that has ever occurred in the history of mankind has chosen our generation as its victim. It is the defenselessness of breath that I would like to now finally speak of. It is difficult to grasp its real significance. Human beings are more receptive for air than for any other thing. They still move within it like Adam in paradise ... Air is the last common property. It belongs to all collectively. It is not pre-portioned; even the poorest may take their share ... And now this last thing that was common to us all is to poison us all ... Hermann Broch's work is positioned between war and war, gas war and gas war. It is possible that he still now feels the toxic particles of the last war somewhere ... but it is certain that he, who understands how to breathe better than we ourselves, is suffocating today on the gas that will take the breath from us others, whoever knows when that will be.[10]

Canetti's impassioned observation shows how information of the gas warfare from 1915 to 1918 had been abstractly translated by the most intensive diagnostician of the 1930s. Broch had realised that after the intentional atmospheric destruction of chemical warfare, social synthesis began in many respects to take on the character of gas warfare, as if atmoterrorism had turned inwards. The 'total war' heralded by old particles and new signs would inevitably take on the characteristics of an environmental war: during this war, the atmosphere itself would become a theatre of war; furthermore, air would become a kind of weapon and a special kind of battlefield.

And, in addition, from the commonly breathed air, from the ether of the collective, the community, in its mania, will in future wage a chemical war against itself. How this can happen can be explained by a theory of 'semi-consciousness' – undoubtedly the most original, if also the most fragmentary part remaining of Broch's mass psychological hypotheses. A state of semi-consciousness is that in which people move merely as trend followers in a trance of normality. As the prevailing total war is waged principally atmoterroristically and ecologically (this in the medium of total mass communication), it spreads to the 'morale' of the troops, who can now hardly be distinguished from the population. Through toxic communions, the fighters and non-fighters, the synchronically gassed and simultaneously excited, consolidate in a collective state of subconsciousness. The modern masses see themselves integrated in an emergency communistic unit that should give them an acute feeling of identity due to their common threatened state. The climatic poisons emanated by the people themselves then prove to be especially dangerous, as long as they are standing beneath sealed communication domes, hopelessly aroused. In the pathogenic air-conditioning systems of synchronically excited publics, the inhabitants breathe in their own breath, again and again. Whatever is in the air is put there through totalitarian circular communication: it is filled with the victory dreams of offended masses and their drunken, far from empirical self-exaltation, followed like a shadow by the desire to humiliate others. Life in a multimedia state is like a stay in an enthusiastic gas palace.

1 See Ian Gibson, *The Shameful Life of Salvador Dalí*, Norton, New York 1998.
2 Salvador Dalí, *Dalí*, translated into German by Franz Meyer, Moewig, Rastatt 1988, pp.229–30.
3 Salvador Dalí, *La Conquête de l'Irrationnel*, Éditions Surréalistes, Paris 1935.
4 Atmoterrorism – exemplified by gas warfare – is carried out by altering the widest environmental background that conditions human life, thus drawing our attention to that background. For more on this, see Peter Sloterdijk, *Bubbles. Spheres Volume 1: Microspherology*, trans. Wieland Hoban, Semiotext(e)/MIT Press, Cambridge MA 2011.
5 The philosophical sources of the definition of the unconscious are illustrated mainly in the works of Odo Marquard, *Transzendentaler Idealismus. Romantische Naturphilosophie. Psychoanalyse*, Verlag für Philosophie Dinter, Cologne 1987; and Jean-Marie Vaysse, *L'inconscient des modernes. Essai sur l'origine métaphysique de la psychanalyse*, Gallimard, Paris 1999.
6 Dalí 1988, p.290.
7 Walter Benjamin, *The Arcades Project*, trans H. Eiland and K. McLaughlin, Harvard University Press, Cambridge MA and London 1999, p.220 [1,4,4].
8 Elias Canetti, 'Hermann Broch. Rede zum 50. Geburtstag', in Elias Canetti, *Das Gewissen der Worte: Essays*, Fischer Taschenbuch Verlag, Frankfurt am Main, 1983, pp.22, 18.
9 Ibid., p.23.
10 Ibid., pp.23–4.

10
Re-presentation of the Repressed: The Political Revolution of the Neo-avant-garde

Peter Weibel

Traditionally, the neo-avant-garde after 1945 is discredited as a purely formalist movement, blinding out the political content of the avant-garde of the 1920s. However, assuming that the avant-garde movements from 1950 to 1970 share the same epistemic field as the cultural theories of their time, from semiotics to psychoanalysis, we can apply these theories to those art movements, to produce a new interpretation of the period. When we do this, we discover that the neo-avant-garde was in fact a political art, not on the level of representation, but on the level of the *dispositif*. It transformed our traditional concept of the image, destroying it and deserting it, extending it into space and time, and redefining it as an arena of action. It thereby expanded our conception of art and art activities, in daily life, on the streets, beyond the studios and museums. There was a political revolution of the neo-avant-garde at the level of the display, the *dispositif*,[1] the tool, negating traditional media of memory and representation, because after Stalinism, Fascism and Hitlerism, it became difficult to believe in the means of traditional culture. To understand this revolution we have to change the dominant model of representation. We have to understand that the neo-avant-garde exchanged the transformation of formal systems of representation for the transformation of *the means and materials* of representation – and the criticism of artistic representation as such. In addition, we have to expand our tools of interpretation and experimentation to include psychoanalytic methods, models and modes of social deconstruction. When we do this, the neo-avant-garde appears as a re-presentation of processes of social and psychic repression, and Viennese Actionism appears in its full, exemplary force.

Wunderblock

One model of representation, of the past but also of reality, is the *Wunderblock*, the 'mystic writing pad'. In 'A Note upon the "Mystic Writing-Pad"' (1925), Freud developed a concept of the unconscious by referring to a child's toy consisting of a thin sheet of clear plastic covering a thick waxed board. The user can write or draw on it with any pointed instrument, pressing through the sheet of plastic, making traces in the surface below. As soon as the sheet is lifted up, the image above disappears, while traces of it remain on the wax surface underneath. Freud suggests that the way the *Wunderblock* records is similar to the way in which the psyche records its material. The psychic system receives sense impressions from the outside world, but remains unmarked by those impressions, which then pass through it to a deeper layer where they are recorded as unconscious memory. The writing technique of pressing through a sheet of plastic to make traces on the surface below mirrors Freud's differentiation between the surface-character of the conscious and the unconscious as a field of traces beneath. The pressing technique is a linguistic allusion to the concept of the repressed. Pressing through the sheet of plastic creates the repressed and dislocates information from the conscious to the unconscious level. The *Wunderblock* illuminates the mechanism by which the repressed becomes the prototype of the unconscious.

This writing of the unconscious, this pressing of the repressed, was the model for Lacan's famous phrase 'the unconscious is structured like a language'. But it also has affinities with the deconstruction of Jacques Derrida, because the *Wunderblock* enables us not only to discover the writing of the unconscious but also to make explicit repressed meanings in the writing. The *Wunderblock* is a means of representation, a representation of the unconscious and the repressed, that corresponds to Derrida's idea that we have to deconstruct writing in order to gather hidden meanings that are deeper than the evident meaning of a text. Both Freud and Derrida look at the text as a pure trace. The concept of the text as a trace, and the trace as representation of the repressed and unconscious, makes a shift from an external representation to an internal one, from the representation of reality to the representation of the psyche. The text is the means to discover the unconscious, the unconscious of a text and the unconscious of the psyche.

This is precisely what Ludwig Wittgenstein reproached psychoanalysis for, in 1946: 'What Freud says about the unconscious sounds like science but in fact is just a means of representation.' Freud's theory of the unconscious and the repressed, as the cornerstone of psychoanalysis, expands the concept of representation. Since psychoanalysis, the concept of representation means more than just representation of the visual on the level of iconography. 'Why does meaning express itself in the dream?' asked Michel Foucault in 1954. The answer is clearly that there exist mechanisms of the mind and the soul that prohibit certain meanings from expressing themselves in ordinary language or in conscious terms. Repression is Freud's term for the mechanism that turns away desires that are unacceptable to the ego and the superego. Those unruly desires are repressed, made inaccessible to our thinking. The unconscious and later the 'id' are the terms Freud uses for this realm of inaccessibility. Our repressed desires appear to us disguised as dreams, symptoms and in other seemingly incoherent, uncontrolled actions. The repressed returns disguised.

In that way, dreams, symptoms and the rest are also systems of representations. The disguise is another way of representation. Representation is not only what is visible and evident; disguise and erasure can also be mechanisms of representation. The traces that are left after the erasing of the writing, even if barely visible, are still telling us their secrets, revealing the truth, the causes and reasons for repressions.

Representation must be read as a system of symptoms. Then the question that Jean-Paul Sartre posed about 'the knowledge that is ignorant of itself' can be answered positively. We can represent the unconscious, the individual unconscious, but also the social unconscious. We can represent knowledge that is ignorant of itself, disguised as dreams, symptoms – and as art. To paraphrase Foucault: why does meaning express itself in art and not in science? The answer is that society itself turns our unacceptable desires, insights, facts and knowledge away from us. There is some knowledge in our society that is repressed by the society itself. Disguised as art, this social unconscious, this repressed, can return to the mind and to reality. Naturally, Freud's concept of the repressed is an attack on the Cartesian conception of a rational mind and subject and therefore also a rational reality. This is why art is always blamed for being irrational, while science is defined as rational. But art is also a rational way to deal with the irrational, the unconscious, the repressed. The popular misunderstanding that art is the expression of drives, of uncontrolled drives, is untrue. Just the opposite is the case. Disguised as art, the repressed, the knowledge ignorant of itself, expresses itself. Art is not only a mechanism of representation of reality but also a mechanism of representation of the repressed.

An iconic understanding of visual representations is a limited tool, because it is more or less a retinal representation. As a model of the unconscious and the repressed, the *Wunderblock* shows us that there are more traces of reality and that the mechanisms of representation are more complex than just the representation of external reality. The dynamic interaction of internal and external mechanisms of representation, reflected in the dynamic interaction of the conscious and the unconscious, shows us that mapping reality includes mapping the mind, and that it is not enough to define a representation isomorphically. This is the meaning of Magritte's famous painting, *This Is Not a Pipe* (1928/9), and the reason it is so attractive to philosophers, like Foucault. If we stick to the conception of a purely visual representation, then we would have to deny the possibility that music and painting can have a political dimension, as Sartre did, when he proposed in *What is Literature?* (1946) that only literature, a complicated text, can have a political dimension, but not music or painting, not the visual arts.

Besides the *Wunderblock*, psychoanalytic theory offers other mechanisms of representation of the repressed to help us construct an aesthetics of symptoms. Among them are the highly effective defence mechanisms of sublimation, displacement and reaction formation. Reaction formation is one of the most powerful concepts for understanding the text of the neo-avant-garde.

Reaction formation

Reaction formation belongs to the category of defence mechanisms of the ego – *Ich*, the 'I'. According to Freud's theory, the ego is situated between biology (represented by the id – *Es*, the 'it') and society (represented by the superego). According to Freud's famous formula *Wo Es war soll Ich werden* (Where 'it' was 'I' shall be), it is the aim of the psychic processes to replace the unconscious restraints of biology by the conscious actions of a sovereign ego. But during this process conflicting demands are made upon the ego and therefore this ego feels threatened, it feels anxiety. And the ego starts to develop defence mechanisms against these demands, be they from society or biology. It unconsciously blocks demands or transforms them into a less threatening form. Among others, Anna Freud in 'The Ego and the Defence Mechanism' (1946) developed a better understanding of these mechanisms and provided us with a list of strategies: denial, repression, regression, rationalisation, displacement, projection, introjection, sublimation and reaction formation.

Denial is the case if a person simply refuses to experience a situation or has blocked this situation from awareness. Repression, on the other hand, is 'motivated forgetting'. A situation or event or person which is or was too dangerous for the ego cannot be recalled or remembered, but this threatening situation is unconsciously effective. Repression is the most famous defence strategy. The repression of a traumatic event, as we know, will always return, but in a different, masked way. Regression happens when we are faced with stress, troubled or frightened. The ego turns back to previous behaviours, more childish or primitive, such as sucking the thumb. We return to a state when we felt saved and secure, as in childhood. Rationalisation is a way to make an impulse less threatening by explaining it in a rational manner, excuses that have a tendency to deny the facts. Acts, thoughts and emotions, the real psychic conditions of which are denied, are legitimised as logically coherent. Displacement is the redirection of an impulse to a symbolic substitute. Some people may have difficulties with love and substitute cats and dogs for human beings. Projection is another technique for displacing unacceptable desires or features onto other people (Anna Freud called it 'displacement outward'). A man who has sexual feelings about his friend but cannot acknowledge these feelings to himself increasingly complains about the presence of homosexuality in society. Introjection or identification is an opposit technique. It not only defends the ego against threatening demands, but supports the integration of the ego into society. It even helps develop our superego. A child that feels lonely tries to act like a mother in order to lessen the fear. Teenagers with a troubled identity imitate their favourite star to establish their own identity. With this example we can understand why Freud saw defence mechanisms as necessary. He even suggested that there is a positive defence, which he called sublimation, which is the transformation of an unacceptable impulse into a form that is not only socially acceptable but even productive. Sublimation was for Freud the source of creation. A person with latent aggression may sublimate it into sport. Freud thought of most creative activities as sublimations predominantly of the sex drive. Reaction

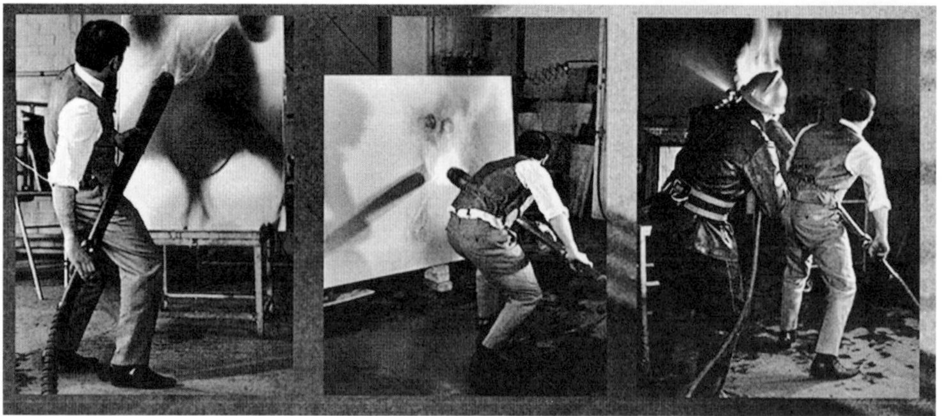

Yves Klein producing a fire-picture, Paris, 1961

formation is comparable to sublimation, because it is a mechanism that also transforms an unacceptable impulse into its opposite, to become socially acceptable. A child abused by its father is naturally unable to accept this traumatic experience and therefore turns even more to the abusing father, which appears rationally inexplicable.

Defence mechanisms are processes by which the ego adapts to the reality principle. The study of defence mechanisms is thus extremely useful for the understanding of cultural productions and the uncovering of the socially unconscious. Reaction formation, described by Anna Freud as 'believing the opposite', is a way of turning reality into its opposite. Adolescents often speak about the opposite sex as being annoying in order to hide their overwhelming desire. Aggression can be transformed into exaggerated tenderness. But reaction formation can also mix with the techniques of displacement or projection. A human being can project their own unacceptable activities onto others, but they can also project other unacceptable activities onto themselves, in a kind of inverse displacement. This projection or displacement happens in a binary code, as positive or negative reaction. Reaction formation is one of the most powerful codes in the encounter of a subject with the social system. In some cases it is more suitable than sublimation for explaining the mechanisms of cultural creativity.

Art

The reduction of representation to purely visual representations of reality is a conceit of modernity. Modern art tried to reduce techniques of representation in the visual arts to the surface of the plastic sheet. Greenberg's modernism was obsessed with the idea of the surface. Until the invention of photography, the main visual form of representation of reality was painting. Painting experienced a crisis when, with the advent of photography around 1840, it was doubled by another technique of visual representation which could imitate reality even better. Modern art is the result of this crisis of representation, which started as a crisis of painting at the very moment when painting lost its monopoly of visual representation. Since before photography there was no visual system of representation other than the painted image, and the painted image reigned over thousands of years, people got used to the idea of comprehensively identifying painting with art itself – identifying the representational system of art, exclusively, with the representational system of painting. But this was wrong because painting was just one visual system of representation. The so-called crisis of representation forced painting to leave visual representation to photography and move to abstraction – that is, the denial of representation. Given that people wrongly believed in the equation 'art is painting is visual representation', it is understandable they would think that the loss of the monopoly of painting was the end of painting; and that the end of painting was the end of art; and the end of art, the end of representation. This delineation follows the logic of modernity. The crisis of representation is just an expression of the loss of the monopoly of representation by painting, because after photography, film, television, video and the computer could also produce images, even moving images, and transmit images in real time. Modern art may thus be seen as a questionable delineation of the transformation of systems of representation through the advent of the technical image. The outcome of this so-called crisis of representation was modern art.

As the cornerstone of modern art in the first half of the twentieth century, abstract art followed the logic of self-dissolution in three steps: (1) *shifting accents* (paint was analysed, and the retinal impression of colour was emphasised, in Impressionism); (2) *declaring independence and autonomy* (paint left behind local object-bound colours and gave colour an absolute status without referential ties to the world of objects, in symbolism and suprematism); (3) *substitution* (paint as a material (*Faktura*) was replaced by other materials – white colour by aluminium, the tissue of canvas by wood – in Russian constructivism). In abstract art not only was the representation of an object omitted but colour and form could also be omitted in a monochrome painting. The monochrome, or even paint-less, easel painting could be cut (Fontana), the surface of the canvas could be replaced by the surface of a skin (Metzger), and naked bodies covered with paint could cover the canvas (Yves Klein). Painting could become an arena of action. The action could take place on the canvas, in front of the canvas or even without the canvas. This is what Rodchenko,

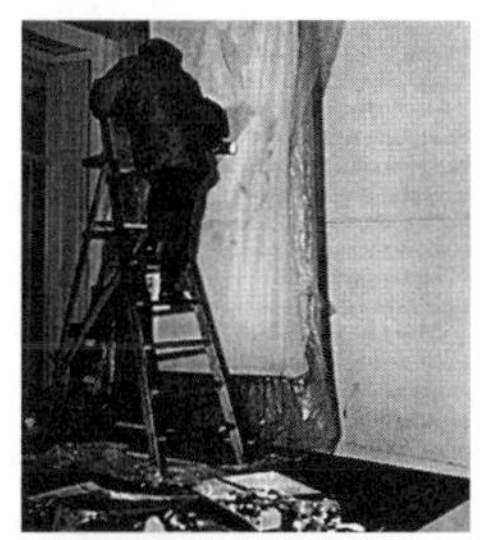
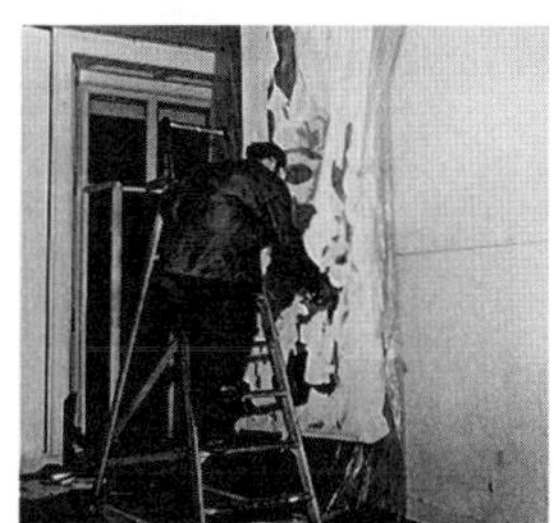
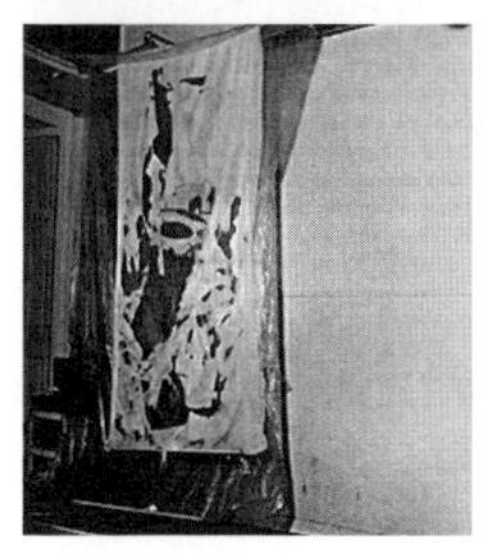
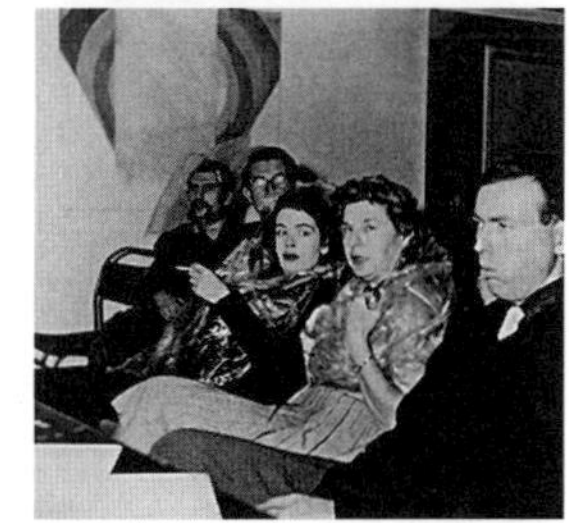

Gustav Metzger's 'Misfits evening', London, 1962

who painted *Black on Black* in 1918, called the 'end of representation', on the occasion of his execution of the first three monochromes in art history in 1921:

> I have brought painting to its logical end and have shown three paintings: one red, one blue and one yellow. I have done this in the knowledge that: everything is over. These are the primary colours. Each surface is a mere surface and there shall be no more representation. Each surface is filled to the border with one singular colour.

These sentences correspond with a placard unveiled by Heartfield and Grosz at the 1920 Dada exhibition in Berlin: 'Art is dead. Long live Tatlin's new machine art.'

Taboo

This formalist view from inside the evolution of modern art is complemented from the outside. The evolution of art corresponds with the evolution of society, and both had reasons to transform the systems of representation. Art had formalist reasons and society imposed these formalist reasons on art for reasons of its own, which were mechanisms of repression. The problem of repression and representation is the problem of the taboo. When something is happening that cannot be accepted, whether by the ego or the superego, whether by the individual or an institution, whether by a subject or a system, then this event is so deeply repressed and so totally denied that it is not possible to speak about it or to hear of it. But, as we know, the repressed has to return even in a disguised form. This is the way to understand the classic formula *speculum artibus*. Art is a mirror of society, not only on an iconic level, but also disguised as a symptom. This encounter of the two different systems of representation, the representation of reality and the representation of the repressed, expresses itself most clearly in the zone of taboo.

The greatest taboo of modernity is the Holocaust. It is completely unacceptable for the modern mind, for the Cartesian subject after the Enlightenment, that in highly civilised Europe the Holocaust was possible. After two world wars and the Holocaust, it became clear that representation had to end. This was expressed most famously by Adorno, in 1949 in his essay 'Cultural Criticism and Society':

> Cultural criticism finds itself faced with the final stage of the dialectic of culture and barbarism. To write poetry after Auschwitz is barbaric. And this corrodes even the knowledge of why it has become impossible to write poetry today.

The Holocaust researcher Raul Hilberg follows the same line in *The Politics of Memory* (1996). Asking himself how Hitler's Germany could be represented, he cannot imagine an adequate visual representation and refers instead to a real enactment to enable the return of the repressed:

> a can of Zyklon gas ... with which the Jews were killed in Auschwitz and Maydanek. I would have liked to see a single can mounted on a pedestal in a small room, with no other objects between the walls, as the epitome of Adolf Hitler's Germany, just as a vase of Euphronios was shown at one time by itself in the Metropolitan Museum of Art as one of the supreme artifacts of Greek antiquity.

To move beyond this crisis of representation we have to change our concept of representation.

We can see this necessity when we compare a sculpture by Polyclitus with a sculpture by Arno Breker. We easily accept the idea that the rise of Greek art corresponds to the rise of democracy. The aesthetic canon and the social canon were mutually determining. The representation of citizens in a shared aesthetic ideal of equality corresponded to the representation of the citizen in the shared social ideal of equality. We easily believe in the parallelism between the emergence of Greek democracy and Greek classicism, between the political and the aesthetic form. This seems to be the meaning of *speculum artibus*. A beautiful art, an ideal body with perfect proportions, is mirroring a beautiful society. The political ideal corresponds to an aesthetic ideal. But we have to remember that Greece was a class society (reportedly, 20,000 free citizens and 400,000 slaves). The ideal body was only the expression of a certain class, the rise and emancipation of the Greek citizen against the former aristocracy. Art and society are interwoven, but not in a purely isomorphic visual form.

In the nineteenth and twentieth centuries, imitating Greek architecture and ideal forms was an attempt to pretend, through the mirror of art, that a social order existed, an order of equality and democracy, that did not actually exist – just the opposite, in fact, a barbarian order of exploitation. The twentieth-century totalitarian systems (National Socialism, Fascism, Stalinism) proclaimed the ideas of Greek classicism and democracy to hide the fact that the social opposite was the case, to hide and disguise the repression. So when we compare Polyclitus and Breker we can see that art is not a visual mirror of society, or we would have to accept that Greece was a barbarian society like Hitler's Germany and Stalin's Russia.

My proposal is to use the psychoanalytic model of representation of the repressed to understand what art is actually mirroring. In the first phase of modern art, artists like Picasso and Bacon tried to show in distorted images of the body – completely different from the ideal body of Polyclitus – the distortion of reality. From Picasso to Bacon, art still followed the classical logic of visual representation. A destroyed city like Guernica is mapped by a destroyed representation. Yet cubism, decades before *Guernica*, had destroyed perspective as a mode of representation. The destruction of classical representation systems by Picasso has nothing to do with Guernica. The public love *Guernica* by a sheer misunderstanding because here the formal destruction of representation systems and the destruction of reality coincidentally correspond. We could also say that the destroyed faces painted by Picasso and Bacon mirror the destruction of human values in two world wars. But when we look at the work of Frankl and music, we see that the victims of the Holocaust can still be represented without distortion of the visual system of representation. The real crisis of representation happened through the neo-avant-garde of the postwar period, when not only the systems of representations were destroyed but the *tools* of representation as well. From Rainer to Fontana to Gutai to Metzger we see destroyed canvases; from the Vienna Group to Fluxus we see destroyed instruments of cultures like pianos; from Happenings to John Latham we see destroyed books, canvases and films.

Opening event for the Vienna Group 'Literary Cabaret', Vienna, 15 April 1959

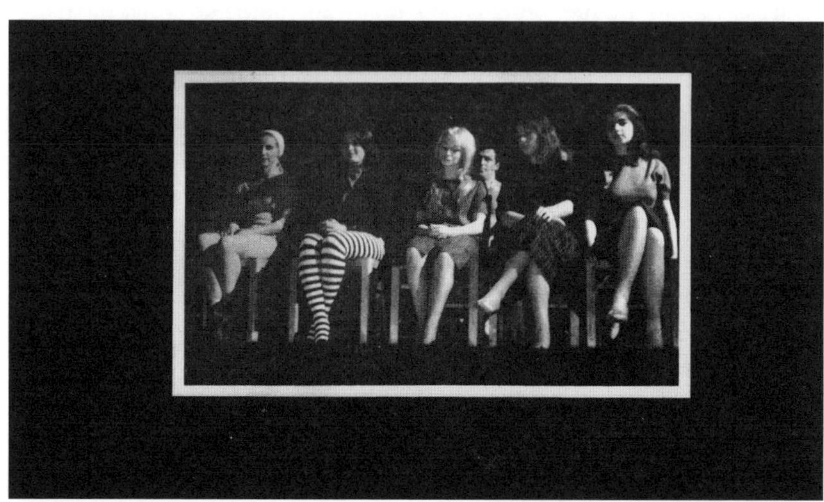

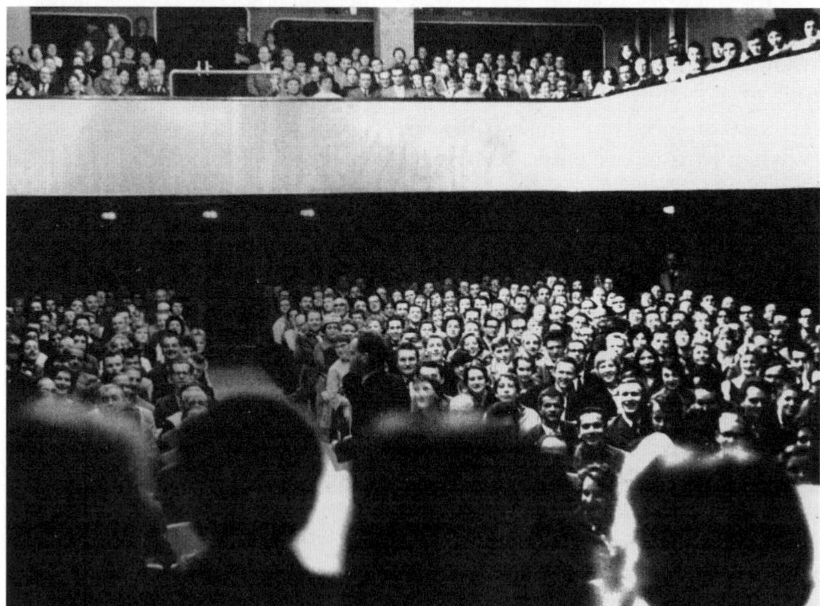

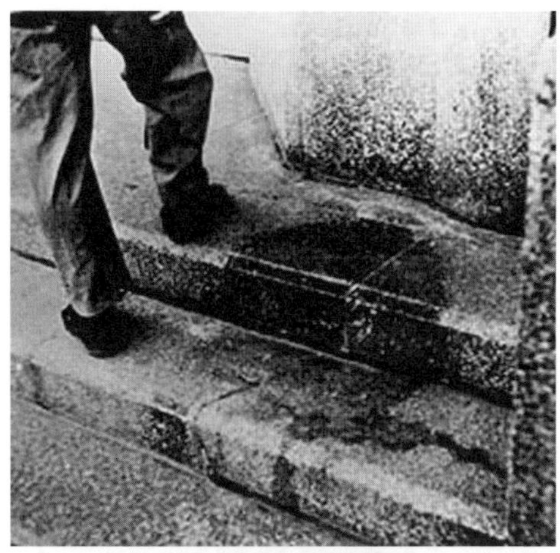

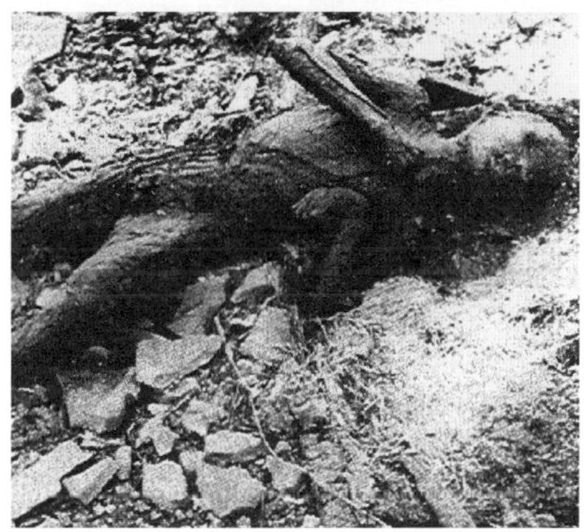

(Top) Traces of victims of the atomic bomb at Hiroshima on the steps of the Sumitomo bank (Bottom) Victim of the atom bomb at Nagasaki

The case of Yves Klein allows us to demonstrate the limitations of formal interpretations of this kind of work, which help to suppress precisely the content against which Klein revolted. The reason for the denial of representation by Yves Klein, his destruction of canvases through fire-guns and his celebrations of bodily traces on canvases, was the traumatic experience of Hiroshima and the atomic bomb. He was, in a certain sense, a disciple of Adorno and Hilberg. In his youth Klein visited Japan and saw the traces of the victims on the ground. He saw the traces of the burned victims and he realised that he could no longer visually represent the horror of an atomic war in the manner of Picasso – by distorting the visual system of representation but not touching the tools of representation, the canvas, the brush, etc. Together with the heroes of the theatre of the absurd and other neo-avant-gardists after 1945, Klein found it difficult to believe in the traditional means of culture, since culture had not prohibited or prevented the horror. Even worse, the horror was executed in the name of culture. So he decided with many others to destroy not only the mechanisms of representation but also the means of representation, the tools, the *dispositifs*, in order to expose as a symptom the horror of the atomic war. His cut is the cut of traces similar to those in Derrida's theory of traces.

The seemingly clean ZERO-group from Manzoni to Günther Uecker also showed the destruction of the means of representation. The reception of this group of artists after World War II was a misunderstanding and a part of the continuing repression. After the war, people didn't want to speak or hear about the war. The war became taboo. But these people saw in the erased white canvases of ZERO their own erased memory. They liked the gesture of erasure in art from Rainer to Rauschenberg because it erased their memory too, their complicity with Fascism. (Fontana even had personal reasons for destroying the means of memory, because he had to hide the fact that he worked for Mussolini and made sculptures for the Fascist movement.)

The shooting at canvases with guns by Niki de Saint Phalle or with arrows like Günther Uecker around 1960, the destruction of screens by the

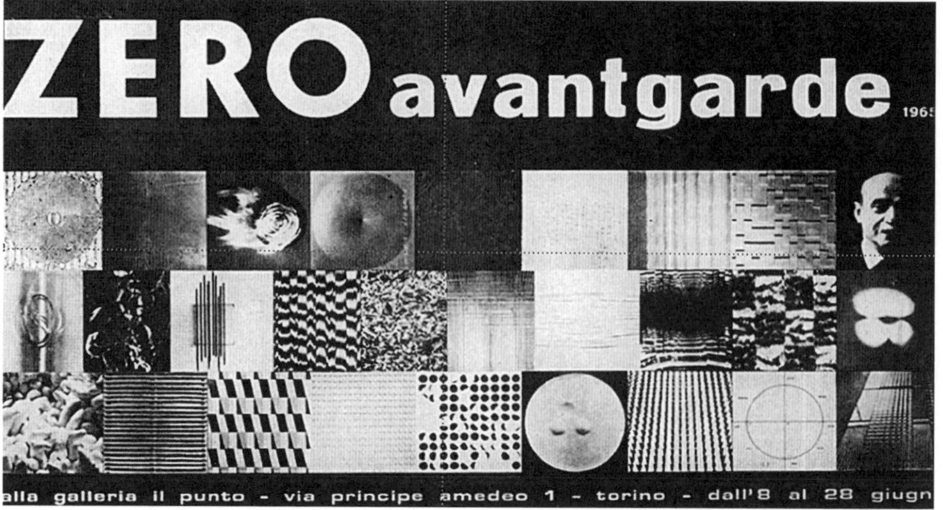

Above: Invitation to *Zero Avantgarde*, Galleria il Punto, Turin, 1965
Opposite (top left): Poster of the Festival 'Kunst und Revolution', Vienna, 1968
Opposite (top right): Otto Muehl, *Apollo 11* 1969
Opposite (bottom): Franz Kaltenbeck lecturing at 'Kunst und Revolution', Vienna, 1968

Gutai group, the destruction of canvases with nails by Guenther Uecker or with acid by Gustav Metzger, the burning of books and canvases by John Latham – these all show a deep mistrust in the means of art, in the means of cultural memory and in culture itself. The Destruction in Art Symposium (DIAS) in 1966 in London and actions by Franz Kaltenbeck and myself destroying public museum windows anonymously at night, and many other similar actions by artists, show the revolt on the level of means of representation. Viennese Actionism with its rituals of self-mutilation, real or simulated (Brus, Schwarzkogler), of violations and victimisations of others, defilements and contaminations, to spatter with colors, dirt, urine and faeces, are clearly an unconscious reaction formation in art against the conscious purification of postwar Austria from its crimes in World War II and its participation in the Holocaust and fascism. After 1945 Austria officially denied having been a part of German National Socialism and its crimes. It preferred to see itself as a victim of National Socialism. This famous *Opfer-Lüge*, the lie of being the victim, was the basis for the foundation of the second Austrian Republic. Since Austria had purified itself so deeply and heavily, its art did the opposite. It bathed in impurity, in blood and dirt. The mirror of art, as we can now see, is not a simple mirror-function. It is a negative mirror, based on comparability. Representation mechanisms in art represent not only what you see consciously, but also what you don't see, even unconsciously. Only the study of reaction formation and similar defence mechanisms of society and its individuals can give you a true representation, a true image.

The re-presentation or, better, the *repetition* of the repressed traumas of two world wars, the Holocaust and the atomic bomb is the content of the neo-avantgarde by way of a reaction formation and an active differentiation of its reality conditions. The neo-avantgarde is not a purely formal repetition of the historical avant-garde. It is a real postwar art, an art about memory, forgetting, repression, trauma and the return of the repressed. As such, the neo-avant-garde begins the critical exploration of the reconversion of the obscure disaster of World War II into the Year Zero of a grey pseudo-democracy. The radical exemplarity of the 'politics of experience' of Viennese Actionism lies in the opposition of its events/actions – polymorphic machinations of the body-psyche – to any artistic representation closed in on itself.

For caption, see opposite

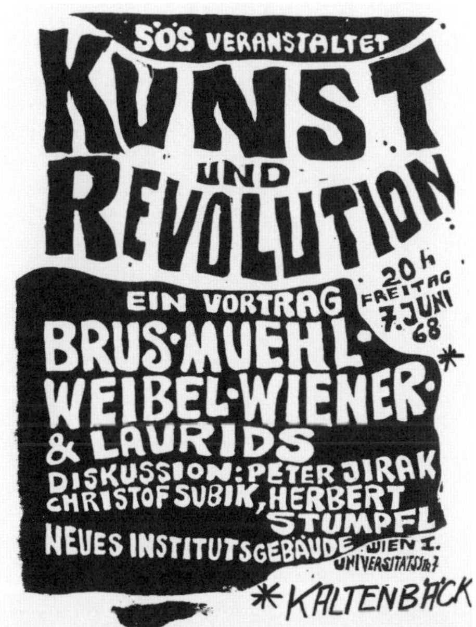

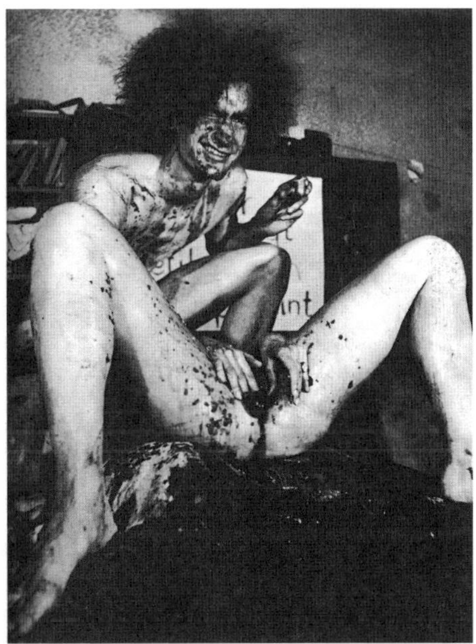

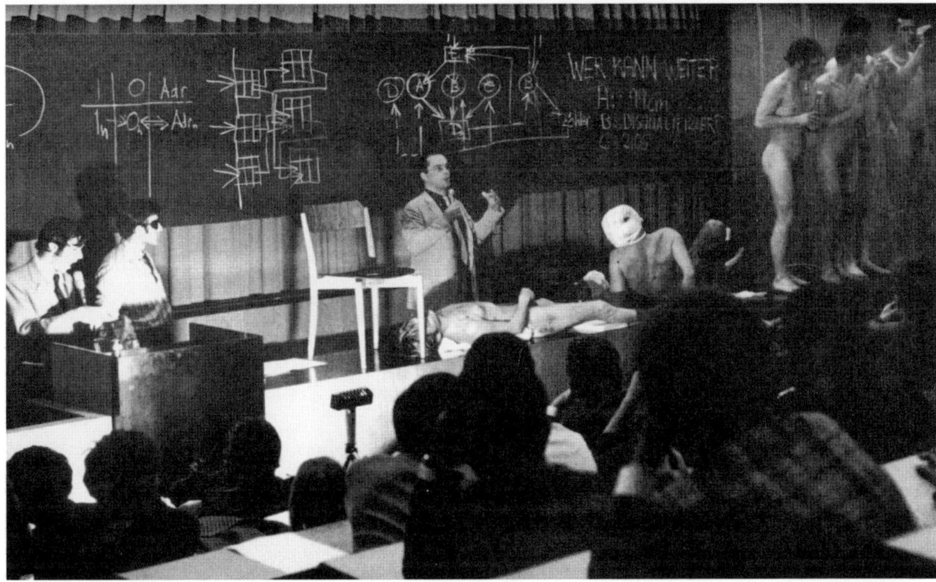

1 *Dispositif* may be translated as 'device', 'machinery', 'apparatus' or 'construction'. Its current theoretical usage is predominantly associated with the work of Michel Foucault, who described it as referring to: 'a thoroughly heterogenous ensemble consisting of discourses, institutions, architectural forms, regulatory decisions, laws, administrative measures, scientific statements, philosophical, moral and philanthropic propositions – in short, the said as much as the unsaid. Such are the elements of the *dispositif*. The *dispositif* itself is the system of relations that can be established between these elements.' Michel Foucault, 'The Confession of the Flesh' (1977) in Colin Gordon (ed.), *Power/Knowledge: Selected Interviews and Other Writings*, Harvester Wheatsheaf, Hemel Hempstead 1980, p.194.

11
The Politics of Equal Aesthetic Rights
Boris Groys

Art and politics are connected in one fundamental respect: both are realms in which a struggle for recognition is being waged. As defined by Alexandre Kojève in his commentary on Hegel, this struggle for recognition surpasses the usual struggle for the distribution of material goods, which in modernity is generally regulated by market forces. What is at stake here is not merely that a certain desire be satisfied but that it is also recognised as socially legitimate. Whereas politics is an arena in which various group interests have, both in the past and the present, fought for recognition, artists of the historical avant-garde have contended for the recognition of all individual forms and artistic procedures that were not previously considered legitimate. Indeed, the historical avantgarde has opened up the potentially infinite horizontal field of all possible real and virtual forms endowed with equal aesthetic rights. One after another, so-called primitive imagery, abstract images and simple objects from everyday life have all acquired the kind of recognition that once used to be granted only to certain privileged images and objects.

Both forms of struggle for equality – political and aesthetic – are intrinsically bound up with each other, and both have the goal of achieving a situation in which all people with their various interests, as indeed also all forms and artistic practices, will finally be granted equal rights. But, clearly, such a condition of total equality has de facto never been attained, either in the political or in the artistic realm. Contemporary art, like contemporary politics, still operates in the gap between formal equality and factual inequality. So the question arises, what are the mechanisms of this inequality – how we can define them and deal with them if we want to keep the promise of equality given by the historical avant-garde?

When the avant-garde started its struggle against aesthetic inequality, it was the museum that was considered the main enemy, as a place of inequality par excellence. The museums were perceived as guardians of the old privileges, as the places of the Romantic iconophilia admiring the masterpieces of the past and preventing the emergence of the new, as the churches of the new religion of art with its strange rituals and esoteric conventions – closed spaces where the initiated few decided the fate of art beyond any democratic discussion and control. Accordingly, the avant-garde understood itself as an iconoclastic movement, as an attempt to secularise and democratise art in the name of equal aesthetic rights. Such appeals and demands have meanwhile become quite commonplace, even to the extent of now being regarded as a cardinal feature of contemporary art – they remain, of course, in many ways still legitimate. But the question arises, is the museum today still the central place of contemporary iconophilia and the origin of contemporary aesthetic inequality? Is the struggle that is directed against the museum – and the art institutions connected with the museum – truly iconoclastic under the contemporary aesthetic regime? Personally, I doubt it.

In the nineteenth century and the first part of the twentieth, the socially dominating tastes were defined and embodied by the museum, indeed. The criteria on which the museum based its choice of 'good' art were generally accepted as the aesthetic norm. But today it is simply not the case any more. Under the dominating aesthetic regime the museum has indisputably been stripped of its normative role. In our time it is the globalised mass media that dictate aesthetic norms, having long since dethroned the museum from its position of aesthetic dominance. The general public now draws its notion of art from advertising, MTV, video games and Hollywood blockbusters. The contemporary mass media have emerged as by far the largest and most powerful machine for producing and distributing images – vastly more extensive and effective than the contemporary art system. We are constantly fed with images of war, terror and catastrophes of all kinds, at a level of production with which the individual artist with his or her artisan skills cannot compete. Nowadays, every major politician, rock star, television entertainer or sporting hero generates thousands of images through their public appearances – many more than any living artist can even imagine. The dominating aesthetics of our time is the aesthetics of the commercialised mass media – not of the museum.

Museum or media?

In the context of contemporary, media-generated tastes the call to abandon and dismantle the museum has taken on an entirely different meaning from when it was voiced during the avant-garde era. Nowadays this protest is no longer part of the struggle waged against prevailing normative tastes in the name of aesthetic equality but is, inversely, aimed at stabilising and entrenching currently prevailing tastes. Characteristically, it is the gurus of the contemporary neoliberal media markets who wonder today – in the style of the early avant-garde – why anyone at all is needed to decide what art is and what it is not. Why can't we just choose for ourselves on the open markets what we wish to acknowledge or appreciate as art without patronising advice from curators and art critics? Why does art refuse to seek legitimation on the open media market just like any other product? From the perspective of the media market the traditional aspirations of the museum seem historically obsolete, out-of-touch, insincere and even somewhat bizarre.

The strategies that are operating behind museum collections and exhibitions are treated in the mass media mostly as the workings of a shadowy conspiracy, as an intrigue masterminded by insiders, as a display of the hidden power of curators and museum directors far removed from any form of democratic legitimation – in other words, as an impenetrable swindle. Instead, artists are invited to follow the enticements of the mass media age, in the quest to be disseminated through media channels. This allows them to address and to seduce a much larger audience; it is also a decent way of earning money – for which the artist previously had to beg from the state or private sponsors. The mass media give the artist a new sense of power, social relevance and public presence within his or her own time. But that means precisely: the critique of the museum has lost today its avant-garde edge. Instead, the call to break loose from the museum amounts de facto to a call to mediatise and commercialise art by accommodating it to the aesthetic norms generated by today's media.

At the same time – and at first glance strangely enough – the mass media also appear as a new space for the true art that was in a certain sense betrayed by contemporary art as a result of its quest for equal aesthetic rights. Certain images circulating in the media become the icons of contemporary aesthetic and political imagination, not only because they are easily accessible, almost omnipresent and conform to the prevailing aesthetic taste, but in the first place because they are regarded as being true, being real and as being true precisely in the very old romantic, iconophilic sense. Kojève pointed out that the moment when the overall logic of equality underlying individual struggles for recognition becomes apparent creates the impression that these struggles have to some extent surrendered their true seriousness and explosiveness. This was why, even before World War II, Kojève was able to speak of the end of history in the sense of the political history of struggles for recognition. Since then, the discourse about the end of history has made its mark, particularly on the art scene. People are constantly referring to the end of art history, by which they mean that these days all forms and things have 'in principle' already obtained the right to be considered works of art. Accordingly, the aesthetic equality of all images that modern art has fought to establish is now frequently considered a sign of their arbitrariness and irrelevance. For if, as is argued, all images are already acknowledged as being of equal value, this would deprive the artist of the possibility of creating the images that could break taboos, provoke, shock or extend boundaries of art. Instead, by the time history has come to an end each artist will be suspected of producing just one further arbitrary image among many. Were this indeed the case, the regime of equal rights for all images would have to be regarded not only as the *telos* of the logic followed by the history of art in modernity but also as its terminal negation. Accordingly, we now witness repeated waves of nostalgia for a time when individual works of art were once still revered as eminently precious, unique and singular because of being in some emphatic sense true

Under these new conditions, in which musealised art has seemingly lost its seriousness and its claim to be true, it is the media that become the space where the quest for the true art takes place. In today's world, the images of terror and of war against terror function primarily as such true images – as authentic icons of the contemporary political sublime. Video art especially became the medium of choice for the contemporary warriors – and because of that the medium of truth. As we know, bin Laden was communicating with the outer world primarily by the means of this medium: we all encountered him as a video artist, in the first place. The same can be said about the videos representing beheadings, confessions of the terrorists, and the rest.

In all these cases we have consciously and artistically staged events that have their own easily recognisable aesthetics. Here we have the people who do not wait for an artist to represent their acts of war and terror. They do not wait for a new Goya, or a new Picasso. Instead, the act of war itself coincides with its documentation, with its representation. The traditional function of art as a medium of representation and the role of the artist as a mediator between reality and memory are here completely eliminated. The same can be said about the famous photographs and videos from the Abu Ghraib prison in Baghdad. These videos and photographs demonstrate an uncanny aesthetic similarity with alternative, subversive European and American art and film-making of the 1960s and 1970s. The iconographic and stylistic similarity is, in fact, striking (for example, Viennese Actionism and Pasolini movies). In both cases the goal is to reveal a naked, vulnerable, desiring body that is habitually covered by the system of social conventions. But, of course, the strategy of the subversive art of the 1960s and 1970s had the goal of undermining the traditional set of beliefs and conventions dominating the artist's own culture. In the Abu Ghraib art production this goal was, we can safely say, completely perverted. The same subversive aesthetics was used to attack and to undermine a different, other culture in an act of violence, in an act of humiliation of the other (instead of self-questioning including self-humiliation) – leaving the conservative values of the artist's own culture unquestioned. In any case, it is worth mentioning that on both sides of the war on terror the image production and distribution are effectuated without any intervention of an artist. The political action becomes here identical with the artistic, aesthetic action – without any need for an additional artistic practice of aestheticisation.

It is important to state that we are speaking here about the images that became the icons of the contemporary collective imagination. The terrorist videos and the videos from Abu Ghraib prison are impregnated in our consciousness or even subconsciousness much more deeply than any work by a contemporary artist. This elimination of the artist from the practice of image production is especially painful for the art system because at least since the beginning of modernity artists wanted to be radical, daring, taboo-breaking, going beyond all limitations and borders. The avant-garde art discourse makes use of many concepts from the military sphere, including the notion of the avant-garde itself. There is talk of exploding norms, destroying traditions, violating taboos, practising certain artistic strategies, attacking existing institutions. The artists of the classical avant-garde saw themselves as agents of negation, destruction, eradication of all traditional institutions of art. In accordance with the famous dictum 'negation is creation', which was inspired by the Hegelian dialectic and propagated by authors such as Bakunin and Nietzsche under the title of 'active nihilism', avant-garde artists felt themselves empowered to create new icons by destruction of the old ones. A modern work of art was measured by how radical it was, how far the artist had gone in destroying artistic tradition. Although in the meantime modernity itself has often enough been declared passé, to this very day this criterion of radicalness has lost nothing of its relevance to our evaluation of art. The worst thing that can be said of an artist continues to be that his or her art is 'harmless'.

Along these lines, Don DeLillo writes in his novel *Mao II* that terrorists and writers are engaged in a zero-sum game: by radically negating that which exists, both wish to create a narrative which would be capable of capturing society's imagination – and thereby altering society. In this sense, terrorists and writers are rivals – and, as DeLillo notes, nowadays the writer is beaten hands down because today's media use the terrorists' acts to create a powerful narrative with which no writer can contend. But this kind of rivalry is even more obvious in the case of the artist. The contemporary artist uses the same media as the terrorist or the warrior: photography, video, film. At the same time it is clear that the artist cannot compete with the terrorist in the field of radical gesture. In terms of the symbolic exchange operating by way of potlatch, as it was described by Marcel Mauss or Georges Bataille, this means that in terms of the iconoclastic rivalry understood as rivalry in destruction and self-destruction, art is obviously on the losing side.

Yet this increasingly popular way of comparing art and terrorism, or art and war, is fundamentally flawed. I will try to show where I see the fallacy. In fact, terrorism is not iconoclastic. Terrorism and war are extremely iconophilic practices. Indeed, the terrorist's or the warrior's image production has the goal of producing strong images – the images that we would tend to accept as being 'real', as being 'true', as being the 'iconic revelations' of the hidden, terrible reality that is for us the global political reality of our time. These images are the icons of the contemporary political theology that dominates our collective imagination. These images answer the postmodern iconophilic nostalgia for a true image and at the same time they draw their power, their persuasiveness, from a very effective form of moral blackmail.

Presentation that presents itself

After so many decades of modern and postmodern criticism of the image, of mimesis, of representation, we feel ourselves somewhat ashamed to say that the images of terror or torture are not true, not real. We cannot say that these images are not true, because we know that they are paid for by a real loss of life – a loss of life that is documented by the images. Magritte could easily say that a painted apple is not a real apple or that a painted pipe is not a real pipe. But how can we say that a videotaped beheading is not a real beheading? Or that a videotaped ritual of humiliation in the Abu Ghraib prison is not a real ritual? After so many decades of the critique of representation directed against the naive belief in photographic and cinematic truth, we are now ready to accept certain photographed and videotaped images as unquestionably true, again.

We are confronted here with a strategy that is historically quite new. The traditional warrior was interested in the images that would be able to glorify him, to present him in a favourable, positive, attractive way. And we, of course, have accumulated a long tradition of criticising, deconstructing, such strategies of pictorial idealisation. But the pictorial strategy of the contemporary warrior is a strategy of shock and awe. And it is, of course, only possible after the long history of modern art producing images of angst, cruelty, disfiguration. The traditional critique of representation was driven by a suspicion that there must be something ugly and terrifying hidden behind the surface of the conventional idealised image. But the contemporary warrior shows us precisely that – this hidden ugliness, the image of our own suspicion, of our own angst. And precisely because of that, we feel ourselves immediately compelled to recognise these images as being true. We see things that are as bad as we expected them to be – maybe even worse. Our worst suspicions are confirmed. The hidden reality behind the image that is shown to us is as ugly as we expected it to be. So we have a feeling that our critical journey has come to its end, that our mission as critical intellectuals is accomplished. Now, the truth of the political has revealed itself – and we can contemplate the new icons of the contemporary political theology without a need to go further, because these icons are terrible enough by themselves. And so it is sufficient to comment on these icons. It makes no sense any more to criticise them in aesthetic terms. That explains the macabre fascination that finds its expression in many recent publications dedicated to the images of the war on terror emerging on both sides of the invisible front.

The source of contemporary iconophilia is not the museum but the mass media. The struggle of the avantgarde against the museum can be properly understood only by keeping that in mind. In fact, art became art originally through iconoclastic practice – of curators rather than artists. The first art museums came into existence at the turn of the nineteenth century, and became established in the course of that century as a consequence of revolutions, wars, imperial conquest and pillage of non-European cultures. All kinds of 'beautiful' functional objects, which had previously been employed for various religious rituals, dressing the rooms of power, or manifesting private wealth, were collected and put on display as works of art – that is, as defunctionalised, autonomous objects of pure contemplation. The curators administering these museums 'created' art through iconoclastic acts directed against traditional icons of religion or power, by reducing these icons to mere artworks. Art was originally conceived as 'simply' art. This perception as such is situated within the tradition of the European Enlightenment, which conceived of all religious icons as 'simple things' – as mere artworks. But the same should be said also about the icons of contemporary mass consciousness. They are simply certain images among other images – nothing more. The art of today can keep its promise of equality of all images only by secularising the icons of today's neoliberal and pseudo-democratic, populist media in the same way as it reacted towards the old icons of religion and power. And by doing so one should not be afraid to be accused of being elitist and undemocratic. The requirement of aesthetic equality of all images is much more radical than the requirement of the democratic, popular legitimisation of certain images by the will of the majority. An allegedly democratically legitimised image is just an image – even if it is functioning as an icon of the mass media. Given our current cultural climate, the art museum is practically the only place where we can actually step back from our own present and compare it with other historical eras. The museum is a place where we are reminded of the tradition of secularisation and of radical egalitarian art projects of the past – so that we can measure our own time against them.

Of course, museums cannot be the places where all possible images are exhibited on a basis of perfect equality. The space of a museum is always limited. That leads to a selection of exhibited images by a curator – a selection that is always questionable and must be questioned. But the work of a curator is primarily not an act of selection. As I have suggested, in our time the work of selection is effectuated by the mass media, not by the museum curators. The work of a curator is an act of presentation – the act of presentation that presents itself. And that is the central difference between the museum, on the one side, and the globalised media and art market, on the other. The curator cannot but place, contextualise and narrativise works of art – which necessarily leads to their iconoclastic relativisation. The museum makes the act of showing, exhibiting, curating images visible; the art market and the media market conceal it, creating the illusion of the autonomy of the image. The museum is a place where the act of curating becomes obvious – even if many curators try to reduce their curating to non-curating, to zero-curating in a tradition of Romantic iconophilia.

Iconoclastic visibility

Giorgio Agamben writes that 'the image is a being, that in its essence is appearance, visibility, or semblance.' But this definition of an artwork's essence does not suffice to guarantee the visibility of a concrete artwork. A work of art cannot in fact present itself by virtue of its own definition and force the viewer into contemplation – artworks lack vitality, energy and health. They are, rather, genuinely sick and helpless; in the museum a spectator has to be led to the artwork, as hospital workers might take a visitor to see a bedridden patient. It is no coincidence that the word 'curator' is etymologically related to 'cure'. Curating is curing. The process of curating cures the image's powerlessness, its incapacity to present itself. The artwork needs external help; it needs an exhibition and a curator to become visible.

Certainly, the hidden curatorial practices of contemporary media create the illusion that the images are per se strong and powerful – because they are able to invade our visual space beyond or even against our explicit consent. These images are presented in the media as, so to say, super-images endowed by supernatural strength and dynamics – and precisely the same super-images are treated by the media as true images, as icons of our time.

But the museum curatorial practice undermines this kind of iconophilia, for its medical artifice cannot remain entirely concealed from the viewer. In this respect, museum curating remains unintentionally iconoclastic even as it is programmatically iconophile. Indeed, curating acts as a supplement or a pharmakon (in Derrida's usage), in that it cures the image even as it makes it unwell. Yet this statement opens the question: which is the right kind of curatorial practice? Since curatorial practice taking place in the museum can never totally conceal itself successfully, the main objective of museal curating must be to visualise itself, by making its practice explicitly visible. Only then can the museum take a stand against the new icons of the popular imagination – in the name of the equal aesthetic rights of all the images. The museum can do so effectively by using – we can say also misusing – the artworks as mere illustrations of art history, by recontextualising images, by making problematic their autonomous status.

Orhan Pamuk's novel *My Name is Red* features a group of artists searching for a place for art within an iconoclastic culture, namely that of sixteenth-century Islamic Turkey. The group are illustrators commissioned by the powerful to ornament their books with exquisite miniatures; subsequently these books are placed in governmental or private collections. Not only are these artists increasingly persecuted by radical Islamic (iconoclastic) adversaries who want to ban all images; they are also in competition with the Occidental painters of the Renaissance, primarily Venetians, who openly affirm their own iconophilia. Yet the novel's heroes cannot share this iconophilia, because they do not believe in the autonomy of images. And so they try to find a way to take a consistently honest iconoclastic stance, without abandoning the terrain of art. A Turkish sultan, whose theory of art would actually serve as good advice for contemporary curatorial practice, shows them the way. The sultan says the following:

> an illustration that does not complement a story, in the end, will become but a false idol. Since we cannot possibly believe in the absent story, we will naturally begin to believe in the picture itself. This would be no different than the worship of the idols in the Kaaba that went on before Our Prophet, peace and blessings be upon him, had destroyed them ... If I believed, heaven forbid, the way these infidels do, that the Prophet Jesus was also the Lord God himself ... only then might I accept the depiction of mankind in full detail and exhibit such images. You do understand that, eventually, we would then unthinkingly begin worshipping any picture that is hung on the wall, don't you?

This subtle iconoclastic strategy proposed by the sultan – turning the image back into an illustration – is actually much more effective than the avant-gardist one. We have known at least since Magritte that when we look at an image of a pipe, we are not regarding a real pipe but one that has been painted. The pipe as such is not there, is not present; instead, it is being depicted as absent. In spite of this knowledge we are still inclined to believe that when we believe that when we look at an artwork, we directly and instantaneously confront 'art'. We see artworks as incarnating art. The famous distinction between art and non-art is generally understood as a distinction between objects inhabited and animated by art, and those from which art is absent. This is how works of art become art's idols – that is, as analogous to religious images, which are also believed to be inhabited or animated by gods.

To practise the secularisation of and by art would mean understanding artworks not as incarnations of art, but as mere documents, illustrations of art. While they may refer to it, these are nevertheless not art. To a greater or lesser extent this strategy has been pursued by many artists since the 1960s. Artistic projects, performances and actions have regularly been documented, and by means of this documentation represented in exhibition spaces and museums. However, such documentation simply refers to art without itself being art. This type of documentation is often presented in the framework of an art installation for the purpose of narrating a certain project or action. Traditionally executed paintings, art objects, photographs or videos can also be utilised in the framework of such installations. In this case, admittedly, artworks lose their usual status as art. Instead they become documents, illustrations of the story told by the installation. One could say that today's art audience increasingly encounters art *documentation*, which provides information about the artwork itself, be it art project or art action, but in doing so confirms the absence of art in the artwork.

The artist becomes here an independent curator and an independent curator becomes an artist. The independent curator is a radically secularised artist. He is an artist because he does everything artists do. But the independent curator is an artist who has lost the artist's aura, one who no longer has magical powers at his disposal, who cannot endow objects with art's status. He doesn't use objects – art objects included for art's sake, but rather abuses them, makes them profane. Yet it is precisely this which makes the figure of the independent curator so attractive and so essential to the art of today. The contemporary curator is heir apparent to the modern artist, although he doesn't suffer under his predecessor's magical abnormalities. He is an artist, but atheistic and 'normal' through and through. The curator is an agent of art's profanation, its secularisation, its profane abuse.

Utopia Station is a good example: curated by Molly Nesbit, Hans-Ulrich Obrist and Rirkrit Tiravanija, this exhibition was presented at the 50th Venice Biennale in 2003. Critical and public discussion of this exhibition stressed the issues of whether the concept of utopia is still relevant in this day and age; whether what was put forward as a utopian vision by the curators could really be regarded as such, and so on. Yet the fact that a curatorial project that was clearly iconoclastic could be presented at one of the oldest international art exhibitions seems to me to be far more important than the above considerations. It was iconoclastic because it employed artworks as illustrations, as documents of the search for a social utopia, without emphasising their autonomous value. It subscribed to the radical iconoclastic approach of the Russian avant-garde, which considered art to be documentation of the search for the 'new man' and towards a 'new life'. Most importantly, though, *Utopia Station* was a curatorial and not an artistic project (even if one of the curators, Rirkrit Tiravanija, is an artist). This meant that the iconoclastic gesture could not be accompanied – and thus invalidated – by the attribution of artistic value. Nevertheless, it can still be assumed that in this case the concept of utopia was abused, because it was aestheticised and situated in an elitist art context. And it can equally be said that art was abused as well: it served as an illustration for the curator's vision of utopia. But in both cases the spectator has to confront an abuse, be it an abuse of art or by art. Here, though, abuse is just another word for iconoclasm.

The space of a museum exhibition or of an artistic installation is often disliked in our day because it is a closed space – contrary to the open space of the contemporary media. But the closure that is effectuated by a museum should not be interpreted as an opposition to 'openness'. By closure the museum creates its outside and opens itself to this outside. The closure is here not an opposition to the openness but its precondition. The media space, on the contrary, is not open because it has no outside – media want to be not open but total, all-inclusive. The art practice that is conceived as a machine of infinite expansion and inclusion is also not an open artwork, but an artistic counterpart of the imperial hybrid of the contemporary media. The museum exhibition can be made into a place of openness, of disclosure, of unconcealment precisely because it situates inside its finite space, contextualises and curates images and objects that also circulate in the outside space; and in this way it opens itself to its outside. Images don't emerge into the clearing of Being on their own accord, in order for their original visibility to be abused by the 'exhibition business', as Heidegger describes it in 'The Origin of the Work of Art'. It is far more that this very abuse makes them visible.

Acknowledgements

The essays in the volume derive from presentations at three conferences held at Tate Britain, London, organised in collaboration with the Centre for Research in European Philosophy (CRMEP), at that time located at Middlesex University, now, since July 2010, relocated to Kingston University London: 'Spheres of Action' (12 December 2005), 'Art and Immaterial Labour' (19 January 2008) and 'Undoing the Aesthetic Image' (24 January 2009). The last of these benefited from the support of the Cultural Services of the French Embassy, for which we would like to thank Dr Philippe Lane, in particular. The editors wish to thank Victoria Walsh and Madeleine Keep of what was then Adult Programmes at Tate Britain, for their help in organising the events; along with all of the speakers involved for their commitment to the project. The essays first appeared, over several issues, in the independent British journal, *Radical Philosophy* (www.radicalphilosophy.com) to which we are grateful for permission to reprint them here.

Notes on contributors

Éric Alliez is Professor of Philosophy and Contemporary Artistic Creation at the University of Paris 8 and Professor of Contemporary French Philosophy in the Centre for Research in Modern European Philosophy, Kingston University London. His writings include: *La Pensée-Matisse: Portrait de l'artiste en hyperfauve* (with Jean-Claude Bonne, 2005), *L'Oeil-Cerveau: Nouvelles histoires de la peinture moderne* (with Jean-Clet Martin, 2007), *Capitalism, Schizophrenia and Consensus: Of Relational Aesthetics* (2010) and *Défaire l'image: De l'art contemporain* (2013).

Franco Berardi is an activist and educationalist working in the Italian autonomist tradition. He teaches social history of communication at the Accademia di belle Arti in Milan. Founder of the Italian magazine *A/traverso* (1975–81), he was on the staff of Radio Alice, the first free radio station in Italy (1976–8). Recent books include: *Félix Guattari: Thought, Friendship and Visionary Cartography* (2008), *Precarious Rhapsody: Semio-capitalism and the Pathologies of the Post-Alpha Generation* (2009), *The Soul at Work: From Alienation to Autonomy* (2009) and *After the Future* (2011).

Georges Didi-Huberman is Professor of Art History at EHESS, Paris. His books in English translation include: *Fra Angelico: Dissemblance and Figuration* (1995), *Invention of Hysteria: Charcot and the Photographic Iconography of the Salpêtrière* (2003), *Confronting Images: Questioning the Ends of a Certain History of Art* (2008) and *Images in Spite of All: Four Photographs from Auschwitz* (2008).

Boris Groys (formerly Professor of Art Theory, Philosophy and Media Theory at the State Academy for Design in Karlsruhe) is Global Distinguished Professor of Russian and Slavic Studies at New York University. He was curator of the Russian Pavillion at the 2011 Venice Biennale. Recent books include *The Communist Postscripts* (2006; trans. 2009), *Art Power* (2008), *History Becomes Form: Moscow Conceptualism* (2010), *Going Public* (2010) and *Introduction to Antiphilosophy* (2012).

Maurizio Lazzarato is an independent sociologist and philosopher who lives and works in Paris. A regular contributor to the journal *Futur Antérior*, he was one of the founders of its successor *Multitudes*. He is widely associated with the concept of 'immaterial labour', expounded in his book *Lavoro immateriale: Forme di vita e produzione di soggettività* (1997). Recent publications include: *Expérimentations politiques* (2009) and *La Fabrique de l'homme endetté: Essai sur la condition néolibérale* (2011).

Elisabeth Lebovici is an art historian, art critic and curator. Her writings include: *Zoe Leonard* (1998), *Femmes/artistes, artistes/femmes: Paris de 1880 à nos jours* (with Catherine Gonnard, 2007), *Olga Kisseleva: Monde croisés* (2008) and contributions to *Agnes Thurnauer* (2007), *Gloria Friedmann* (2009), *Martine Aballéa: Roman partiel* (2009) and *General Idea* (2011).

Antonio Negri is the foremost political philosopher of the autonomist and post-autonomist movements in Italy. Founder of Potere Operaio, in 1969, he was a leading member of Autonomia Operaio during the 1970s. His many books in English include: *Insurgencies* (1999), *Time for Revolution* (2004), *Political Descartes* (2007) and, with Michael Hardt, the trilogy *Empire* (2000), *Multitude* (2004) and *Commonwealth* (2009).

Peter Osborne is is Professor of Modern European Philosophy and Director of the Centre for Research in Modern European Philosophy at Kingston University London, and an editor of the journal *Radical Philosophy*. His books include *The Politics of Time: Modernity and Avant-Garde* (1995; 2011), *Conceptual Art* (2002), *Marx* (2005), *El arte más allá de la estética* (2010) and *Anywhere Or Not At All: Philosophy of Contemporary Art* (2013).

Jacques Rancière is Emeritus Professor of Philosophy at the University of Paris 8. His many books in English include: *Disagreement: Politics and Philosophy* (2004), *The Politics of Aesthetics: The Distribution of the Sensible* (2004), *Film Fables* (2006), *The Future of the Image* (2007), *Dissensus: On Politics and Aesthetics* (2009), *The Aesthetic Unconscious* (2009) and *The Politics of Literature* (2010). His latest book is *Aisthesis: Scènes du régime esthétique de l'art* (2011).

Judith Revel is a political theorist and translator. She teaches at the University of Paris 1. She is the author of *Michel Foucault: Expériences de la pensée* (2005), *Dictionnaire Foucault* (2007), *Qui a peur de la banlieue?* (2008) and *Foucault, une pensée du discontinu* (2010).

Peter Sloterdijk is Professor of Philosophy and Aesthetics and (since 2001) President of the State Academy for Design at the Centre for Art and Media in Karlsruhe. He is the author of the bestselling work of postwar German philosophy, *Critique of Cynical Reason* (1983; trans. 1988). His other writings include *Derrida, An Eygptian* (2009), *Terror from the Air* (2009) and the vast triology *Sphären* (1998–2002), of which the first volume has been translated into English as *Bubbles: Microsphereology* (2011). Since 2002, he has co-hosted the German television discussion programme, 'Philosophical Quartet'.

Peter Weibel is an arist and curator and (since 1984) Professor for Visual Media at the University of Applied Arts in Vienna. From 1993 to 1999, he was chief curator at the Neue Galerie am Landesmuseum Joanneum in Graz, Austria. Since 1999 he has been Chairman and CEO of ZKM, the Centre for Art and Media Technology, Karlsruhe. His numerous publications include: *Bildkompendium Wiener Aktionismus und Film* (with Valie Export, 1970), *The Vienna Group: A Moment of Modernity, 1954–1960* (ed., 1997), *Beyond Art: A Third Culture* (2005), *Contemporary Art and the Museum: A Global Perspective* (co-ed., 2007) and *Peter Weibel: The Open Work, 1964–1979* (2008). In 2011, he co-curated *The Global Contemporary: Artworlds After 1989* at ZKM.

Photographic and collection credits
p.3 and front cover Photograph courtesy the artist, collection Camille Oliver-Hoffman, Washington
p.21 Photo © Tate Photography, 2013
p.22 Collection of the Center for Creative Photography, University of Arizona. Gift of the Laura Volkerding Estate
p.28 Photo © 2013 The Museum of Modern Art/ Scala, Florence
p.33 © Harun Farocki 2006
p.37 Courtesy the artist
p.42 Courtesy Makhmalbaf Film House
pp.48–63 Photographs courtesy the artist
p.66 Courtesy the author
p.68 Courtesy Stiftung Hans Arp and Sophie Taeuber-Arp e. V.
p.69 © D.R.
p.70 ©Mathieu Bertola/Les Musee de la Ville de Strasbourg
p.73 Courtesy the artist
p.74 Photo Kenrik Gaard
p.75 Photo Markus Tollhopf
p.123 © Demart proarte B.V.
pp.132–9 Photographs courtesy the author

Copyright credits

Index

Page numbers in *italic* type refer to pictures.

V

W

Z

Also available from Tate Publishing:

@ Earth
Peter Kennard

Expanded Cinema: Art, Performance, Film
Edited by David Curtis, A.L. Rees, Duncan White and Steven Ball

Film and Video Art
Edited by Stuart Comer

Land Art
Ben Tufnell

The Life and Death of Images: Ethics and Aesthetics
Edited by Diarmuid Costello and Dominic Willsdon

Live: Art and Performance
Adrian Heathfield

Installation Art
Claire Bishop

Manet and the Object of Painting
Michel Foucault, with an introduction by Nicolas Bourriaud

The Possibility of Life's Survival on the Planet
Patrick Keiller

September: A History Painting by Gerhard Richter
Robert Storr

In association with The Open University:

Art & Visual Culture: A Reader
Edited by Angeliki Lymberopoulou, Pamela Bracewell-Homer and Joel Robinson

Art & Visual Culture 1100–1600: Medieval to Renaissance
Edited by Kim W. Woods

Art & Visual Culture 1600–1850: Academy to Avant-Garde
Edited by Emma Barker

Art & Visual Culture 1850–2010: Modernity to Globalisation
Edited by Steve Edwards and Paul Wood

In association with Afterall:

Art and Social Change: A Critical Reader
Edited by Will Bradley and Charles Esche

Art and the Moving Image: A Critical Reader
Edited by Tanya Leighton